Using
Instructional
Media

Using Instructional Media

James S. Kinder
California State University at San Diego

 D. Van Nostrand Company

New York Cincinnati Toronto London Melbourne

D. Van Nostrand Company Regional Offices:
New York   Cincinnati   Millbrae

D. Van Nostrand Company International Offices:
London   Toronto   Melbourne

Published by D. Van Nostrand Company
450 West 33rd Street, New York, N. Y. 10001

Published simultaneously in Canada by
Van Nostrand Reinhold Ltd.

10 9 8 7 6 5 4 3 2

Preface

This capsule text provides an overview of the effective utilization of media at all levels of instruction. Directed primarily toward prospective and in-service teachers, it should also be of use to industrial, armed-services, and other personnel engaged in training activities where audiovisual components can enhance program effectiveness.

Emphasis throughout is on using media in a school or classroom context wherein media must be integrated into a total instructional plan. The discussion assumes that the reader may be working with students in small groups, large groups, and individually as well as in the familiar "class of thirty." It assumes no previous knowledge of mediated instruction or experience in operating equipment.

The book aims, in short, to acquaint teachers with the basic principles, procedures, and possibilities of media in any teaching situation. For only teachers having this broad base of understanding will become competent and ultimately creative in taking intelligent advantage of the growing resources and technical expertise now available in most school districts.

The first two chapters make explicit the book's concern that media be viewed not as educational adjuncts but as primary instructional tools which, in order to be optimally useful, must meet the criteria of any instructional product: they must answer student needs; they must help to fulfill the teacher's objectives; and they must be subjected to thoughtful planning, preparation, utilization, and evaluation. In Chapter 2, the review of media in the light of current theories of instructional communication and of learning is especially pertinent in this regard.

Subsequent chapters explore the nature, advantages, and disadvantages of specific media ranging from the simplest graphics to the most elaborate multimedia systems. Discus-

v

sions here are braced with classroom examples and suggestions for ensuring that each use of media complements the teacher's content or skill objectives. Later chapters broaden the focus to include total learning environments and the learning resources center, which has become an integral part of so many modern schools.

Although the present text constitutes a revision of the author's earlier *Using Audio-Visual Materials in Education*, it is in effect a new work. An advancing technology and a host of recent educational innovations have brought us to a point at which a wholly new conception of the field is necessary. The outlines of that new view are still emerging, but certainly we need to get on with the task of introducing all teachers to the essentials of instructional media.

JAMES S. KINDER

Contents

Chapter 1 Media As an Outgrowth of Social and Technological Change 2

Chapter 2 Communication As Part of the Learning Process 32

Chapter 3 Using Pictorial Media 50

Chapter 4 Using Graphics 86

Chapter 5 Using Auditory Media 114

Chapter 6 Standard Instructional Materials 144

Chapter 7 Mediated Instructional Procedures 178

Chapter 8 Creating a Learning Environment 220

Chapter 9 The Learning Resources Center 242

Selected References 254

Index 267

Using
Instructional
Media

Chapter 1

Media as an Outgrowth of Social and Technological Change

BEHAVIORAL OBJECTIVES*

After studying this chapter, the reader will be able to:

1. Cite two reasons why education must keep up with social change, especially with reference to gifted and culturally different students, and suggest two instructional procedures by which schools can accomplish this goal.
2. Identify two influences of technological development upon education.
3. List seven guidelines for effective media use and three goals underlying them.
4. Compare the terms *instructional media*, *learning resources center*, *multimedia*, *systems*, *hardware*, and *software*.
5. List five advantages of instructional media.
6. Cite one instance of participation by each of the following in the development of instructional media: federal government, state government, industry, and professional associations.

---

*The behavioral objectives at the beginning of each chapter in this book are statements of significant operations that readers ought to be able to perform after studying a given chapter. Limitations of space preclude listing all the objectives around which each chapter was constructed, however; a particular reader or class of readers may wish to pursue objectives more specifically derived from a particular perspective. (See the *Selected References* list at the conclusion of the text for references on Accountability in Education.)

It is commonplace today to remark that a revolution in education is taking place. This observation has been made many times in the history of education, as schools have responded to the fertile thinking of such leaders as Quintilian, Locke, Rousseau, Pestalozzi, Montessori, Dewey, and scores of others, as well as to social changes occasioned by historical events such as the Industrial Revolution, the Declaration of Independence, the current "space race," the emergence of cybernetics, and many more. Change is always with us, and it is always mirrored in the schools.

Among the most significant thrusts for change in recent years has been Americans' expanding consciousness of social—and corresponding educational—inequities in our nation. Also significant is the technological sophistication we now possess, for this sophistication not only affects our lives in profound ways but also seems to hold a tantalizing promise for increasing our efficiency in education.

Men and women preparing to teach today will probably teach for the next three decades or longer. Their careers will carry them into a new century. Some will teach in communities where the schooling pattern is conservative. Others will work in more progressive communities, with strikingly modern facilities and differentiated programs. During their careers, most can be expected to make several moves from district to district. They will need to grow considerably in their private and professional lives. As Margaret Mead has pointed out, no one now alive will live all his life in the world where he first reached maturity. The best teachers are those who remain vitally alive to the dynamic world around them.

School administrators have long acknowledged that social change originating outside the school exerts an impact upon education that is probably more profound than actions initiated within the school. Educators who are sensitive to the larger world in which students live, yet mindful of their professional responsibility to provide the structured learning experiences that students need in order to live meaningfully in that world, must be more creative today than ever before. For it is probably harder today than previously to make schooling "relevant" for the diversity of students who flood our institutions of learning. But a second form of change, the dazzling evolution of technology that is now only a few decades old, may help educators to meet the new challenges of a dynamic society.

Instructional media, which form the subject of this book and are increasingly the subject of many preservice and in-service education programs, are a fascinating instance of the school's utilizing techniques and concepts from the world at large to do a job which is uniquely the school's. Today's students are "media oriented." It is to the advantage of today's teachers, therefore, to become acquainted with ways in which media can be used to improve instruction. Recent years of experimentation, implementation, and evaluation have yielded important new developments in instructional media, which this book will explore. At the same time, we shall return to the many more commonplace uses of pictorial and other materials which skillful teachers have always employed effectively to enrich their programs.

Because we know that no aspect of education ought to be approached without reference to other aspects and to society at large, this chapter will trace some of the outstanding social and technological factors which bear on today's schools and some of the principles and practices which educators are now putting forth in response to these factors. Finally, we shall set forth some guidelines for effective media utilization in schools.

SOCIAL CHANGE

Social change brings social problems. In a period of high economic prosperity, many people possess low earning capacity, reside under poor housing conditions, live with below-average health and medical services, and/or try to function in broken homes; each of these factors may handicap the development patterns of children. Educators and, indeed, all of society are becoming increasingly aware that many school problems stem from the economic and cultural backgrounds of students.

Not all social woes can be laid at the doorstep of the school, yet the school must share in some measure problems such as school dropouts, unemployment of younger wage earners, delinquency, lack of motivation, and loss of ambition. The school dropout problem reached alarming proportions in the early sixties with figures ranging from 35 to 50 percent. Currently, contrary to public opinion, the trend has leveled off, so that Silberman concluded, after an extended national survey subsidized by the Carnegie Foundation, that "the proportion finishing high school has risen from 58 percent as recently as 1955 to the current rate of 75 percent or thereabouts, and is expected to reach 85 percent by the mid-1970s."[1]

Many people of age eighteen and older are illiterate. According to the U.S. Office of Education, 30,000,000 young men and women will be looking for employment in the 1970s; 2,000,000 of them will have spent no time at all in high school, and 7,000,000 of them will not be high school graduates.[2]

Cultural Pluralism and the Schools

Students from subcultures outside the so-called mainstream of America are of considerable interest and concern to many educators today. Some have variously been tabbed as "disadvantaged," "underprivileged," "behavioral deviants," "slow learners," "alienated youth," "underachievers," or "nonachievers." They may be found almost anywhere, but they are more likely to reside in the inner city and in various low-income rural areas.

Many social scientists have suggested that the present educational system is turning "poor children into poor students," and that much governmental aid to schools cannot even compensate for failures of the system. A large number of youths from impoverished environments become disillusioned at school and many become hostile. They feel that their

1. Charles E. Silberman, *Crisis in the Classroom* (New York: Random House, 1970), p. 18.
2. John L. Burns, *Our Era of Opportunity*, in *Instructional Technology: A Book of Readings*, ed. Frederick G. Knirk and John W. Childs (New York: Holt, Rinehart and Winston, 1968), p. 22.

goals and those of the school are antithetical. Their efforts at success appear to be useless. Morale is low and failure is high. To many, the subject matter in junior and senior high schools is anything but relevant. The conventional curriculum does not seem to prepare them for the lives they expect to lead. Teachers and students often reach points of conflict.

Large numbers of educators contend that the schools have, over the years, exerted a profoundly positive social influence, whereas certain critics feel the influence has been far below what it should have been. One critic has even remarked, "No one can say that the school cannot win its difficult battle for the street. It has never really tried!" In a similar vein, some believe that, rather than teaching the young, inner-city schools only try to pacify them, substituting social conformity for a sense of personal worth. Certainly it seems reasonable to acknowledge that many of the verbal and bookish skills of the conventional school are in conflict with the values of the culturally different students whom today's schools serve. One educational director laments, "What do you do when the reading materials in your classroom tell how Dick and Jane or their slightly updated cousins visited Grandfather's farm, and you know that half of your students not only have never seen their grandfathers but are embarrassed by the topic?"[3]

What is being done or can be done to make education meaningful for all groups? A host of innovative projects, experiments, and new organizational plans are under way. Although it is not within the scope of this book on instructional media to probe school organization per se, it will be useful for our purposes to sketch in five types of administrative alternatives for meeting the needs of the culturally different. Each alternative offers possibilities of media utilization.

The first alternative, *compensatory education*, is another term for any of many types of remedial teaching. Not a "new" approach, it has already produced positive results in varying degrees. Just now, with our concern for the cul-

3. Daniel U. Levine, "The Reform of Urban Education," *Phi Delta Kappan*, 52 (February 1971): 328.

turally different, compensatory education has received new emphasis. Potential dropouts and underachievers can often be identified early and given special assistance before trouble appears. Programs such as Headstart (discussed further in Chapter 6) and Follow Through are essentially compensatory in nature. Remedial work in many forms appears anywhere from preschool years on through the entire school program.

Adaptations in *teaching methods* according to students' needs are always in order, but in the case of culturally different students new methods are often imperative. Through method or otherwise, schools must convince culturally different students that they are capable and can take a hand in shaping their own destinies. Studies show that many of these youths have immense potential.[4]

Methods which incorporate immediate feedback concerning progress, short-term tasks or learning "contracts," active learner involvement, concretion, functionalism, and sensory manipulation, offer promise. Motivation, an overused word, can bring about substantial improvement in the potential dropout or underachiever. In this connection, creative use of media coupled with imaginative leadership, tailored programs, and sensitive new approaches can do much to assist youth who may otherwise flounder. Involvement in learning makes students participators instead of spectators.

Student-centeredness instead of teacher- or subject-centeredness provides another key. The methods employed must not, however, lose sight of the fact that students should at some time in varying degrees be led to new language patterns, and that they must see the need for and achieve reasonable skills in reading, computation, and socially useful activities. The learner's set of values must in some way be compatible with society. Here, counselors and guidance personnel need support from classroom teachers.

Curriculum adjustment (not necessarily curriculum differentiation) is a third approach to more acceptable pro-

4. Elinor F. McCloskey, *Urban Disadvantaged Pupils: A Synthesis of 99 Research Reports* (Portland, Ore.: Northwest Regional Educational Laboratory, 1967).

grams for the culturally different. Curriculum adjustment is not to be confused with assignment of students to tracks (college preparatory, general, or vocational, for example). This approach may call for a different set of courses or modified content of many existing courses. The curriculum must reflect the subcultures of those whom it serves. So-called academic subjects are not necessarily dropped, but may be removed from first priority. Conventional scholastic interests are preceded by the diversity of interests, needs, and talents of students in a heterogeneous society.

Numerous writers have stressed that a majority of *teacher preparation programs* tend to emphasize middle-class values. Strom writes:

> Were the future teachers in any academic major to receive some training in urban sociology, psychology of motivation, culture pattern and personality, human development and the teaching of reading, our circumstance within the slum might be markedly improved in terms of instructional quality, pupil progress, home-school relations, and teacher morale and tenure.[5]

Modern teacher training programs might provide some sort of incentive plan in order to identify, recruit, and train teachers for work with culturally different students. Special compensation is now being talked of seriously, as are in-service programs that include visiting arrangements. Paraprofessional aides (parents and young people from the neighborhood), too, would be helpful, as would cooperation with representatives of outside civic and social organizations such as youth agencies, police, churches, welfare organizations, and administrators of national groups and programs.

School reorganization is yet another approach to effective education in the inner city. Back in 1961 Conant contended that "big cities need decentralized administration in order to bring the schools closer to the needs of the people in each neighborhood and to make each school fit the local situation."[6]

5. Robert D. Strom, *Teaching in the Slum School* (Columbus, Ohio: Charles E. Merrill, 1965), p. 33.
6. James B. Conant, *Slums and Suburbs* (New York: Signet Books, 1961), p. 127.

Issues involved in decentralization are hotly debated among educators. Some believe that school systems of more than 20,000 pupils with thirty principals or so do not serve the best interests of their communities. Accordingly, they advocate subsystems within the big cities. It is argued that these subsystems would provide greater freedom to experiment with curriculum, teacher selection and placement, methods of teaching, and administration. Civil rights and minority groups generally support this approach, but other individuals contend that decentralization of schools leads to high costs, lowered educational standards, and local conflict.

The five avenues for improving education described above seem to apply to all schools: from the inner-city school, often characterized by a tense, ethnically mixed population, to the suburban school with its increasing numbers of youth who drop out or apparently reject everything their teachers stand for. In between is a vast number of schools afflicted with similar problems but not as acutely. The students do not rebel nor do they drop out; many just seem to turn off the teachers and routinely go through the motions of being students.

Encouraging the Gifted Student

Too many schools in the past seem to have reasoned that the gifted, by their very nature, can shift for themselves, whereas slow learners or the "underprivileged" cannot. (For purposes of this discussion, "gifted," "talented," and "creative" students are discussed jointly, although we should point out that important differences exist among them.) Such a philosophy may have dire results for the gifted, besides violating the principle of equal educational opportunity. No one knows how much potential leadership is lost because talented students have been permitted to waste their time and to develop bad work and study habits. Boredom and frustration with unchallenging tasks may result in laziness, apathy, daydreaming, hostile and disruptive behavior, and eventually dropping out of school. Studies show numerous high-ability students among the dropouts.[7]

7. Daniel Schreiber, ed., *The School Dropout* (Washington, D.C.: National Education Association, 1964).

Efforts to effectively handle the teaching of these students have been sporadic. During the sudden drive to win the "space race" occasioned by Russia's launching of its Sputnik satellite, a flurry of excitement about gifted students and their possible contribution to this "race" occurred. This excitement has since ebbed, but gifted students remain objects of interest for conscientious educators.

Schools which attempt to serve the gifted usually follow one of three patterns: acceleration, enrichment, or special classes (in a few cases special schools). Acceleration is not generally favored because of the fear of creating an imbalance in social, emotional, or physical development. Some studies, however, show that with proper instruction bright students are able to take acceleration in stride and still maintain superior levels of academic performance.

Enrichment is favored in theory, but practical difficulties are encountered in providing students with enrichment programs while they remain with their age- and grade-peers. Extra burdens are likely to be placed on the teachers. Students frequently question why they should be asked to do more than their classmates when the rewards seem to be the same. To be successful, any enrichment program needs careful planning. It needs teachers who have sufficient time for the extra tasks. Furthermore, students and parents must fully comprehend the move. Special classes or schools for the gifted are impractical except in metropolitan areas. Such arrangements are expensive and in some cases are open to public criticism.

Regardless of the manner in which the gifted are taught, they need to be identified early in their careers and encouraged. It must also be recognized that there can be inverse results if the student is pushed or driven beyond his limits by overzealous parents or teachers.

Although the foregoing paragraphs dealt with the culturally different and the gifted more or less as groups, it must be remembered that there are all sorts of gradients in these groups. Consequently, the various problems discussed have so many ramifications that the only reasonable method of dealing with them is that of treating learners on an individual basis. More and more educational theories and programs are based on this premise, and it is the underlying thread of much of this volume.

TECHNOLOGICAL CHANGE

Part and parcel of the social factors we have been discussing is the whole panoply of modern technology. A chart of recent advances in mass communication alone would show a line of development paralleling that of the scientific knowledge explosion, then shooting off in many directions. The last seventy-five years have seen the development of, for example, steam-driven, high-speed rotary presses, advanced optics, films, wire and tape sound recordings, simple and complex duplicating and copying machines, radio, television, computers, and communications lasers.

This technological escalation has bestowed upon education a proliferation of equipment and materials which can assist in the reorganization and redefinition of educational experiences. Curriculum revision for improvement in education leans heavily on the materials and devices of instruction. From unrelated types of materials (ungraded readers, arithmetics, geographies, etc.) we have moved to complex systems for the teaching of basic reading, arithmetic, science, languages, and other subjects. Curriculum groups, notably those of the sciences, foreign languages, and mathematics, have evolved organized teaching systems with instructional units including everything from texts and workbooks to library carrel listening-viewing stations with facilities to "dial" for data. The once bulky, clumsy, finicky tape recorder is now available as a pocket foolproof cassette recorder which is as practical for home study as use in the classroom. The 8-mm film serves in much the same way, having a range and latitude of uses far beyond its 16-mm predecessor.

Once technology enters the school building, dramatic renovations usually begin. Not just schoolhouses, modern school plants become systematized learning centers. Much is being written today about a "systems approach" to instruction. (*System* here may be defined as a set of organized, integrated techniques and theories with accompanying practical knowledge for designing, testing, and operating instruction. We shall discuss this topic more fully in Chapter 7.)

Educational "systems" provide not only conditions for effective learning but a sort of educational engineering, drawing upon many disciplines (architecture, science, psychology, sociology, administration, etc.) for design of buildings and working space. Facilities are tailored to fit programs and educational theories such as tutorial instruction, team teaching, and other patterns. Flexibility is a key word in school buildings which often feature modular design. Several areas of learning, notably those where repetitious skills and oral-aural drill are the foundation, have been emancipated from the $20' \times 20'$ classroom to a learning laboratory. Box-shaped buildings are giving way to imaginative designs tailored for sophisticated learning use. Plastic and rubberized inflated health and physical education centers, some with artificial turf surfaces, are not uncommon. The buildings and facilities expansion might well be a volume by itself.

The Concept of Innovation

Innovation and educational technology are closely related. This is true not simply because much of present-day educational innovations are indeed technological but because the schools have adopted from modern technology the working hypothesis that a sort of engineering effort is effective in solving practical problems by research, design, and development.

Although innovation has always been employed in teaching, it is only within the last decade that the cry for new ideas and methods has reached thundering proportions. Today, schools, in general, experience better financing through federal assistance and local effort. Industry, too, has assisted. Along with this increased support, larger sums have been channeled into research and development (R&D), although only about one tenth of 1 percent of the budget goes for this category. The National Education Association (NEA) Project on Instruction has recommended that school systems should allocate an appropriate proportion of their annual

Fig. 1. A bold R & D program in the Pittsburgh schools utilizes a computer system operated under Project PLAN in Iowa City, Iowa. Here, fifth-grade students at the John Morrow School feed individual test cards into an "electronic brain" for transmission via telephone to Iowa City. An immediate response showing complete test grades is returned. (Photo, courtesy Pittsburgh Public Schools.)

operating budget—not less than 1 percent—for the support of research, experimentation, and innovation.

The push for R & D has been spearheaded by various private foundations, the National Science Foundation, industry, the National Education Association, and the Elementary Secondary Education Act of 1965. Innovation has been felt in such matters as the following:

- —new patterns of school organization as in team teaching, flexible scheduling, and nongraded schools
- —new methods of utilization of the proliferating equipment and materials

Fig. 2. Mathematics can be learned in more ways than one, as shown in this well-equipped math center in a British primary school. (Photo, courtesy Drs. Clarence Calder and Vincent Rogers, of the University of Cincinnati. Reprinted through the courtesy of *Phi Delta Kappan*.)

- experimentation with simulations and games
- library expansion and closer coordination with the school program
- development of programs for exceptional children
- development of community educational services
- experimenting with and testing exciting new curricula especially in reading, arithmetic, science, high school mathematics, foreign languages, creative writing, to name only a few
- methods of teaching and curricula in teacher education, notably in microteaching, minicourses, and simulations
- attempts to revitalize rural schools and to bring them into the mainstream of modern education

Currently, a broad range of new and tested educational "products" along the above lines is in actual use. One innovation, "Sesame Street," the most thoroughly researched television program in history, is estimated to have influenced six million preschoolers to learn ABC's and rudimentary number understandings. Through computers and leased telephone lines, arithmetic programs based at Stanford University have reached rural children as far away as Kentucky and Mississippi. Computers, too, have been employed to monitor individual and group performance in schools across the country. Additionally, diagnoses, followed by prescribed individual tasks to help students master basic skills, have been fostered by innovation. As one example, the University of Pittsburgh's R & D Center has designed a method called Individually Prescribed Instruction (IPI), which is now being tried out in 252 schools in thirty-nine states.

Despite important new departures by many school systems, however, the gap between invention and use/acceptance is enormous. Even in the matter of ideas emerging in hardback book form, the gap is five to eight years. Finn says, "The current timespan between the development of a new process and its adoption by a substantial majority of units of the system has been estimated at about 35 years. During the next 10 years this timespan will be reduced to about one-quarter of that length, or from 8 to 10 years."[8] The traditional resistance to change is mellowing.

On the credit side of the ledger, nevertheless, one finds throughout the country numerous comprehensive programs involving all aspects of print materials, conventional audiovisual materials, radio-television-videotape services, preparation facilities, and leadership to implement the use programs.

As a general rule larger districts have greater facilities and programs, but even smaller districts have either independent services and centers or have integrated services with a county or parish media center.

The employment of numerous and varied forms of equip-

8. James D. Finn, "The Emerging Technology of Education," in *Instructional Processes and Media Innovation*, ed. Robert A. Weisgerber (Chicago: Rand McNally, 1968), p. 325.

ment and materials is not based on whim. Use grows from research, and hardheaded school boards and administrators have carefully pondered values before committing appropriations. But, in many respects both the research and utilization of modern media by the schools lag behind industry, the armed services, agriculture, medicine, advertising, and other groups.

Whether bold innovation will continue to burgeon or whether it will settle down to gradual change is moot. However, it seems reasonable to expect that an increasingly large group of intelligent education leaders will lean more and more toward an overall scientific-technological pattern in education.

THE MEDIA TERMINOLOGY MAZE

What are instructional media and what can they contribute to an educational program? At the risk of being pedagogically unorthodox, let us begin by clarifying what these media are *not*.

Media materials and techniques are *not* educational "fads and frills." They are an integral part of the school experience. Such materials are used by industry for serious purposes. The same is true of their use in the armed services. Children go to school for the serious business of learning—to obtain information, to master skills, to develop appreciations and to be able to react to people and to their environment in appropriate ways. Media are tools for learning.

Are *instructional media* the same as *audiovisual materials*— a term perhaps more familiar to many? The trend today seems to be toward use of the broader term *instructional media* rather than the somewhat more narrow *audiovisual materials*—in keeping with educators' broadening concepts about the many forms that teaching tools can take. The term *audiovisual* was popular when technological advances first began to yield a wider array of nonprint materials for classroom use. It emphasized the two senses basic to learning, and, through long and wide use, became standard.

As the use of A-V materials became more widespread, the *Dictionary of Education* defined audiovisual instruction as

(1) that branch of pedagogy which treats of the production, selection, and utilization of materials of instruction that do not depend solely on the printed word; (2) instructional techniques employing materials and procedures not dependent solely on the printed word.[9]

But a field in rapid transition, such as the A-V world was during the 1960s in this country, tends to cast about for new terminology. *New media*, a more recent term, began to be used with increasing frequency. UNESCO used the term regularly, as did the Association for Educational Communications and Technology (formerly known as the Department of Audiovisual Instruction) of the National Education Association and the United States Office of Education, although the term was not used to the exclusion of all others. *New media* seemed to be related in some way to educational television (ETV), programmed learning, and possibly language laboratories, connoting only recent innovations in the field—although, as Edgar Dale has pointed out, audiovisual tools and techniques can be new in the sense of recent origin, new in the sense of being untried, or new in the sense of occurring afresh.

Instructional (or *educational*) *media* seems, in turn, to have come into use as an offshoot of the term *new media*. In a generic sense, *media* refers to all information or instructional content regardless of the form of storage. In 1963 the newer term was given official recognition by the Association for Educational Communications and Technology of the National Education Association as follows:

Educational media are defined here as those things which are manipulated, seen, heard, read or talked about, plus the instruments which facilitate such activity. Educational media are both tools for teaching and avenues of learning. . . . [10]

9. Carter V. Good, ed., *Dictionary of Education*, 2nd ed. (New York: McGraw-Hill, 1959), p. 290.
10. Barry Morris, ed., "The Function of Media in the Public Schools" (A Task Force Position Paper), *Audiovisual Instruction* 8 (January 1963): 1.

The term *media*, however, is still not universally used. *Instructional materials* and *curriculum materials* are two broad terms often employed to refer to both print and non-print media. Many public schools use one or the other to refer to departments and centers in which *learning materials* of many types are stored. Such collections are often called *learning resources centers.* Somewhat more sophisticated is the term *instructional technology*, frequently used in university and higher education circles. *Technology* usually connotes hardware, while *resources* suggests services and a totality of materials.

Educational communications and *audiovisual communications* fit into modern educational theory when the emphasis is on the concept of message. The Association for Educational Communications and Technology defines the latter as:

> That branch of educational theory and practice concerned primarily with the design and use of messages which control the learning process. . . . Its practical goal is the efficient utilization of every method and medium of communication which can contribute toward developing the full potential of the learner.[11]

In this book the term *multimedia* will be used at times. It is a generalized term which connotes not only several media but the employment of a planned integration of media so that they reinforce learning in a systematic fashion. The term is not new, but its more recent use implies something of a *systems* point of view.

The *systems* approach can be described as a molding of man-machine instruction into a unitary process involving behavioral goals, functions, procedures, resources, guidance, and evaluation. A discernible trend has been from kits to multimedia to systems. In a *systems* approach both hardware and software are thoroughly intertwined to maximize the intended educational purposes. (*Hardware* generally refers to mechanical and electronic equipment. *Software* refers to

11. Donald P. Ely, ed., "Alphabetical Listing of Terminology," *Audiovisual Communication Review* 11, Supp. 6 (January 1963): 36.

instructional materials such as books, films, slides, posters, tapes, and the like.) The term *multimedia* has now pretty much replaced the older term *cross media*.

Multisensory materials is an older phrase not to be confused with multimedia. It came into use to broaden the original term *visual education*.

The military and some branches of industry use the phrase *training aids*, though few schools do.

Aids, devices, tools, equipment, and other nouns are employed with the adjectives mentioned above. Cynics add the word *gadgets*. Some of these terms if narrowly construed imply crutches or impersonal mechanization—but such need not be the case, because in a broader sense the intended meaning is something that assists, or a resource.

Many of the above terms will be used throughout this book. The emphasis, however, will be *instructional media* as used in our title. Many of the media overlap in values and uses, whether used for motivation, communication, the building of concepts, or other purposes. In this book, *media* will refer to devices and materials; *methods* will refer to techniques of media usage in an instructional context.

VALUES OF INSTRUCTIONAL MEDIA

Whereas teachers once had to rely almost entirely on a single textbook, a chalkboard, or possibly an out-of-date political map for their materials of instruction, the modern teacher has access through the school district's learning resources center to a large array of proven instructional materials.

Modern educators recognize in instructional media such basic values as concreteness, enrichment, and dynamic interest. Instructional media also show inaccessible processes, materials, events, and things. They help us to study changes in time, speed, and space, while giving all members of a group the opportunity to share an experience. They provide integrated experiences varying from the concrete to the abstract, and they bring experts and multiple resources to the classroom.

Attitude and behavior changes are facilitated by means of

instructional media, as are the getting and holding of many students' attention. Instructional media have been shown to induce greater acquisition and longer retention of factual information and to stimulate interest in voluntary reading. Furthermore, they provide objectivity in the study of a delicate or controversial subject, as well as providing for direct contact by students with the realities of their social and physical environment. Finally, they are valuable for all age and ability groups.

More specifically, instructional media illustrate and clarify nonverbal symbols and images, quantitative relationships, complex and abstract relationships, temporal and spatial relationships, and specific details. They reinforce verbal messages in nonverbal ways. (It should be borne in mind that these values obtain only when the materials are well designed and when they are used appropriately to achieve specific learner objectives.)

CURRICULUM SPECIALISTS   Recognition of the values of instructional materials and techniques has stimulated increased attention to the many materials, source lists, reading references, filmographies, and other supplementary aids available to teachers, as well as to the production and preparation of materials by teachers and students. Effective utilization and preparation of instructional media are of special concern today to the *curriculum designer*. He or she is directly or indirectly concerned with *what* is taught, *why*, and *how*. And media are especially important in the *how* area. Whether the curriculum design in a particular school is subject-matter- or experience-oriented, instructional materials and methods help teachers provide clearer explanations, more stimulation, and, in most cases, more active student involvement.

PUBLIC ACCEPTANCE AND SUPPORT

As media departments have become more and more an accepted part of the school scene, values of the type outlined above have become more apparent. In and out of the classroom, media have played a pronounced role in educational change.

Public acceptance of media since the 1940s has ranged from cautious parochialism to almost evangelical espousal. Advertising, agriculture, manufacturing, sales, personnel training, and other occupations and groups, as well as education, rely upon the employment of one form or another of media to accomplish their objectives. No businessmen's meeting is complete without "visuals." Luncheon, dinner, and evening lecturers make extensive use of the ubiquitous media.

The National Level

The National Defense Education Act of 1958 gave a pronounced boost to education in general and to educational technology in particular. The law specifically provided for grants and contracts for "research in more effective utilization of television, radio, motion pictures and audiovisual aids for educational purposes." Subsequent federal enactments have made huge sums of money available for research and the purchase of equipment, materials, and services.

The Economic Opportunity Act of 1964, the so-called War on Poverty Act, provided for numerous centers for the training of youth. In several of these centers, often farmed out to private industry, the provisions for conventional and sophisticated equipment and materials within the instructional programs were significant.

The Elementary and Secondary Education Act of 1965 was the boldest approach of all. During the first year of operation alone, its various titles made the following appropriations:

Title I, Education of Children of Low-Income Families: $965 million, of which about 29% went for equipment, books, and various aids

Title II, School Library Resources (instructional media of all kinds): $100 million

Title III, Supplementary Educational Centers and Services: $98 million

Title IV, Educational Research and Training: $103 million

Title V, Strengthening State Departments of Education: $14 million plus

Altogether, the United States Office of Education has under its administrative jurisdiction twenty-three legislative programs and acts. ESEA, detailed above, is the most far-reaching. Nolan Estes has summarized its impact well:

> The PACE (Projects to Advance Creativity in Education) design for innovation puts an end to the excuses of our school districts that they lack the capacity to change. We live in an age where we cannot afford a continued lag in the implementation of ideas in education.[12]

Former President Johnson's January 1965 State of the Union Message reflected the new national attitude toward education and instructional techniques. In 1972 the appropriation for USOE was boosted $1.175 billion from $4.951 billion to $6.126 billion. Some federal programs were reduced or eliminated while others 'were increased. Project Headstart and television's "Sesame Street" were upped $17 million and $3 million respectively. Much of the overall increase in the budget is slated for aid to poor students, emergency school districts, and student loan or grant assistance. Trends following the 1972 election have not been definitely established; however, there are some indications of shifting or even decreased allotments in federal assistance.

Although President Nixon has as yet made no strong and specific commitments to education, he has on several occasions expressed concern for schools with "integrity, independence, and creativity." He has stated an interest in student loans and a continuing federal commitment to preschool programs such as Headstart and Follow Through as well as a National Teachers Corps. Excerpts from his speaking and writing provide only these details: "I consider education a federal concern, a state responsibility, and a local function. . . . Local school systems should be responsible for developing specific projects and programs. . . . "

In connection with another education concern he has stated:

12. Nolan Estes, "ESEA: Dimensions '67 of Title III," *Audiovisual Instruction* 11 (December, 1966): 795.

A second necessary move is to employ a variety of means to bring the schools closer to the people in order to relax the tense atmosphere of alienation and mistrust that prevails in some urban neighborhoods among students, parents, and teachers. Within limits curriculums should be tailored to the needs of different groups. . . .

The President's final thought, although again lacking specificity, is interesting to media-minded educators:

Create a National Institute for the Educational Future to serve as a clearinghouse for ideas in elementary and secondary education and to explore the revolutionary possibilities that modern science and technology are making available to education.[13]

The Commission on Instructional Technology, in a report to President Nixon and Congress in January 1971 entitled "To Improve Learning," made sweeping recommendations for a massive effort in the use of new educational media. Part of the federal concern for education has centered on efforts to reduce the tragic waste of human resources occasioned by economic and cultural deprivation. Numerous programs and projects have been launched in this connection, of which VISTA, Headstart, Job Corps, and Community Action Program are perhaps the best known. Educational media play a prominent role in all these programs.

For nearly a decade the federal government has subsidized media institutes, conferences, and workshops across the country. It is not possible to assess their worth quantitatively, but their value appears to have been considerable. They have brought in-service and preservice teachers together for new and refresher instruction in media devices and principles. A significant number of individuals have been trained as media specialists and technicians able to provide instructional services to their respective school systems. In addition, no discussion of the part the national government has played in media education can overlook the establishment of the National Educational Television Network System and the

13. *Today's Education* (January 1969): 21–22.

many types of support for instructional television at the local level.

Industry and Private Foundations

Even before the educational alarm precipitated by Russia's preceding the U.S. in outer space, several foundations began boosting technological capability in education. In 1954, for example, the Ford Foundation made significant early contributions toward the development of educational television.

The expenditure of billions for education from local, state, and national sources whetted industry's interest considerably. Industrial giants such as Columbia Broadcasting, IBM, General Electric, Raytheon, Westinghouse, and Xerox have entered the educational market. Companies which once confined their efforts to book publishing, educational film production, or the manufacture of recording devices are now joined in large conglomerates which research, design, develop, sell, service, and operate instructional projects in foreign languages, arithmetic, reading, or other subjects. Today industrial groups are bidding for the operation of Job Corps training centers, vocational training centers, and high-level technological training at or near the professional engineering stage.

PERFORMANCE CONTRACTING School systems faced with failure to achieve what might be called average progress in such areas as reading and mathematics are now willing to farm out certain teaching activities to industry. *Performance contracting* is the term applied when a school system contracts out to a private instructional firm certain instructional tasks on the basis of guaranteed student performance. This pattern of instruction is now employed by more than thirty school districts across the country. Usually the contracts are limited to a few subject areas and to a brief period of time, as one year. One school district (Gary, Indiana), however, has turned over to an instructional firm the entire school program of an entire school for a period of four years. Doubts exist as to the ultimate legality of such a move. Nevertheless, performance contracting has grown until it is estimated that for the current year between $100 and $150 million dollars of school funds will go to contracting firms.

This development appears to be a way of linking new outside forces onto the existing educational system. Some observers see the instructional corporations bringing up-to-date expensive equipment and instructional methods to bear on educational problems in a more forceful manner than the schools have been able to do. Examples include vital and effective in-service training programs for teachers and staff, wide use of instructional materials, the disappearance of "classes" and the substitution of "learning centers" coupled with nongraded scheduling, meaningful and challenging evaluation measures, and an introduction of genuine innovative processes. Performance contracting may become the educational development of the 1970s. At the moment there is much confusion and some bickering with offstage political shadows. A recent article highlights the issue in this manner: "Performance contracting in schools, like a crystal dropped into a stream of light, acts as a prism, displaying a colorful spectrum of fundamental educational issues and requiring they be examined."[14]

Industry not only has its own resources to draw upon but, having worked with government in billion-dollar defense budgets, also has a great deal of know-how in obtaining new federal money for education. Should educators welcome this new entry into their field or should they oppose it? Perhaps it is well neither to accept uncritically nor to condemn outright.

The State Level

Some states have passed statutes prescribing some knowledge of instructional media as a condition of teacher certification. Many more have a *de facto* prescription, and others have established regulations concerning media materials in

14. James A. Mecklenburger and John A. Wilson, "The Performance Contract in Gary," *Phi Delta Kappan*, 52 (March, 1971): 409. (It might be noted that the entire issue of this journal is devoted to performance contracting.)

connection with the granting of permanent certification, often as a part of the preservice education programs of colleges and universities. Some regulations extend down to the inclusion of the materials and techniques in method courses and student teaching. Such regulations do not necessarily call for the pursuit of separate media courses, but rather require integration of media instruction into the total program or by blocks in core programs. (This book is particularly designed to meet these preservice conditions.)

The Professional Level

Over the years professional associations and societies have sought directly or indirectly to improve media services in the schools, in areas including libraries, audiovisual materials, curricula, public relations, building design, and educational broadcasting. In addition, organizations concerned chiefly with the needs of the handicapped and the atypical, as well as numerous subject matter specialties, have become intrigued with the possibilities inherent in media.

For the most part, the efforts of these groups have been poorly coordinated. In many instances they have seemed to work competitively, each seeking a larger domain of service. In 1969 the Department of Audiovisual Instruction of the National Education Association and the American Library Association joined in a commendable attempt to bring some order to the chaos by producing a handbook entitled *Standards for School Media Programs*. This bulletin is important not only for the contribution it makes toward universal guidelines for media programs but because it documents the common interest of both groups in new modes of learning. On the other hand, *standards*, no matter who formulates them, are likely to be soon outmoded, in our rapidly moving society.

NEW POSSIBILITIES BRING NEW PROBLEMS

No educational innovation—no matter how promising—can be truly effective if divorced from instructional theory, the backbone of education. We have already noted that instructional technology is more than the sum of its parts, and that characteristic is the basis for the new *systems* approach to education which involves designing, carrying out, and evaluating both teaching and learning. It is a combination and integration of human and nonhuman resources.

As we approach the end of the twentieth century, technology in education is desirable and inevitable. Yet technological systemization presents problems of financing, teacher education, administrative organization, and integration with basic theories of learning. Technology must not outrun our wisdom to use it.

Technological proliferation carries secondary problems such as lack of standardization and inadequate techniques in bibliographic control, cataloging, housing, and distribution. But, the same acumen that invents the technology can devise solutions to these hurdles. Today's corps of teachers, aides, prospective teachers, and other instructional personnel must be educated intelligently in instructional media concepts. In earlier days, teaching was a unidimensional art, and teacher effectiveness rested on a knowledge of content. A second dimension was added when method—the knowledge of how to organize and present content meaningfully—became important. The third dimension resulted from the idea that, to be most effective, teachers needed to understand something about those being taught—what makes a person act as he does, what makes him "tick." The fourth and most recent dimension has developed through a recognition that people learn through a synthesis of content, method, and psychology (conditions for effective learning), and materials with a "systems" approach as a catalyst. Conditions of teaching have changed, but the above four dimensions show a progression which indicates a new and more complex concept involvement in the teaching process.

Although prospective teachers are supposedly facing the "stuff" of modern-day learning realistically, not infrequently one meets new teachers who are inadequately prepared for the tasks ahead. Schools and colleges of education, as well as the teachers of teachers, need to concern themselves with up-to-date theory, technology, and method. No less in need of a

firsthand acquaintance with new instructional media concepts are the in-service teachers. How to bring them into the
mainstream of modern education is an ever-growing problem.
A truly contemporary education for prospective teachers, an
upgrading for all in-service teachers, and plans for the self-
renewal of all disciplines are tasks of great magnitude—
especially as we become more aware that the *means* of education must never overshadow or determine its ends.

Effective instruction embraces the questions not only of
how, *where*, *when*, and *who*, but, above all, *what* and *why*.
"How" questions must not become an end in themselves.
"Where" questions must address the issue of sequence, or at
what point various experiences and understandings are best
taught. "When" questions must lead us into considerations
of time-duration. "Who" questions must go beyond traditional assumptions, to embrace new views of the individual
student as well as new instruction personnel including not
only teachers (alone or in teams) but curriculum designers,
tutors, aides, paraprofessionals, consultants, and community
resources. The "what" questions of effective instruction will
be more easily answered if buttressed by these questions.
But the fundamental question—"why?"—must always take us
into the realm of *objectives*: what we want to accomplish.

Planning and sub-planning are the very keystones of effective learning in organized formal education. Some critics
today are saying that formal education as currently practiced
is virtually obsolete; nevertheless, formal learning promises to
remain as our educational mainstay. The big questions then
are how to make it pertinent, interesting, and effective.

SOME GUIDELINES FOR EFFECTIVE UTILIZATION OF MEDIA

Before turning to specific instructional media in the chapters that follow, some general guidelines for the effective
utilization of media are appropriate. We shall, of course, provide suggestions for utilization at many points in this book,
with reference to the particular media under discussion. And
it should be pointed out that *no* universally acceptable guide-

lines for media utilization have as yet been formulated and accepted by the profession. The suggestions that follow here are broad, and not intended as definitive. Not all of them apply in all situations, and some situations will require others which considerations of space prevent our listing here. The following guidelines are intended merely as useful principles, suggestive of the many dimensions of effective media utilization in instruction. Underlying all of these guidelines is the rule that to be effective, instructional media should be *properly prepared, wisely selected, and intelligently used.*

GUIDELINE 1: Choose instructional media which fit specific objectives of the instruction. By listing your objectives first, then selecting materials that best further the attainment of those objectives, you avoid using materials merely for the sake of using materials.

GUIDELINE 2: Prepare yourself in advance. Once you have selected the media you will use for your lesson, thoroughly familiarize yourself with them (for example, preview the slide, filmstrip, or film you have chosen) and consult study guides and manuals. Further, integrate the materials you have chosen into your lesson plan, considering sequence, timing, and proper coordination of all learning materials used.

GUIDELINE 3: Prepare the class in advance. Student readiness ensures an "atmosphere" for association and assimilation. Discuss with the class in advance the materials to be used, by name, type, source, and other pertinent information. Make the students aware of the reasons for using those particular materials, things to look for, associations to be made or considered, and new or unusual words, phrases, or symbols. Explain beforehand, too, any negative features of the material.

GUIDELINE 4: Prepare physical facilities in advance. Although students are a captive audience, they are entitled to the use of all learning materials under optimum conditions. All equipment and media should be ready before the class assembles and should be in good working order.

Alternative materials should be available in case of break-downs. Schedule student operators, if used, and be sure that you and/or the student operator know how to operate the equipment easily. Attend to seating arrangements, speaker's location, screen placement, light control, volume of sound equipment, and similar factors.

GUIDELINE 5: Ensure student participation either before, during, or after presentation. The actual degree of student participation will depend on the type of materials used, their purpose, and the students' age or grade levels. Audio material does not necessarily eliminate student discussion during preparation, for example.

GUIDELINE 6: Follow up use of instructional materials with related activities and an evaluation of the materials by the class. Facilitate the students' forming of associations and conclusions which have resulted from the use of the instructional materials, encouraging them to summarize the content imparted by the materials, set forth generalizations based on that content, or discuss the materials in the light of the purposes for which they were used. You might test the students on the lesson or repeat the use of the media. Follow-up projects which involve individual students, committees, the entire school, or even the community may result from the use of the materials. If time permits, such projects may involve extended research and a challenge to creativity.

GUIDELINE 7: Evaluate the materials you have used. Judge how well the materials did the job for which they were intended, also considering whether or not the students responded positively to them. You might then ask yourself what other materials, if any, might do a better job.

The teacher who follows these guidelines flexibly and faithfully will in all likelihood maximize media values.

In the following chapter, we shall explore the question of *communication* as an aspect of the learning process. Much will be said about the *why*, *where*, and *when* of instruction.

Subsequent chapters will analyze the media themselves. The book's concluding chapters will emphasize personnel, facilities, and the preparation of instructional media by teachers so that appropriate devices and materials will be utilized at the right place, at the right time.

Chapter 2

Communication as Part of the Learning Process

BEHAVIORAL OBJECTIVES

After studying this chapter, the reader will be able to:

1. Draw and explain a diagram of the communication act.
2. Given a videotape, tape recording, or other transcription of an actual lesson, identify four instances each of factors that obstructed communication and those that enhanced communication (including redundancy).
3. List three reasons for today's emphasis on the communication process as part of learning.
4. Identify three ways in which a teacher might implement Gagné's theory about dynamic learning processes.
5. Explain two ways in which instructional media can facilitate each of the following: individualized instruction, extrinsic motivation, and learning via the senses.

Parallel to the shift from a unidimensional to a systems concept of education which we traced in Chapter 1, there has developed a new focus on the learner, the learning process, and the broad question of how instruction is best *communicated.*

Some see these new concerns as part of education's attempt to be more responsive to new types of students, from backgrounds not formerly present in large numbers. Others attribute them to new knowledge of child development. Alternatively, today's emphasis on communication in the classroom may be part and parcel of an emphasis on communication by American society at large. Or perhaps the movement is a logical outgrowth of our new sophistication with instructional media and attendant curriculum design, wherein the "receiver" of any instructional message communicated via media is considered no less important than the "message" or the "medium." Certainly, too, the gradual growth of general psychology into specialized applications, particularly operant conditioning and social psychology, has moved us in this direction, as experimental studies have come out of the static laboratory into such dynamic areas as the classroom, playground, home, and community.

LEARNING OBJECTIVES AND THE NEW EMPHASIS ON LEARNING

At the turn of the century, the objectives—or "goals," or "aims"—of education were very general and fantastically broad: "to learn to speak French" or "to increase English vocabulary." Subsequently, from about 1918 to 1925, objectives became minutely detailed: e.g., "to learn when to use *i* before *e* in spelling *ie* and *ei* words" (objectives and rules were often one and the same), or "to memorize the addition combinations through 10." Then the pendulum swung back to broad objectives until 1948, when the American Psychological Association began focusing attention on educational objectives in terms of *behavioral change* which was definite, attainable (in the near future), observable, and measurable.

Objectives—alternately called *behavioral objectives, learning objectives, performance objectives, instructional objectives*—came to be expressed in terms of the actions, or behavior, that students demonstrate as the result of instruction. It became important that the student, as well as the instructor, be able to evaluate his own progress and thus organize or reorganize his efforts to align them with his goals. From these developments have come new concepts in *task description* and *task analysis*, as well as new developments in testing such as *item analysis, difficulty indices, validity,* and general *test building.*

With the learner as central figure, modern educational researchers have undertaken investigations into methods of instruction, motivation, guidance, peer influences, and other sometimes neglected aspects of learning. Educational psychologists, for example, have formulated new theories concerning dynamic learning processes. Among these is Robert Gagné, who has suggested that there are eight discernible kinds of learning, which occur in a hierarchical fashion and which should influence the structure of instructional design. Gagné's kinds of learning, from the simplest level, are: (1) signal, (2) stimulus-response, (3) chaining, (4) verbal association, (5) multiple discrimination, (6) concept, (7) principle learning, and (8) problem solving.[1] For each type, Gagné has established a set of *conditions* necessary for its achievement. Media are considered integral to the establishment of such conditions and to what Gagné calls the "events of learning," as: (1) gaining and maintaining attention, (2) insuring recall of previously learned knowledge, (3) guiding learning by use of verbal and pictorial hints or "cues," (4) providing the learner with feedback, (5) providing situations in which applications may be made through recall and transfer, and (6) evaluating outcomes.[2]

1. Robert M. Gagné, *The Conditions of Learning* (New York: Holt, Rinehart and Winston, 1965), pp. 33–57.
2. Robert M. Gagné, "Learning Theory, Educational Media, and Individualized Instruction" (Paper delivered at the Faculty Seminar on Educational Media, Bucknell University, November 16, 1967).

Thus, teachers today see their professional role increasingly as that of stimulating, organizing, and guiding behavioral change. They do so through such activities as: formulating learning objectives, organizing a variety of learning experiences and situations, choosing an instructional method, selecting and preparing instructional materials, encouraging student involvement, evaluating performance, and carrying out follow-up procedures. Learning is acknowledged as so complex an activity that it can no longer be assumed to have occurred via a single lecture, a single textbook, or a fragmentary homework assignment. Increasingly, effective learning is believed to result from the planned use of many materials and types of learning experiences, sometimes employed when several teachers (a "team") combine their talents and efforts to plan learning activities and guide student effort.

Individualizing Instruction

Advocates of the team teaching type of organization hold that students fare best if their activities are structured so that part of their work is in large groups, part in small groups, and part individualized. Thus, a student might spend 40, 20, and 40 percent of his time respectively with the above arrangements. These percentages oversimplify the matter, because individual student needs are much too variable to be structured in hard and fast schedules.

Many other plans for dealing with individual differences are being tried across the country, such as nongraded schools, flexible scheduling, and differentiated staffing assignments, with unique building arrangements to accommodate each plan. As society increases in complexity, the amount and variety of both students and material to be learned increases. However, while heavy emphasis is given to individualized instruction, abolition of group learning is by no means advocated. It has been hypothesized, indeed, that attitudes can be learned only through group (social) contact. Peer influences not only stimulate behavioral change but set many of its conditions.

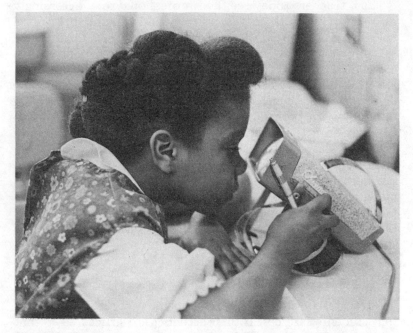

Fig. 3. Individualized instruction is facilitated by individualized equipment such as filmstrip and slide projectors that "even a child (like this first-grader) can operate." (Photo, courtesy Pittsburgh Public Schools.)

More and more instructional procedures tend to be individualized, with a noticeable fostering of self-learning and self-correction. Although these concepts have always played some part in education, at least in principle, it is only within the last few years that they have become central foci. It is important, though, not to stop with the observation that individualized instruction can and does take place under many conditions. We must remember that it is only when an individual reacts as *he* needs to react that instruction has been individualized. Although people can and do profit from shared experiences, each person, in order to learn, must make those experiences his own by repeating or interpreting them according to the particular pattern in which he reacts.

Instructional media, accordingly, are being designed or

Fig. 4. Small-group instruction can be an exhilarating change of pace for students and teacher, as in this scene in an "open classroom" at Harris Hill School. (Photo, courtesy Penfield, New York, Central Schools, Department of Educational Media. The teacher is Mrs. Wilma Comstock.)

modified so as to accommodate large, small, and individual learning patterns. Apparatus for projecting slides, filmstrips, and films are available for large-group use, and appropriate machines have been designed especially for seminars and individual study. Some are even suitable for check-out from school for home study. Practically every move toward individualizing instruction emphasizes the importance of media in the process; hence the task of instructional designers to individualize media becomes more challenging.

New Attention to Motivation

Any move in the direction of bettering instructional communication and individualizing learning takes us, sooner or later, to the question of motivation. This issue is a lively one today, because some critics of the schools have charged that the motivations of many present-day students are not sufficiently tapped by current educational procedures.

Motivation can be described as an inner drive, implying an emotion or desire that energizes the will. An *intrinsic* form of motivation is one originating or existing within the student that causes him to respond, whereas *extrinsic* motivation originates outside the student. Teacher-created incentives are essentially extrinsic, although the student must eventually supply intrinsic motivation if the external incentive is to take hold. When the latter is lacking or is weak in a student, the teacher hopes to kindle and build it by starting extrinsically.

The instructional media repertoire is replete with motivational assistance. As only one example, *simulation games* have been increasing in favor because they provide almost unprecedented participation opportunities, as students assume and act out roles having a bearing on material to be learned. Teachers, or teachers and students jointly, focus their attention on a problem or situation and, after proper stage-setting, attempt an analysis bolstered by facts and realism. Simulation games are particularly helpful in certain areas of the curriculum which are social in nature yet sometimes difficult to make "lively"—such as social studies, guidance, vocational opportunities, and community problems. Discovery-inquiry-report with due regard for all points of view is the three-pronged equation which characterizes simulation games. Many student talents which are often untapped can be brought into play with this approach. (Simulation games will be discussed in more detail in Chapter 6.)

We have already noted that nonprint experiences ranging across field trips, resource persons, videotapes, films, and a host of others can supply excellent motivation. Each "medium" has its own advantages and limitations within instruction, as we shall see throughout this book.

The Senses and Learning

Interest in the role of the senses in learning was already afoot in educational circles when instructional media began their ascendancy. It had long been recognized that the various senses condition the reception of messages in the communications act. One writer went so far as to state that

> we learn about 1 per cent through taste and another 1½ per cent through the sense of touch. The sense of smell provides about 3½ per cent, and hearing provides about 11 per cent of what we learn. An overwhelming 83 per cent of our learning is through visual experiences.[3]

Retention of what is learned is likewise related to sense experience. Observation and research tend to show, holding time as nearly constant as possible, that people generally remember:

10 percent of what they *read*
20 percent of what they *hear*
30 percent of what they *see*
50 percent of what they *hear* and *see*
70 percent of what they *say*
90 percent of what they *say* as they *do* a thing

These figures on the relative importance of various senses to learning and retention (developed at the University of Texas, Industrial Education Department, about 1950 by the late P. J. Phillips) are, of course, only approximations. Yet it is clear that learning and retention are inextricably interwoven with the mode of instructional communication used. Communication theorist Marshall McLuhan's dictum that "the medium" itself (book, film, recording, television) is much more than a mere transmission channel but is indeed "the message"[4] is but a striking expression of an old idea, yet it has bold implications. Media are important in their own right, not just as transmission vehicles. This being true, the design and production of media—both software and hardware—assume an importance rivaling that of their utilization.

3. Ted C. Cobun, "Media and Public School Communications," in *Instructional Process and Media Innovation*, ed. Robert A. Weisgerber (Chicago: Rand McNally & Company, 1968), p. 93.
4. Marshall McLuhan, *Understanding Media: The Extension of Man* (New York: McGraw-Hill, 1964).

Equally important, it now appears, is direct instruction in learning via the senses. As one example, a movement for *visual literacy* has recently emerged, aimed at improving the extent to which students, and others, can respond to and derive information from visual stimuli. Visual and verbal literacy can be combined in this way to provide greater initial learning and extended retention afterward. Visual literacy will be treated further in Chapter 3 on pictorial media.

COMMUNICATION SKILLS AS PART OF TEACHER COMPETENCE

In the past most teaching depended almost entirely on verbal communication between teacher and student, or written communication to the student from printed materials. Although these communication channels continue to play important roles in the learning process, today's students are learning facts, skills, concepts, and appreciations from various types of pictures, television, recorded words, programmed lessons, and other media.

Teachers want to foster students' communication abilities, of course. They teach the basic communication skills: voice improvement, reading, clarity of expression in writing, and, in recent years, listening skills. After developing or presenting an idea, the teacher usually asks the class, "Does everyone understand?" "Are there any questions?" "Is this clear?" But on the next test there is usually ample evidence that a few, perhaps many, did not understand. Why?

For one thing, communication, regardless of the medium, is a two-way process. Students often ask one another, "What are we supposed to do?" "What did the teacher mean?" Communication from teacher to students has failed. Ideas that were thought to have been presented clearly only befogged and confused the students. Has the teacher taught? Whose fault is it?

Understanding is a developmental process which can be conceived of as occurring on three successive levels. The first level is the experience level: the grass roots level of experiencing, where misunderstanding is at a minimum. But all learning cannot be presented at this level because conceptualization and generalization do not occur in experience but are extrapolated from it.

Vicarious experience, the basis of the second level of understanding, is used extensively in the modern school, where there are many substitutes for "real-life" experience. In addition to reading, vicarious experiences can be gained from still pictures, films, filmstrips, resource persons, simulations, mock-ups, television, and the like. How these vicarious experiences are used will be the theme of much of this book. The more concrete and realistic the vicarious experience, the more nearly it approaches the learning effectiveness of the first level.

Of course, misunderstandings can result from vicarious experience, too. Unless the learner realizes that he is dealing with a substitute, his learning may not square with real-life learning. For example, pictures of a dog and an elephant may lead the child to think that the animals are of the same size. Films, through close-ups and long shots, or because they are out of date, biased, or unrealistic, may also give false impressions.

Understanding on the third level depends on abstraction. It is illustrated by words (written or spoken), formulas, schematics, and symbolization. Especially in the type of civilization in which we live, abstraction or symbolization represents shortcuts in thinking and experiencing which help us condense ideas.

An example of the above is a term like *orange*, which has gradient meanings all the way from perceptions of color, size, odor, and texture, to pictures, words, and colored styrofoam models, to a vast conglomerate concept of citrus, fruit, nutrition, geographical distribution, and myriad other associations.

It is an oversimplification to say that learning can be characterized as taking place at three levels. Obviously there are many levels, but in broad terms the three stages treated above appear to stand out. The Stanford Revision (by Terman, in 1916) of the Binet-Simon individual mental abilities tests recognized these three stages of thinking by including a set of pictures among the subtests. Children could score normally at three age levels if they could first *enumerate* items in the pictures, second *describe* the items, and third *evaluate*, conceptualize, or provide associations with the pictures. It is useful to imagine an inverted spiral as a graphic example of this development of a concept: beginning with rudimentary perceptions and then broadening outward and upward through vicarious learning and abstract symbolization. At their best, communication and learning employ media at *each* level. Efficient integration of all levels is the goal of effective teaching, for teaching is essentially a communications process. The youth of each generation acquire skills and information stored up by their predecessors, through an act of transfer, an impartation, a dialogue. The general view of communication as interchange of ideas by words, letters, or messages, therefore, is a narrow one. The broader view, and clearly the only complete one, includes the interchange of ideas through many media.

THE COMMUNICATION ACT

From the foregoing it is clear that communication, the very heart of instruction, is a complex process. Teachers communicate symbols which have meaning for them, and they can hope that there is a common understanding of the symbols by the students. This is the assumption every teacher makes in every presentation, regardless of the media employed. This writer makes such an assumption as these lines are written. The artist makes it as he places various symbols on a canvas. If the art form is extremely modern, the intent of the artist may very well never be conveyed. Signs, words, or pictures, or other forms of communication, must be underlaid with a oneness of understanding. Signs such as \$, $\mathcal{c}$, &, and X take on meaning with rudimentary instruction; others, such as δ, $\circ$, $\cong$, ∞, $\oint$, and $\supset$, come with much more instruction. Formulas, such as $F = M_1 M_2 / D_2$ or $A = (a + b)/2 \times h$, require extensive understanding before they communicate anything. A proofreader's marks such as $\subset$, #, $\overset{..}{\vee}$ convey no more meaning than a foreign language unless they are understood by both sender and receiver.

In written composition, the sentence structure, vocabulary, syntax, idea density, and other factors may not be shared by writer and reader. The result is poor communication. It accounts in large measure for many present-day students' poor understanding of the writings of Shakespeare, Chaucer, Wordsworth, or Emerson. The so-called readability formulas of recent years were designed to assess the degree of communication from an author to a given audience. Congeniality in social communication rests on the same basis.

Communication theorists view communication as an act that can be represented by a formula with three factors: *A*, *B*, and *C*. The *source* is represented by *A*, the *medium* by *B*, and the *receiver* by *C*. The teacher may be *A*, the spoken word *B*, and the student *C*. Specialists speak of the parts as the *encoder*, the *signal* (or *sign*), and the *decoder*. An idea is put into words, pictures, symbols, or some other form for transmission. To be received, the destination (person or class) must not only receive the message clearly but must be able to understand the words, pictures, or other symbols involved. Although communication appears at times to be simple, it is actually more complex than the above explanation implies. Kemp has suggested a model that allows a more complete explanation of what takes place (see Figure 5).

According to Kemp, his model illustrates how a *message* is originated by a *source* or *sender* and is then *encoded—*

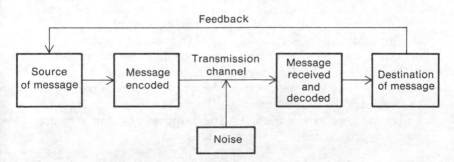

Fig. 5. The route of the message during the communication act. (Reprinted by permission from Jerrold E. Kemp, *Planning & Producing Audiovisual Materials*, 2nd ed. San Francisco: Chandler, 1968, p. 11.)

converted into transmittable form. For Kemp, the message is mental, the source is the sender's brain, and the transmittable form is a verbalized thought:

> The message then passes through a *transmitter* (print, film, television) via a suitable *channel* (air, wire, paper, light) to the *receiver* (a person's senses—eyes, ears, nerve endings), where the message is *decoded* (within the nervous system, conversion into mental symbols) at the *destination* (brain of the receiver).[5]

The significance of the "feedback" aspect of the model is that

> effective communication depends upon the receiver being active. He reacts by answering, questioning, or performing, mentally or physically. There is then a return or response loop of this cycle, from receiver to sender. It is termed *feedback*. Feedback may enable the originator to correct omissions and errors in the transmitted message, or to improve the encoding and transmission process, or even to assist the recipient in decoding the message.[6]

Certainly all sorts of things can happen to a message between source and receiver! There may be distraction, interference, distortion. The theorist calls this sort of thing *noise*, a term applying to anything that happens to a message to change it from what the sender *encoded*. Chief among "noises" are sounds, faint images, poor print, voice irregularities, vibration, temperature, mechanical defects, competing thoughts, and body discomforts.

One factor not noted in the communication act as represented in Kemp's model is an attempt to forestall or bypass any noise that might occur. The term commonly applied to this bypass factor is *redundancy*. The sender reiterates the encoding by mere repetition—by encoding and transmitting it through multiple forms and contexts. At times the *redundancy* element may be anticipatory, or it may be a follow-up to feedback. In common parlance, much redundancy is known as "good teaching"! The implications for a multimedia approach are, of course, extensive.

5. Jerrold E. Kemp, *Planning & Producing Audiovisual Materials*, 2nd ed. (San Francisco: Chandler, 1968), p. 11.
6. Ibid.

As an example of positive use of *redundancy* in teaching, let us consider the teacher of a high school health class who has just finished talking about folk medicine. Students have seemed attentive, yet only one or two perfunctory questions have been asked. The teacher feels that his feedback indicates he has had little impact on the class. Accordingly, he asks if anyone has ever heard of a home remedy for the removal of warts. There are several affirmative answers and the discussion moves into treatments for swellings, hiccups, acne, colds, fever blisters, sterility, and a host of other ailments. Someone brings up the oft-accepted efficacy of vinegar, molasses, honey, apples, wine, toddy, hours of retiring and arising, etc. At an appropriate point, the teacher asks if someone can define voodoo, thus tying the propitiation of evil spirits to students' understanding of folk medicine. Before the class period ends it is agreed that tomorrow students will bring in actual examples of folk medicinal agents; records and poems about voodooism, witchcraft, and incantation; and books on these subjects so that the class can focus its attention on scientific research and method along with its vicarious experiencing of certain aspects of folk medicine.

Such an illustration will generally be accepted as an example of good teaching. It is also an example of redundancy, in which students are reached through several channels rather than a single one—in this case, a lecture.

Barriers to Effective Communication

Industrial training personnel, who are sometimes faster to jump at new theories (not always to their advantage!) than educators, have held for some years now that "the key to effective management is communication." Only consider *your* last "misunderstanding" with someone, and how things might have turned out differently if the two of you had actually communicated effectively in the first place.

We have already noted the detrimental effect of *noise*, in many forms, upon communication. A number of other factors can interrupt the communication act to such an extent that the receiver (student or class) does not receive the original message as it was intended. For one thing, poor communication is frequently occasioned by the fact that the communicator makes unwarranted assumptions about the receiver's ability to understand the message. Among the many possible barriers to effective communication, certain major ones are particularly worthy of note.

Poor Physical Reception Clear understanding depends first of all on clear, unhampered, undistorted reception of the message. Unless a student hears the teacher distinctly, he cannot possibly receive a sound message clearly. The same is true of visual messages. Written or drawn material placed on the chalkboard, for example, must be large enough for all in the class to see it. Other simple physical interference factors may include light value, glare, room temperature, chalkboard location, cleanliness of writing surfaces, quality of textbook paper and print, vocal volume, enunciation, and distracting mannerisms on the teacher's part.

Inaccurate Reading of Feedback Because communication is a two-way process, there is necessarily feedback. The teacher does receive some kind of return message from the students. In simple face-to-face communication the message can be perceived from their physical expressions and actions. But beyond this, the teacher needs evidence of actual understanding. Is there evidence of association? Is there evidence of the ability to apply and generalize? None of these must be assumed on the basis of students' *assurances* that they have understood, or through questioning one or two students. In non-face-to-face teaching, as in television and programmed learning, effective ways of "reading" feedback are especially critical.

Dissimilar Background Experiences Different backgrounds of sender and receiver can destroy communication. The teacher may describe an act, scene, or principle so clear to him that he wonders how anyone could misinterpret it, yet the student may find much of the message unfamiliar. He hears but does not understand. Such expressions as *oligarchy*, *one-party system of government*, *pi*, *improper fractions* can easily be misunderstood because of differences in background between teacher and student. How often has an algebra teacher been guilty of combining two, three, or more operations into one with a perfunctory "therefore X equals . . ."? The beginning student needs to go through the steps one by one: collect, combine terms, and transpose. We can say that an effective teacher is one who, among other things, uses his imagination to put himself in his students' places, seeing the learning problem as *they* see it.

There are some ideas or concepts so commonly referred to that everyone in our culture is assumed to understand them. Frequently, however, ideas such as freedom, individual initiative, right to vote, personal property, and labor are not actually understood. Using these ideas without first arriving at a definition that all present can accept may cause a breakdown in communication.

Jargon   Teachers, like most people, may fall into the habit of using jargon in their speech. Indeed, educational jargon is very noticeable in the classroom, at professional meetings, in social gatherings, in conversations with parents, and on many other occasions. A friend of the writer has two pocket notebooks filled with jargon passed for true coin at educational meetings. Sometimes jargon is even used purposely to prevent understanding, or for effect, but more often it is used thoughtlessly. In each case, the receiver does not get a clear message.

Verbalism   To some people verbalism is not a cause of poor communication, but a result. Whichever it is, teachers must be unusually alert to avoid it. Too often mere words pass for mastery. We live in a word-centered world; much of our communication is word-centered. Words, however, are meaningless unless they rest on a firm foundation of experience.

Media materials and techniques can help dissipate much of the verbalistic confusion in learning. They are not a panacea, and because they promote vicarious learning, they, too, must be watched so that an appropriate association—grounded in his own experience—is made by the student. There is less excuse for verbalism today, in school or out, because of the many new communication media and new teaching aids. Insofar as possible, when two people use a word it should connote the same meaning to each. Alice could not accept the semantics of Humpty Dumpty, who said, "When I use a word, it means just what I choose to mean—neither more nor less." Neither can we.

Differing Conceptions of Time and Space The present school population was born after World War II. Their time dimension can be a barrier to communication. A visitor on the Plains of Abraham above the city of Quebec asked a small Canadian boy what he knew of the famous battle. The boy honestly replied, "Not much. You see, I wasn't born then."

Space, no less than time, can cloud classroom communication. Books, films, and various types of pictures can assist in space orientation. Surely it is unwise to depend solely on verbal accounts of what happened early on the morning of April 19, 1775, at Lexington, or for an understanding of how one carries on life processes in the hot, dry environment of the Sahara. Travel can help break the space barrier, but not the time barrier. The teacher will need the assistance of every available teaching aid.

The Generation Gap The factor of the generation gap is more than the time and space barriers mentioned above, although it is related to them. A significant sociopsychological phenomenon today is the ever-widening gap between older and younger people. How much of the gap is caused by age differences (time) and how much is a convenient excuse for other communication barriers is unanswerable. Nevertheless misunderstandings occur because the two groups live, in some respects, in two different worlds. The differences are observable in fashions, speech, value systems, and life-styles. A few sentences from a letter of Lord Chesterfield to his son in 1748 are ironically instructive in this regard:

I have this moment received your letter of the 4th, N. S., and have only time to tell you that I can by no means agree to your cutting off your hair . . . your own hair is, at your age, such an ornament, and a wig, however well made, such a disguise, that I will upon no account whatsoever have you cut off your hair. Nature did not give it to you for nothing . . .

Often the generations seem to speak different languages. Currently words such as *bag*, *thing*, *pad*, *pig* have taken on, for some, meanings not yet found in dictionaries.

How can teachers use instructional media to deal with the challenges posed by the communication act, the learning process, and the learner? We can find the answer by studying the individual media.

Chapter 3

Using Pictorial Media

BEHAVIORAL OBJECTIVES

After studying this chapter, the reader will be able to:

1. Given a learning objective, and given three possible types of pictorial media, select on type that would best meet the objective, and support this choice.
2. Given a flat picture, rate its instructional effectiveness according to at least six criteria and specify the criteria used.
3. Given the content objectives of a unit, devise a student production exercise that involves pictorial media and contributes to the achievement of the objectives.
4. Given any item requiring projection in the classroom (an object, a student paper, a map, etc.), determine whether opaque, overhead, or some other form of projection is appropriate, and prepare and present the item accordingly.
5. Given a learning objective, construct a lesson using a film, following the seven guidelines for effective media use set forth in Chapter 1.
6. Design a lesson in a specific subject in a way that will increase the visual literacy of students at a specific age/grade level.

Among instructional media, pictures are probably the oldest and most common form. Pictures of one kind or another have been part of man's attempt to communicate and clarify knowledge since the time of the cave dwellers. The glamour of more modern pictorial media, such as films, should not lead us to overlook the enrichment that even the simplest "flat" picture, such as a photograph, can lend to instruction. Indeed, the newer media, far from rendering simple pictures obsolete, only capitalize upon the inherent power of a single picture.

FLAT PICTURES

The commonest of all pictorial media, the so-called flat picture, is the least expensive and most readily available. Long before children start school, they enjoy pictures, and throughout life in our media-filled culture they continue to look at or "read" them. Modern advertising alone testifies to the ability of pictures to communicate as virtually a universal language.

Advantages of Flat Pictures

Teachers use pictures to motivate and vitalize learning simply because students like them. Pictures also clarify vague or incorrect ideas about things, places, customs, and ideas removed from one's immediate environment, as well as within one's locale. Moreover, pictures are affected relatively little by time, at least not to the same degree as many written media. Pictures often show the events of the past most clearly. Concepts and abstractions, too, can be made more meaningful through pictures, as with the use of photos of successive generations of one family, to illustrate the concept of population growth. Pictures have value for all school levels, though possibly not to the same degree or in the same way.

Naturally, the number of pictures needed to do the job, whatever it may be, varies widely and will be dependent upon the learner, the nature of the learning task, and the amount of information to be conveyed. For example, one well-selected picture can provide a sufficient idea of what an astronaut's "spacesuit" looks like. But a series may be required to show, for example, the evolution of communication via mechanical devices, ranging from the Gutenberg printing press to the latest electronic computer.

Useful Types of Flat Pictures

Of the three types of flat pictures discussed below, each can be used in color or black and white. (It is worth noting, of course, that the field of pictures is so enormous that detailed categorization by type, beyond the three categories discussed below, is impractical. Any picture—from an expensive glossy color study print to an insignificant newspaper clipping—may have instructional value if utilized appropriately. On the other hand, bulging files of dog-eared, unsorted clippings from magazines are usually of interest only to the collector.) In general, as we have mentioned, a few "good" pictures are more useful in the long run than many mediocre ones. Also, the value of pictures is usually enhanced by tasteful mounting and display. Any picture that finds its way into a teacher's permanent collection should reflect more than merely passing interest. Its instructional merit should be assessed just as books, films or recordings are assessed.

STUDY PRINTS   Study prints are unified sets of photographic reproductions, usually mounted to facilitate longer use. The pictures often contain pertinent information on their reverse sides: information about the picture, sometimes the source of the picture, lists of questions, suggestions, problems. In some cases, the data on the reverse side are an abridged teachers' manual. There is no limit to the number of pictures, of course, except that too many cannot be effectively used at one time; experience has shown that one really effective picture is worth more than many which only attempt, with varying success, to present the same idea.

Study prints are either purchased or produced locally by a school district's learning resources center. Sometimes the sets circulate from the center; at other times they are stored for long periods of time in individual school buildings. Public libraries also collect pictures on topics of general interest—recent political conventions, for example—and are usually willing to allow teachers to borrow such sets for a specified time.

The new teacher should make it a point to determine, as early as possible, the study print resources of his district, either in his own learning resources center or in the district or county instructional materials center. In some states—California and New Jersey, for example—the county office provides many instructional media resources for teachers in smaller communities. If sets are available in a district office, they will usually be listed in a catalog of instructional materials. In one large metropolitan school district, for example, the catalog of study prints contains lists of more than 9,000 sets totaling 100,000 prints. Some sets contain only two items, others as many as thirty-five. Duplicate sets are available for many topics because the learning resources center serves more than 100 schools with 4,000 teachers. A topic such as "The Harbor and Harbor Activities" is represented in this coastal city by as many as thirty separate sets, containing between six and thirty-one pictures each. In all there are 210 pictures of the harbor, in multiple sets. These pictures are all mounted, most of them laminated between plastic sheets to ensure longer life and to give them a more inviting appearance.

PHOTOGRAPHS   Photographs are not particularly different from study prints, except that they can be somewhat more unique in that they are ordinarily made from original negatives or copied from existing non-copyrighted pictures. Processed on photographic paper in either a mat or a gloss finish, photographs can have a great deal of warmth and definition. Many large school districts today employ photographers and maintain equipment to provide teachers with photographic service. This service is limited, however, because funding only allows for a small percentage of the possible needs to be handled.

More and more teachers, as a result, are doing their own photographic work, and some are involving their students in the activity as well. Many school districts lend cameras and provide raw film stock to teachers. In one school located in a prosperous farming community, a fourth-grade teacher, dissatisfied with the pictures available on truck farming, decided to make her own pictures of lettuce and carrot farming utilizing local "settings." The school media director assigned a photographer to work on the project. The teacher prepared a list (her "shooting script") of the "shots" she would like to have, and the photographer did the shooting and processing. The pictures were printed in duplicate and became a set of study prints available to all teachers in the district.

One's budget and the anticipated function of a photo will govern whether the finished product is prepared as, for example, a $2'' \times 2''$ slide, or a paper print in $4'' \times 5''$ or $8'' \times 10''$, $11'' \times 14''$ or larger form. In connection with a unit on modern architecture, for example, a junior high school social studies teacher could justify the small expense of twenty-six large glossy photos of local architecture, representing types from classic Greek and Roman to functional modern.

All pictures are valuable, but teacher- or student-produced pictures have special value. Tailored for specific purposes, they usually fill a void where no adequate commercially prepared pictorial materials exist. A home economics teacher, for example, could locate only a few incomplete and unsatisfactory textbook illustrations relating to the making of buttonholes. With the help of selected students, she arranged cloth, pictures of hands, and scissors to show the various steps in making a buttonhole. Each step was photographed with a standard press camera, and the developed film was enlarged to $8'' \times 10''$ prints. Fourteen prints told the buttonhole story very clearly. During this project student interest and performance were high, for the teacher was at once creating a teaching resource and motivating her students.

Teachers find photos interesting to prepare and, in terms of student response, well worth the effort. Both elementary and high school students have the ability to assist in taking and processing photographs. Their creative imagination, in fact, usually adds vitality to such projects. On field trips student photographers are every bit as important as reporters who will "write up" the excursion.

In addition to their value in providing important material directly connected with key learning objectives—like learning to make a buttonhole, or identifying the characteristics of modern architecture—photos have always had rich supplemental value. In connection with a study of the short stories of Bret Harte, for example, an American literature teacher assembled photos of frontier-style buildings, settlements, dress, inhabitants like cowboys and miners, dance halls, posters, billboards, newspaper headlines and mastheads, and an enlargement of a lonely eye-shaded editor setting hand type by the dim light of a kerosine lamp. A colleague in industrial arts contributed photocopies of artists' sketches of some of the characters in "The Outcasts of Poker Flat." This teacher elected to gather her collection over a period of two weeks prior to the introduction of the Bret Harte unit, with the assistance of several friends and a helpful librarian. She might, alternatively, have involved her class in the search for appropriate photographs, in which case the display itself would have developed with the unit rather than preceding it.

Encouraging students to make a *collage*, a collection of pictures, words, and other materials assembled on a sheet of paper to express a single theme, is another way of capitalizing on pictorial media in order to meet basic learning objectives.

Fig. 6. Senior high school students in an American literature class discuss a collage made to illustrate a short story. (Photo, courtesy Chula Vista, California, High School.)

One inventive teacher used the following strategies to instill an appreciation of the short story in her students:

Basic Learning Objective:
Students will be able to identify the theme of a short story.

Basic Teaching Strategy:
Students read various short stories from the text.[1] Along with the reading assigned in class, students are allowed to go to the library for additional reading of personal choice, which is summarized in students' "journals." Some of the stories which they read are Stephen Crane's "The Open Boat," John Steinbeck's "Travels with Charley," William Faulkner's "A Rose for Emily," and Katherine Anne Porter's "Rope." The teacher proposes a project for the culmination of the unit. Students are divided into groups of five for the development of the project, which consists of each student group selecting any short story which it has read and then preparing a 24" X 36" verbal-pictorial collage to summarize it.

Specific Learning Objectives:
Given the assignment of making a collage that symbolizes the story, students will be able to:

– show at least ten images in the story, which can be validated by rereading the story

– show at least two symbols in the story

– show how the symbols contribute to the theme of the story

Specific Teaching Strategy:
One of the preconstruction activities of the project requires each student to jot down a page of phrases which express his images of the story that are capable of being rendered pictorially. To a certain extent this list might even be called a verbal collage, montage, or script. Each student tries to visualize what the collage will look like; the irony of "Rope" is hard to portray, whereas the descriptive "Travels with Charley" is much easier and results in lists of two dozen or so phrases, many more

1. *The American Experience: Fiction*, ed. Marjorie Wescott Barrows, et al. (New York: Macmillan, 1968). Curriculum Manual: *Course Notes and Suggestions for English 11X and English 11Y*. Sweetwater Union High School District, 1969.

than it is possible to place on the collage. Students prepare the collage from pictures taken from magazines, newspapers, and other sources. Depth is added by original sketches and cutouts from construction paper. Captions (original or slogans cut from advertisements or other printed copy) help tie the collage together so that it becomes a symbolic interpretation of the author's theme.

Follow-up:

Each student is asked to write an evaluation of his group's collage: how well the project carried out the theme of the story, what elements of the story were impossible to pictorialize, to what extent the collage was truthful or fanciful, what difficulties were experienced in finding proper materials, and what was the personal significance of the collage. One student writes the following description of the collage from "Rope," typifying the depth of understanding which can be gained and expressed with such use of pictorial media:

The left side of the collage was done in black and white to symbolize an argument and a generally dark and gloomy atmosphere. This side of the collage has pictures of a broken egg, a steak, a messy table, people arguing, and comments like "Money," "Involved," "Come Back to Your Senses," "Hot Line," and "Get Out of Town" all of which symbolized the husband and wife argument. In the center of the collage we have a piece of rope curving from the top of the picture to the bottom to indicate tension and a kind of break in the marriage. The rope caused the big argument. On the right side of the collage we try to show how the couple got back together again by pictures in color of a pretty kitchen with roses, fruit, and comments like "A Few Kind Words," "Lovers," "That's What I Like," "His and Hers," "Good Match," and "It's Up to You." The collage is intended to indicate that if two people love each other they can get back together again after an argument. The squiggly piece of rope itself signifies the tension that is built up in the story, and at the bottom of the collage, the end of the rope points to the colorful side with LOVE.[2]

2. Description of the collage by Gloria McMahon. Project reported by Barbara Dean, Student Teacher, Chula Vista High School, Sweetwater (California) School District.

TEXTBOOK ILLUSTRATIONS   Most of today's textbooks are generously illustrated. Color is not always necessary, but its psychological effect makes it a valuable asset. Most authors and publishers exert every effort to include meaningful and appropriate pictures along with verbal material. Teachers who ignore textbook illustrations lose the benefit of an important instructional aid. Yet, observation suggests that relatively few teachers discuss textbook illustrations in class, and that even fewer consider an understanding of illustrations a legitimate objective in a unit of study. Very few teachers appear to use illustrations in testing.

Criteria for One's Own Collection

Experienced teachers report that a personal collection of pertinent pictures is an asset. Preservice teachers can begin their picture collection while they are still in college. They will be able to use it during student teaching, and it will be useful for many years afterward. In-service teachers, with the assistance of students, can develop a file of effective pictures. Teachers who are asked to teach a new course or a new subject should gather pictures as part of planning their new work.

Picture sources are ubiquitous. Many school districts furnish their teachers with extensive collections, as we have seen. On the other hand, every imaginative teacher continually "scrounges" interesting pictures related to a specific topic or concept. Often these are "one-shot" materials, to be used once and discarded. Some, however, can beneficially be stored for later use.

Picture selection should be done critically. Not every picture is worth saving. Eight useful criteria to insure authentic instructional pictures should be kept in mind (the order of importance may vary, depending on one's instructional objective):

Authenticity   Pictures should be truthful and accurate. Erroneous information is as bad as no information, perhaps worse.

Simplicity   To be most effective, pictures should be simple and uncluttered.   Not only are simple pictures more valuable from a teaching standpoint—they are often superior aesthetically.

Relative Size of Items   The best teaching pictures include a familiar object so that students can obtain a correct perspective for new objects.   Pictures of marine animal life, for example, can be made more valuable if a coin is placed in the picture to show relative size.   Similarly, a human figure is frequently a useful guide to *scale*.

Action   Unless the picture is one of purely static items, it should show action.   Posed pictures of people are of little value unless their purpose is to bring out a detail, such as costume, hair style, or facial expression.   Although pictures are flat and without motion, they should *imply* action.

Camera Work   Good camera work adds to the value of any picture.   Pictures that are properly exposed and developed, with good contrast, depth of field, and clear detail are most desirable.

Artistry   Effective arrangement of objects, color values, camera angles, and "human interest" are important in every picture.

Condition   Pictures should be free from smudges, blurs, scratches, or blemishes.

Identification   Good captions or apt descriptions are helpful.

KEEPING THE COLLECTION FUNCTIONAL   Several examples of the creative use of pictorial media have already been given. At this point, it may be useful to consider the underlying principles according to which teachers determine that pictures of one kind or another are desirable.   Essentially, the teacher needs to identify the learnings he regards as most essential for a given unit of study.   Following this, he needs to determine which of these requires a *visual component* in order to insure mastery on the students' part.   Let us take three typical units as examples: (1) rice-growing among the cultures of Southeast Asia; (2) a novel by Charles Dickens; and (3) a study of primitive man.

The unit on Southeast Asian rice-growing entails the following understandings, each of which can be fostered with a picture:

planting methods, manual and mechanical: *photographs of each*

watering methods: *photographs of pumps, levees, plants growing in water, the land being dried up*

harvesting, manual and mechanical: *photographs of each*

types of rice: *photographs of long-grain, medium-grain, and short-grain rice*

rice production: *photographs of polishing and packaging rice*

use of rice: *photographs of diverse people eating rice with indigenous utensils*

geographic distribution of rice production: *map of the world showing principal rice-growing areas, including parts of the U.S.*

Through this kind of analysis, the teacher insures that he obtains visuals essential to students' learning.

Study of a novel by Dickens, say, *A Tale of Two Cities*, on the other hand, entails historical, political, socioeconomic, and philosophic understandings, many of which can be assisted through pictures:

social conditions in eighteenth-century Paris and London: *period photographs of the two cities, emphasizing affluence and squalor existing side by side*

means of transportation utilized by characters in the novel: *photographs of tumbrels, carts, coaches, ships of the period*

aspects of the French Revolution: *photographs of the Bastille, torture devices, a guillotine, fortresses, and prisons* the author: *photographs or reproductions of portraits of Dickens*

Here again, pictorial media are brought into the unit not merely as interesting supplementary materials but as items directly related to instructional objectives of the unit.

A unit on primitive man suggests the following objectives and correlated use of pictorial media:

artifacts suggestive of daily life: *photographs of excavated grinding stones, knives, fish boxes, weapons*

living arrangements: *photographs of excavations of formerly inhabited trenches, caves*

religious dimensions: *dramatic photographs of "Stonehenge," England, with captions indicating the presumed significance of the placement of the massive stones and something of the ceremonies assumed to have occurred there*

aesthetic and communications dimensions: *photographic reproductions of cave paintings from France and Spain*

primitive man as an evolutionary milestone: *photographic reproductions of artists' sketches of prehistoric men, compared with artists' sketches of man at other evolutionary stages*

Too often, textbook illustrations of historical or anthropological relics, artifacts, and artists' sketches of the period suggest to the student, nonverbally, that other men at other times lived in such a *bizarre* manner that they must somehow have been grossly inferior to modern man. Rarely are the beauty, the spiritual depths, and the very real struggle for physical survival conveyed in a way that present-day students can identify with. Great photographs have the capacity to inspire awe and a deep interest in and respect for one's fellowmen—whether on the other side of the world or in a time long past. Certainly the power of well-conceived pictorial media can greatly assist our more verbal teachings about man in his many dimensions.

Procedural Suggestions for Utilizing Pictorial Media

Students of art and art history have long known that detailed study of a work of art can yield a surprising number of insights into both the subject of the work and its creator. Although most of the pictorial media utilized in contemporary classrooms do not classify as "works of art," they should, if selected and utilized according to the criteria we have been discussing, nevertheless reward concentrated study. If the teacher, in short, has selected materials that will reward prolonged examination, why should he or she simply mount them, tack them on the bulletin board, and forget them—hoping that students will pass by and linger? Why not, rather, make pictorial media every bit as important as verbal media in extending students' understanding of a given topic or period or question?

As you accumulate pictorial media to enhance your teaching units, therefore, bear in mind the following alternatives to the "post-and-forget" option:

Individualized instruction   Any time you individualize instruction, consider a wide use of pictorial and other visual media. They are especially effective for students with artistic abilities. Individual researching of questions, writing of stories or reports, and compilation of materials on a particular topic may be effectively stimulated by use of visual media.

Small-group instruction   This very promising alternative between total individualization and standard large-group instruction is as amenable as its two alternatives to concentration on the study of pictorial media. Here, committees or groups work on a topic or question that may well be illuminated by the study of pictorial media.

Large-group instruction   Class—or large-group—instruction can utilize pictorial media perhaps less effectively than the two aforementioned systems because every member of the class must be able to see the picture in question clearly. For this reason, it is vital that pictures be displayed prominently—or projected on a screen.

Home study   Creative home study use of pictorial media is not common at present, but, as in the case of many plausible educational alternatives, there is no reason why it cannot be employed to considerable advantage. Why should not students check out pictures to analyze as "homework" assignments, just as they check out supplementary books or periodical articles?

In short, the use of visual media appears to hold considerable potential, thus far hinted at but not yet fully established by research, for increasing and extending verbal learnings. As just one example, we might cite the work of Horiuchi, of Kyoto University, Japan, who found, in teaching 1200 students from the second, fifth, and seventh grades about vocabulary, that a *visual* method—in which *verbal labels* (such as "glasses," "chair," "coat") were presented via flash cards, was less effective than *pictorial representations* of the same objects presented by the same method. This was true especially with younger, less verbal students.[3]

Classifying, Mounting, and Storing

A drawer or filing cabinet overflowing with unclassified pictures of varying quality is practically worthless. To be effective, pictures must be put into some kind of order: by topic, subject, activity, or any other meaningful system. Along with collecting and classifying goes the task of keeping the materials up-to-date. The criteria to be kept in mind are *timeliness*, *relevancy*, and *vitality*.

Pictures may be said to fall into two categories: *temporary* and *permanent*. The former should be used once and then, staunchly, discarded! The latter should be durably *mounted* to increase their usefulness. Mounting is best done as the pictures are collected, so that no damage occurs to the pic-

3. Hideo Horiuchi, "The Effects of Educational Media on Retention," in *New Media for Instruction, No. 3, Survey of Educational Media Research in the Far East*, ed. Benjamin C. Duke (Washington, D.C.: U.S. Department of Health, Education, and Welfare, Office of Education, 1963), pp. 146–147.

ture and mounting does not become a chore. As pictures are mounted, thought should be given to artistic placement, color of mounting stock, size of margins, relevant captions, and proper identification. The two principal methods of mounting involve wet and dry processes.

Although wet and dry mounting are the commonest types used by teachers, students, and learning resources centers, there are other types such as rubber, cement, and adhesive lamination.

WET MOUNTING   This is the oldest and cheapest of all mounting processes. It is simple but exasperatingly messy at times, and potentially destructive to certain clay-coated stocks and photographs. Wallpaper or library paste, vegetable glue, or flour-and-water paste are satisfactory for most work. Rubber cement may be used, but it may dry out and it tends to yellow. The following simple directions will result in a good wet mounting job:

1. Turn the print face down on spread-out newspapers. Brush the paste evenly over the reverse side of the print with a back-and-forth motion until it is well coated. Let it dry for a minute or two, until the paste becomes sticky but has not begun to harden.

2. Place the print on a piece of cardboard that has already been prepared to size. Using a soft cloth for smoothing, start in the center of the print and work outward to the edges with a rotary motion, pushing out the excess paste and pressing the print tightly against the board. (When the excess paste has been worked out, the print may be further smoothed with a rolling pin.)

3. In the same manner, paste backing paper to the reverse side of the board to lessen the danger of warping.

4. Place the print under a weight. Let it dry thoroughly for at least twenty-four hours.

5. After the print is dry, it may be coated with a light synthetic resin varnish or a clear plastic spray.

DRY MOUNTING   This process is more satisfactory, although slightly more expensive than the wet process, as it gives more attractive and longer-lasting results. The materials needed, other than the mounting board, are dry mounting tissue, which can be purchased at a photo supply store, and an electric iron. To make the process more economical, ordinary food-wrapping plastics can be substituted for mounting tissue. Professionals replace the electric iron with a regular tacking iron and a dry mount press, which heats electrically. There are six steps in the dry mounting procedure:

1. Turn on electric current for the tacking iron and dry mount press.
2. Tack the dry mounting tissue to the back of the picture, leaving the corners free.
3. Place the picture on the mounting board. Adjust the margins so that the top and sides are equal, with the bottom margin one inch larger than the other margins.
4. Place the assembly in press, with the picture uppermost. Cover the picture with a cardboard or sheet of paper as large as or larger than the picture.
5. Press the platen down. The time ordinarily required for good adhesion is thirty seconds at 175° F.
6. Remove the picture from the press. Trim the edges in a paper cutter if required.

Pictures which belong to the school should be catalogued and filed at the learning resources center, if there is one, or in the libraries of individual schools.

Storing pictures can be a problem unless the teacher is fortunate enough to have plenty of space. Even then, proper containers are needed. The best storage is a pressed paper or metal filing case. Cardboard packing boxes or orange crates will serve, though they are not so satisfactory. Manila folders or envelopes help keep the pictures in order.

FLASH CARDS

Flash cards involve words, pictures, numbers, or all three. They must be large enough to hold up before a class for drill purposes (see Ch. 4 for lettering techniques), unless they

Cartel Nº4

Nuestro comedor

Una mesa grande	Una silla grande

el plato	la taza	el cuchillo	el tenedor

la olla	el jarro	el cántaro	el balde

Fig. 7. Flash cards can facilitate instant recognition of material, such as the quick survey of words connected with dining room use shown here.

are being used for individual instruction. They have long been used in developing vocabulary in both the native language and in foreign languages. Look at Figure 7 and think how a language teacher might use this picture as it is, or as ten separate enlarged flash cards.

Word-picture language cards may be purchased for most foreign languages. Actually, it takes a teacher only a short time to prepare a large number himself. Flash cards are also useful in mathematics drills, among other subjects.

PROJECTED STILL PICTURES

Advantages of Projected Still Pictures

Depending upon one's objectives, projected pictures may have several advantages over unprojected pictures. For one thing, they can be enlarged, via the projection screen, to almost any size. Their novelty captures students' attention. As a rule, projected pictures are used in darkened or semi-darkened rooms, a condition which is in itself unique and results in greater attention.

Although projected still pictures are slightly more expensive than flat pictures, they are considerably less expensive than motion pictures. Additionally, the teacher has almost complete control over their presentation, a condition less true of motion pictures. A picture may be held on the screen for as long as necessary while students raise questions and express points of view. Furthermore, many still-picture projectors are equipped with remote-control accessories, facilitating teacher-student interaction during viewing. Incorporated in many remote-control accessories is a light which the teacher can direct on certain parts of the screen like a mobile pointer.

Projected still pictures have the same general advantage as all pictorial materials—that is, they help students visualize things, skills, processes, and ideas, thus making concepts more concrete. They are used by teachers of all subjects and at all levels. A primary school teacher may use them to assist in teaching the names of animals, to visualize a story or poem, or to provide common experiencing as a springboard in language arts. In senior high school they can provide richer, more dynamic presentation of information, promote rapid and clear perception of data, and stimulate feelings and attitudes about subjects presented.

A moment's thought will disclose the almost infinite possibilities for teaching via a projected, sequenced series of still pictures, in a host of subject areas:

business/commercial education: *Getting a Job, Today's Office Machines*

communication: *Uses of the Comma, Using the Library, Shakespeare Country*

fine arts: *Instruments of the Orchestra, Making a Silk Screen Print*

foreign languages: *A Trip to France, Visualizing Basic Vocabulary*

health/physical education: *Learning the Square Dance, Basics of First Aid, Blocking in Football*

home economics: *Principles of Food Preparation, Design and Pattern Making*

mathematics: *Algebra in a Typical Day, A Bank Account*

science: *How to Use Balances, Basic Photography, Mendel and Mendelian Law*

social studies: *Community Resources, County Government, A Political Campaign*

vocational education: *How to Finish a Piece of Lumber, Shop Safety, Steps in Constructing a House*

A particular advantage of projected still pictures is the ease with which they can be coordinated with the "single concept" notion of instruction, whereby only one clearly circumscribed topic is presented at a time. In this respect they differ from many mediated learning materials based on multiple concepts, which can be confusing to students.

Types of Projected Still Pictures

The types of pictures to be considered here are those projected by any of the following: slide projector, filmstrip projector, opaque projector, overhead projector, stereoprojector, microprojector, and tachistoscope. These devices are non-motion, though attempts are being made to put motion into some or all of them. Practically every school in the nation is equipped with projectors for most types of still pictures. Every teacher should understand the advantages and uses of each.

SLIDES AND FILMSTRIPS   The most widely used projected still pictures, slides and filmstrips, are very similar. A filmstrip is a series of related pictures arranged in a fixed sequence; the sequence of slides is determined by the teacher. The filmstrip is more popular than the slide, but this preference may be based on convenience rather than on merit.

Many slide sizes are available, but only the 2″ × 2″—and to a lesser extent the 3¼″ × 4″—are used to any extent by teachers. The 3¼″ × 4″ slide is limited in use and is usually tailored for a specific purpose by the teacher. Most school systems have standardized on the 2″ × 2″ slide. Custom had it that only a few of the large—or "Lantern"—slides were used at a time, in contrast to many of the 2″ × 2″ being used on one occasion. This need not be so. Both sizes may be purchased commercially, lend themselves to teacher and student production, and are inexpensive.

The filmstrip is available in two sizes. By far the most popular is the *single frame*, having a picture size of ¾″ × 1″. With the width of the picture across the film, projection takes place vertically in the projector. The *double frame* contains a picture size of 1½″ × 1″ and is photographed with the width of the picture along the length of the film, so that projection takes place horizontally in the machine. Single frame filmstrips are almost universally used by school systems.

Slides and filmstrips serve a variety of learning purposes, including enrichment experiences, the introduction of study units, and another approach to drill.

Although slides have been used mainly with large groups, they are becoming more popular with small groups or in individual work. Some schools are fitting out individual study areas so that slides may be used in individual study. This is very practical, since the slide projector can be used with a low light level.

Notwithstanding the ease with which filmstrips can be

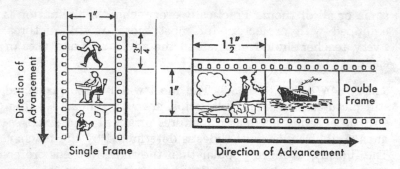

Fig. 8. Single-frame (left) and double-frame filmstrips, showing direction of projection.

used, some teachers experience problems. The film can jam in the machine and the sprocket holes can be stripped. During the early 1970s sprocketless filmstrips appeared in an experimental stage, holding great promise for solving one of the major problems in this area. A relatively soft, pliable substance, film is easily scratched. Filmstrip rolls should always be handled by gripping the edges so that fingerprints do not smudge the film surface. The roll should be curled lightly, never cinched tightly, to insure that scratching does not occur.

Although filmstrips cost only a few dollars, some learning resources centers prefer not to circulate them. Accordingly, they cut the filmstrips and mount the frames as slides. This is a questionable practice because of the low cost of filmstrips, the implication that teachers would otherwise ruin filmstrips, and the fact that a well-sequenced and structured medium is mutilated. In certain instances, of course, this procedure may be justified, though certainly not as policy. If, of course, a school system purchases, or already has in stock, a filmstrip which is adjudged to be poorly sequenced, the filmstrip might then be converted to slides. In general, however, remaking filmstrips into slide units and/or sets is time-consuming, and the values will not in most instances justify the costs.

Although slides and filmstrips are discussed here under the heading of pictorial materials, their audio adjunct should be noted here. New equipment makes it possible to synchronize sound recording with slides or filmstrips without difficulty. Not only are tape and record audio accompaniments possible, but they influence profoundly the learning experience promoted by the picture. In one sense, audio accompaniments restrict the uses of filmstrips, e.g., by controlling the speed of presentation, thus allowing the teacher little chance for extension or clarification of a point. For slides, however, the so-called sound-on-slide device is a new and relatively expensive arrangement by which a flat tape is adhered to the 2" × 2" cardboard frame. A special projector then permits recording, playback, and image presentation simultaneously with this unitary device. The tape allows reuse, all types of revisions, and a full thirty-five seconds, maximum, for commenting on each picture (sufficient for most pictures), and is always in synchronization. Audio may act as a satisfactory replacement for scripts and/or spontaneous verbalization.

Our question whether sound slides and filmstrips are *pictorial* or *audio* media reflects questions now being asked by professionals as well. Indeed, the matter of bibliographic control and appropriate shelving is raised by many nonprint media. Librarians and administrative personnel are now striving for new methods to handle the "sound filmstrip" or the "illustrated record/tape." As the problem is mainly an administrative one, teachers are concerned only indirectly. The ALA-DAVI bulletin on "Standards" leaves the matter open:

> Rigid adherence to the numerical sequence of a classification scheme is not necessary if other groupings of resources make the materials more easily used, more accessible, or more inviting for exploration. A *multimedia arrangement with printed or audiovisual resources on similar subjects shelved together* is proving successful in some schools. (Italics added.)[4]

Thus, we appear to be moving toward a view in which the *function*, rather than the *form*, of a particular medium determines its classification.

4. *Standards for School Media Programs* (Chicago: American Library Association; Washington, D.C.: Department of Audiovisual Instruction of the National Education Association, 1969), p. 26.

Preparing a Slide Set or Filmstrip   Proper preparation is especially important for all projected pictures, still or motion. As an efficient first step in the preparation of a slide set, the teacher or student should determine just what pictures will be needed to tell a complete story. The use of either a "shooting script" or a "storyboard" prevents waste of time and film.

The 2″ × 2″ teaching slides are usually photographically prepared. Simple film shooting with a 35-mm camera and some raw film stock (a tripod is helpful, but not necessary) is followed by laboratory processing. Slides are ordinarily returned mounted in cardboard masks and are ready for use. Hand-drawn slides are possible, but are not practical except for an occasional "fill-in" slide.

Lantern slides, 3¼″ × 4″, have usually been handmade. These slides are made on glass or acetate with such media as colored pencils, India ink, crayons, ceramic pencils, typing on cellophane, and similar simple devices and materials. This slide is easily prepared by students. Its surface area is more than three times that of the 2″ × 2″ slide.

Filmstrip preparation is limited largely to commercial studios, particularly if single frame strips (most commonly used) are desired. In recent years, however, a new copy camera has been developed which makes local production easy. This special camera is not recommended for individual purchase because of its specialized nature, but it is practical for learning resources centers. Teachers who work in a district with such a camera simply take their slides to the center and a filmstrip can be made in a few minutes. The process is inexpensive.

All in all, teacher-made photographic materials—slides, filmstrips, and prints—have become much simpler with new developments by the photographic industry. Instamatic cameras relieve teachers and students of virtually all the guesswork of timing, focus, and other minutiae. Completed pictures, color or monochrome, are pulled from the Polaroid camera a few seconds after exposure. Slide-making kits provide for easy copying of pictures or the photographing of small objects. Even lighting arrangements have been standardized and calibrated.

Now that cheaper and simpler projection equipment has made the creating of slides and filmstrips, particularly slides, so simple, many schools across the country indicate worthwhile results in slide shows produced for virtually all subjects with many types of students from age seven upwards. In some schools, for example, workshops are scheduled for photographic activities. It has been found that the use of cameras cause students to observe, analyze, and interpret. Very soon after students begin camera work they progress from snapping posed pictures of family and friends to composing pictures of person-thing relationships. They see previously unseen pictures and new points of view; they cease to point and snap aimlessly. As work progresses most students show more poise and more satisfaction with school. Through picture making, still or motion, many students are able to communicate more clearly than through verbal methods. As Marshall McLuhan might suggest, the medium becomes part of their message.

Here, too, the visual literacy movement stands to become a part of the regular school curriculum, from kindergarten through the twelfth grade and on into the colleges. Some visual literacy projects, workshops, and conferences have been funded through the Federal Office of Education with assistance from the Eastman Kodak Company. Advocates of visual literacy maintain that "visuals are a language," that visual communication, no less than verbal communication, requires that young people learn to "read" and use visuals accurately and skillfully. Proponents of visual literacy speak of the *syntax* of pictures, of vocabulary, and of the relationships between visual and verbal communication. Emotions, for example, can be communicated by words and phrases, but a picture or pictures can communicate the same emotions equally well. When words join together in sentences they become subject, predicate, object, and possibly modifiers. Pictures, too, can show subject, action, object, and modifiers. Subjects and objects are tied together with actions (for example, *cried, stumbled, pointed, sped*). Concrete objects may be modified (as in *howling dog, haunted house, muddy road*, or *angry clouds*). Furthermore, modifiers and nuances may be added by the "writer in photography" if he

refines his communication by sharp focus, appropriate lighting, skillful close-ups, good cropping, deft angling, effective
contrast, and thoughtful use of color and texture.

Two important uses for slides are worth reviewing before
we leave this popular medium. One is the potential that
slides hold for interdisciplinary work. A good example is the
senior high school teacher who, wishing to explore the
rhythms shared by poetry and music, produced a slide set
with tape accompaniment entitled *Animals in Poetry and
Music*. Using the music of Camille Saint-Saens together with
the poetry of Ogden Nash, Rainer Maria Rilke, and William
Blake, he limited his production to fifteen slides, illustrating
ten poems. All slides were made from photos taken in a local
zoo. A rhinoceros flashed on the screen to accompany
Nash's "The Rhinoceros," with appropriate music from
Saint-Saens' "Carnival of the Animals." As the music shifted,
a tiger appeared, accompanied by lines from William Blake's
"The Tiger":

> Tiger! Tiger! burning bright
> In the forests of the night,
> What immortal hand or eye
> Could frame thy fearful symmetry?

Other pictures, poetry, and music presented a panther, a tor-
toise, a wild jackass, a kangaroo, a gazelle, birds, and cocks
and hens. Others might have been used, but these were sufficient to vitalize the study of rhythm in verse and music.

When used with younger students (in which case one would
use simpler poetry), this kind of multidisciplinary approach
introduces the additional value of *mimetic*, or imitative,
work. Primary students might be asked, "Can you tell from
this picture and this music how an elephant walks?" Such an
activity develops rhythm, intrigues young children, and can
be used to stimulate a desire to draw or finger-paint.

A second effective use of slides is with students not highly
motivated or secure in verbal work. Under a creative history
teacher in the Watts community in Los Angeles, for example,
a group of students produced an unusually compelling slide

show on *The U.S.A.: Land and People*. The slides were divided into two sets: one shot in color, showing beautiful, bright, joyous subjects; the other in monochrome, for drab, cheerless, wasteful aspects of American life. Because field trips and actual photography were not possible for these students at the time, the entire project was accomplished using only books, magazines, and other sources of pictures.[5]

Opaque and Overhead Projections

We have seen how slides and filmstrips bring otherwise inaccessible subjects into the classroom. Opaque and overhead projectors facilitate classwork by making it simple for the teacher to enlarge both accessible material and pictures of inaccessible subjects so that the entire class may view them at once. For example, remarks and corrections written on themes in English composition classes can be projected for the entire class, so that all students can discuss and learn from the errors and strengths of an individual student's paper.

These projections can be used in innumerable other ways in other subject areas. In fact, the following remark made by one teacher after extensive use of the opaque projector (also applicable to the overhead projector) is well taken: "If there is a limit to suggestions for use of these opaque projectors, it is the limit of the imagination!"

OPAQUE PROJECTIONS   Opaque projections are so named because they project opaque material (material through which no light can pass) by means of reflected light. All the other projected materials discussed in this book, in contrast, involve transparent or translucent material. Because opaque projection lacks some of the luminosity of the other forms, it requires the use of a darkened room. The advantage of opaque projection is that there is no need for processing the materials to be projected. Pictures, book pages, charts or

5. Project reported by Thomas Brown and Sam Cockins, Media Coordinators, Department of Teacher Education, University of Southern California.

graphs, postcards, or flat materials of any kind can be projected as they are. Even small three-dimensional materials, such as coins, shells, or tools, may be projected in silhouette. If mounting is necessary, it is simple. Elementary school teachers can project illustrations from supplementary readers so that an entire class can study the picture at one time during the story hour.

In addition to projecting pictures on a screen for class use, opaque projectors enable teachers to enlarge small pictures, maps, and graphs. For example, a small map from a current magazine can be enlarged and copied for group use.

A high school teacher of the author's acquaintance has had splendid success in using pictures in the opaque projector for German conversation. Flat pictures, sometimes supplemented with stick figure drawings, are projected in the opaque projector. A taped recording eliminates the placement of words on the pictures or chalkboard and a consequent translation step. Handout sheets with the German words are used from time to time.

Any familiar situation that can be illustrated pictorially and captured in conversation adds to student interest. Pictures may consist of magazine clippings, $2'' \times 2''$ slides, stick figures, or hand-drawn flash cards. Before showing the pictures, playing the tape, and repeating the conversation, the teacher calls attention to new vocabulary and unusual word structure.[6]

OVERHEAD PROJECTIONS   Unlike the opaque projector which employs reflected light, the overhead projector sends the light through the medium to be projected, hence the name *transparencies* for the materials to be projected. The name *overhead* comes from the fact that in operation the machine throws a picture over the head of the operator. Thus, the machine is used from the front of the room, whereas most projectors are used from the rear of the room. The front-of-the-room position allows the instructor to face

6. From ideas in a lesson plan by Melvin Steinfield, San Diego City Schools.

the class at all times. Eye-to-eye contact is maintained and the teacher has complete control over the presentation as regards timing and sequence of materials.

The overhead projector is widely used. It made its debut with World War II, but improvements in the equipment itself, the great versatility of the method, and a growing list of new ways to prepare materials have resulted in expanded usefulness. Probably no single piece of media equipment has had the growth and impact of the overhead projector in education, industry, the armed services, and all contexts where illustrated presentations are made.

It is even possible to add details by marking with a water soluble felt pen or wax-based pencil directly on the transparency. The markings can be removed easily with a soft cloth. The machine employs an efficient optical system and delivers up to 2000 lumens of light with an incandescent or a new (quartz iodide) bulb. This strong white light makes darkening of the room unnecessary. The projection surface or "stage" is a flat open glass plate over the lamp housing. Stages are large: 7″ × 7″, 8″ × 10″, and sometimes 10″ × 10″. The large stage permits more freedom in the preparation of projection materials, especially when hand-drawn or typed. The projected image is also large. Materials placed on the projection surface are completely visible to the instructor at all times, allowing him to point or otherwise focus attention on specific areas. Additional transparencies can be overlaid on the original so that step-by-step developments or complex information can be shown. On the overhead machine, too, small opaque objects can be projected in silhouette. Parts of transparencies may be covered and used as needed. Color can be abundantly employed. There are so many uses and advantages of this projector that it is no wonder it has received nearly universal acclaim.

Projection materials for the overhead projector are easy to prepare, either in advance of use or by writing directly on acetate sheets or plastic rolls on the spot. A multitude of high quality commercially prepared transparencies are also available. The following outline shows the methods of preparing transparencies either in class or prior to class:

Impromptu (in class): *writing or drawing on single acetate sheets (clear or frosted), writing or drawing on plastic rolls, placing three-dimensional objects on the "stage"*

Handmade (prior to class): *writing or drawing with felt-tip pens or wax-based pencils on transparencies, applying tapes or dry-letter transfers to transparencies, typewriting on transparencies, pasting cut-outs (silhouetted) on transparencies*

Machine-processed: *by spirit duplicator, by thermal copy, by diazo (ammonia process) system, by lift or picture transfer, by electrostatic film, by photocopy film*

Commercially produced: *finished transparencies and overlays, from paper masters*

Processing transparencies with one's own machine requires a certain amount of skill, though it can be acquired readily. Therefore, many teachers have become extremely creative at producing their own handmade transparencies.

Additionally, as a corollary to the rapid rise of overhead equipment, dozens of commercial companies are now producing educational transparencies either as single units or sets. Among the producers are projection equipment manufacturers, textbook publishers who have correlated transparencies with their book publications, film producers, and independent concerns. For the most part, preparation of the transparencies is supervised by technical experts and people involved with curricula. Commercial transparencies are usually in color and of high quality, and include materials such as overlays and sophisticated representations which are beyond the production capabilities of individual teachers or most schools' learning resources centers. Among the commercially prepared materials are packaged *masters* (originals) which are ready for local copying. Prepared on bond paper or translucent tracing paper ready for use in one's own copying machine, these masters are inexpensive and relieve teachers of the burden of detailed preparation.

Transparencies should be mounted in cardboard frames if

they are to be used more than once. Overlays for successive or cumulative use must of necessity be mounted, so that each successive transparency is properly aligned with the previous ones. Data concerning the transparency should be noted on the frame before it is put away. Inasmuch as most transparencies will not exceed $10'' \times 12''$ they can best be filed in standard filing cabinets.

Students, as well as teachers, can learn to prepare transparencies ahead of time and to make use of them in presenting material to the class. Students often feel more comfortable in front of a group of peers if they have "support." Some of the eye focus is diverted from the speaker to the visuals, yet the attention is on the ideas being discussed. And, many students prefer the more sophisticated use of the projector to the chalkboard. In group interaction activities students can mark or diagram their ideas and reactions on sheets of acetate with felt pens or pencils. As other students take turns in the discussion, they, too, can use the transparency to help them present, expound, and defend ideas. Teachers who take turns in instructing the large groups in team teaching pointed out in Chapter 2 find the overhead projector an almost indispensable tool, giving presentation more variety and clarity and helping to hold attention. Transparencies may even be used around the study table.

More evidence of the value of overhead projection is apparent in *Standards for School Media Programs*, which recommend one machine for every ten teaching stations (where *teaching station* is usually synonymous with a classroom), plus one machine for every school learning resources center for schools with "basic" media programs. For schools with "advanced" media programs, the bulletin recommends one machine for every five teaching stations, plus two machines for every school learning resources center.[7] (See Chapter 8, for a further discussion of *Standards for School Media Programs*.)

7. *Standards for School Media Programs* (Chicago: American Library Association; Washington, D.C.: National Education Association, 1969), p. 45.

Other Projections

As opposed to the widespread and versatile projections previously discussed, the stereoprojectors, microprojectors, and tachistoscopes are specialized and limited in use; therefore the preparation of materials for use in these machines is not common among teachers. Stereoprojectors are employed in clinics, laboratories, graduate seminars, and analytical study. Microprojectors are used in the biological sciences. The tachistoscope is a still projector equipped with a controlled, shutter-like mechanism which permits flash exposure. This equipment is used to increase reading rates, recognition rates, and attention spans. The apparatus is specialized, and teachers other than reading specialists will rarely be called on to use it.

FILMS

Almost all the advantages of flat pictures and projected still pictures inhere also in films. In addition, films can show movement, and, because they use so many individual pictures (frames), their coverage of progress or development is especially valuable. Most students find the selective use of films more challenging and dynamic than any other form. By its very nature the film is the best possible bridge available for spanning the time-space gap which we have already cited as an important obstacle to learning.

Although it is not within the scope of this book to discuss all the many exciting innovations that have occurred in educational films in recent years, certain major developments are so important that every teacher needs to be conversant with them.

Full Course Films

In several subject areas—biology, physics, and chemistry, for example—entire courses have been filmed. The films were not made to replace teachers, but to enable teachers to do a more effective job. One distinguished series is a course in high school chemistry consisting of twenty-six study films.

Known as the CHEM Study Films, the series is the result of a study by a committee of the American Chemical Society. The National Science Foundation collaborated in the production, and Atomic Energy Commission Chairman Dr. Glenn T. Seaborg headed the committee responsible for the films. Some were photographed in radiation laboratories, in giant cyclotrons, and in industrial laboratories, with the assistance of the nation's leading chemists. The films show the use of rare, expensive equipment and modern experimental techniques. In the film *Gases and How They Combine*, for example, the film's action is stopped to allow discussion after a significant question has been raised. The projector is then started and the film scientist who posed the original question presents the answer. This technique promotes active student participation.

Several studies of the values of full course films have been made, but they have been inconclusive. In some cases they seem wholly acceptable; other studies, however, show that students in massed film classes tend to dislike the course. To be used to fullest advantage, full course film units usually need to be supplemented with other, integrated instructional materials such as records, student workbooks, and textbooks. These materials are often considered as "kits" with films taking a primary place.

16-mm and 8-mm Films

Instructional motion pictures are almost universally produced in 16-mm width. Both smaller and larger sizes are also possible, however. Recent developments have resulted in increased use of the 8-mm width. Years ago this width was used without any sound accompaniment and was generally limited to home use. The 1960s and early 1970s, however, saw unusual film and optical developments in the narrow width. Currently, 8-mm films can carry either magnetic or optical sound tracks. *Optical sound* is produced when the audio part of a motion picture is "photographed" on film at the same time that the picture is being photographed. Through the action of light and electricity, the soundwaves can be activated simultaneously with the projection of the moving picture. *Magnetic sound*, on the other hand, is recorded on a magnetic stripe running the length of the film and can be recorded either simultaneously with the picture or at another time (it can also be erased and edited). It is activated by a magnetic recording device attached to the projector. Magnetic sound can be converted to optical sound in the laboratory. Overall, the 8-mm development looks like this:

image size: *Standard 8*, *Super 8*, *Format M*

audio: *magnetic sound*, *optical sound*

loading projector: *cartridge load*, *reel load*, *continuous loop*

Despite their identical widths, Super 8 film is 50 percent larger in image area than Standard 8 film, which makes Super 8 films about 10 percent longer than Standard 8 for the same number of frames.

Clearly, standardization is needed, because at the moment the ratio of use of Standard 8 (sometimes called Cine 8) to Super 8 is about 50:50, although Super 8 seems more and more to be the favored size. Format M is practically dead. Approximately the same ratio holds between optical and magnetic sound, as well as between reel and cartridge loading. One 8 mm directory lists more than 500 titles which cover almost every subject from arithmetic to zoology. Several film producers have begun to issue all their releases in both 16 mm and 8 mm. Many educators look to Super 8 for truly revolutionary developments in the future.

Although 8-mm films can be of almost any length, they tend to be relatively short, running from thirty to forty seconds to four or five minutes. Recently, they have tended to confine themselves to one topic and have thus been labeled *single-concept* films. *Shortfilm* and *brief-film* have also been suggested as labels, inasmuch as these films are both short in length and limited in subject matter. They might also be called *target films*, for their unity, emphasis, and coherence enable students to focus upon one problem or idea.

A great backlog of films in other widths—even including

some classic commercial productions—is now being converted to 8 mm. This cutting-down process was inaugurated a quarter of a century ago by a subsidiary of certain Hollywood producers, formed and operated as an educational adjunct. The company's 16-mm releases attempted to abbreviate the commercial releases from two hours or more to the fifty minutes or less necessary for convenient classtime viewing. The single-concept film, on the other hand, utilizes only short segments of classics: for example, a dustbowl sequence from *The Grapes of Wrath* might be five minutes. It should be borne in mind, of course, that no reduction of a previously produced film will automatically result in the transformation of a worthless film into a worthwhile one!

Educational television has become another source of both 8- and 16-mm films. Videotape playback equipment is not always available and is also expensive; hence there is a need for films for use in standard projectors. Any helical scan videotape in half-inch, one-inch, or two-inch format can be duplicated in 16- or 8-mm (Standard or Super 8 film).

Another development in design of 8-mm film is the *modular film*. A modular film contains several segments which can be connected, each of which can also stand alone. Pioneer work on this type of film was done by Robert Wagner of Ohio State University on a grant from the United States Office of Education (OE-3-16-020, 1966). Wagner produced a four-and-one-half-hour "galaxy" film entitled *Communications Theory and the New Educational Media*. The galaxy was broken down into four titles: (1) *The Information Explosion*, (2) *Perception and Communication*, (3) *The Process of Communication*, and (4) *The Teacher and Technology*. Each title was then divided into a series of thirty-one *modules* or subsections, each module essentially a single-concept film of two to eight minutes. The modules could be rearranged into 900 possible combinations. While the administration and distribution of such a galaxy at the district media center level becomes a nightmare of cutting, assembling, rearranging, and maintaining a record of modules, this pattern (one of the most startling in recent years) does provide the teacher with more flexible materials.

A decided boost to 8-mm use came with the self-rewinding, cartridge-loaded 8-mm film projector, which makes it unnecessary to handle the film or to fumble with threading or rewinding. After a film cartridge is snapped into a slot in a projector, the machine is operated automatically by buttons. The projector is simple, inexpensive, and lightweight. Whether this same type of innovation will spread to the 16-mm projector remains to be seen.

A Canadian educator set down, some years ago, a blueprint for the future of 8-mm development which has yet to come to pass:

> ... we want a sound projector as portable as a typewriter, the price of which is to be under a hundred dollars; we want foolproof cartridge loading that will allow for individual operation, unaided, by a five-year-old child; we want thousands of single-concept films, silent and sound, in three- to ten-minute continuous loops, and we will personally supervise the visual treatment in accordance with our professional experience and objectives, these clips to cost no less than cheaper textbooks, no more than the best reference books.[8]

How have we been doing along this line since 1962?

STUDENT PRODUCTION   One sign of progress in 8-mm film use has been the burgeoning numbers of student filmmakers across the country. We have already noted that students are using still cameras, Polaroid and Instamatic, in significant learning situations. Equally notable is student work with film, usually with the 8-mm format. Students of all ages, including primary school children, have proved capable of producing an 8-mm motion picture. In Los Angeles, one kindergarten group made a two-minute film with an Instamatic 8-mm camera and titled it *Travel.* It was done with large building blocks stacked to represent cars, trains, boats, and planes. Although the children received considerable adult help, they felt that they had made a film.

From the age of six upwards, acceptable short film produc-

8. Mark Slade, "Eight Millimeter: The Eighth Lively Art," *Audiovisual Screen and Audiovisual Guide*, 41 (October 1962): 599.

tions are possible, with battery-powered cartridge-loaded Instamatic Standard or Super 8 cameras. Production starts with a storyboard and systematic planning. From the planning stage to final production the participants face realistic problem-solving, but students are accomplished innovators and quickly invent intelligent solutions. Polished production, however, is not as important as student motivation, growth, and the fostering of creativity. In producing a film, students soon learn that they must cooperate, assume responsibilities, and make decisions. Teachers without prior experience are soon able to direct satisfactorily. It is helpful if they have had an opportunity to attend a short film production workshop. Expenses are surprisingly nominal and student growth is well worth the costs.

As the examples in this chapter document, the success and versatility of all pictorial media depend largely on *proper preparation, wise selection, and intelligent use*. The guidelines for effective utilization which have been set out in Chapter 1 apply here as they do in all media, and they will continue to be stressed throughout the following chapters.

Chapter 4

Using Graphics

BEHAVIORAL OBJECTIVES

After studying this chapter, the reader will be able to:

1. Identify the distinguishing feature which makes each of the following a *graphic:* graphs, diagrams, sketches, cartoons, comic strips, posters, graffiti fences, maps, globes, and charts.
2. Describe five types of graphs and draw one example of each.
3. Given four actual learning situations, select from among the following a medium especially well suited to each, supporting the choices: diagrams, cartoons, posters, graphs.
4. Support, and then attack, the statement: "The graffiti fence is an effective instructional medium."
5. Compose a lesson plan for teaching map study skills, incorporating five types of maps.
6. Design a chart summarizing types of charts.
7. Explain, listing the readability criteria for lettering, how lettering in classroom use of both projected and non-projected materials can be made most effective.

Graphics (or *visual symbols*) is a term signifying words, pictures, drawings, or any of a great variety of arbitrary or conventional signs whose purpose is *to render visible something that is invisible.* Graphics simplify and present complicated information (i.e., operations, quantities, qualities, elements, and relations) in condensed form. Someone once defined graphics as "visual shorthand."

Among the commonest communication media, graphics are widely used in industry, advertising, and government to catch attention quickly, present facts succinctly, or "sell" an idea. When graphics are employed in schools, of course, they are used to facilitate student learning. Students must therefore be taught to "read" graphics, much as they are taught to "read" other forms of communication. The present-day teacher or student who cannot read graphics suffers, in fact, from a form of illiteracy. Similarly, the teacher or student who cannot produce graphics lacks one kind of ability to communicate. Simple forms of graphics can be taught as early as kindergarten, later becoming more complex as they are used, in arithmetic and social studies, to represent size, quantity, proportion, and relationship. At the college level they grow in variety and complexity of uses. Today's graphics show startling new technical advances in color reproduction, design, and other attention-getting elements.

We shall not enumerate all the subsidiary graphic forms here. Attention will be focused on seven major forms: graphs, diagrams and sketches, cartoons and comic strips, posters, graffiti fence writing, maps and globes, and charts. Technically, it can be difficult to distinguish one form from another—for example, the differences between a chart and a graph, a diagram and a chart, or a cartoon and a comic figure, are not always easily discernible. At times two or more forms are combined into one representation. As we define each type, we will point out its effective use in instruction.

GRAPHS

A graph is a flat representation employing dots, lines, or pictures to visualize statistics or relationships. Graphs are constructed according to exact specifications. They depict specifically quantitative and numerical data for analysis, interpretation, or comparison. In most instances even very complicated data can be graphed. While the purpose of a graphic representation is to simplify, a good graph will indicate titles and sources of data so that the reader can locate and study the original information. Five common types of graphs will be presented here.

CIRCLE GRAPHS   Circle graphs, sometimes called "pie" or sector graphs, have been found to be the most easily read of all graphs. A quick glance at the relative sizes of portions of a circle graph can disclose the way in which a total entity, be

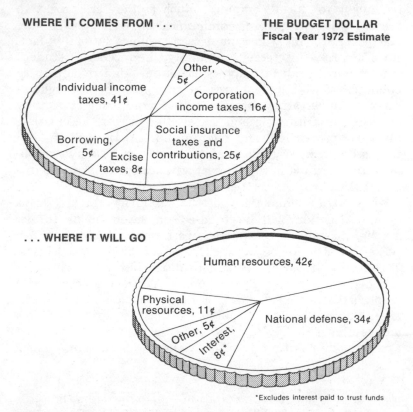

WHERE IT COMES FROM . . .

THE BUDGET DOLLAR
Fiscal Year 1972 Estimate

Other, 5¢

Individual income taxes, 41¢

Corporation income taxes, 16¢

Social insurance taxes and contributions, 25¢

Borrowing, 5¢

Excise taxes, 8¢

. . . WHERE IT WILL GO

Human resources, 42¢

Physical resources, 11¢

Other, 5¢

Interest, 8¢*

National defense, 34¢

*Excludes interest paid to trust funds

Fig. 9. President Nixon's budget message is succinctly summarized by this circle graph.

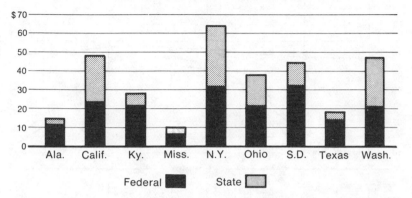

AID TO FAMILIES WITH DEPENDENT CHILDREN
Average monthly payment per recipient

Fig. 10. This bar graph shows not only the average monthly sum received by families with dependent children, but also the source of the funds.

it the U.S. government budget, population of Los Angeles, or drug abuse in New York, is divided into its component parts: i.e., a drug abuse "pie" and its components of heroin, marijuana, "speed," and other drugs.

BAR GRAPHS Bar graphs, arranged vertically or horizontally, are used for comparative purposes. Two or more single bars, to represent, say, political candidates, may be lined up on a graph next to a scale of numbers (total votes) and compared as to which bar (candidate) reaches the higher number of votes. Another use of the bar graph would be, as in the circle graph, to indicate parts of a whole, such as division of votes in a general election, by showing a bar divided into parts with quantities written on each segment. Bar graphs may be arranged to run in two directions to show change in two dimensions, such as profit and loss or decrease and increase.

LINE GRAPHS Line graphs, sometimes referred to as *profiles* or *frequency polygons*, are precise and extremely useful in plotting trends, such as price fluctuations, pollution readings, traffic deaths, and other information, of a time-

CORRELATION BETWEEN MEAN TEMPERATURE, LOCATION, AND ALTITUDE

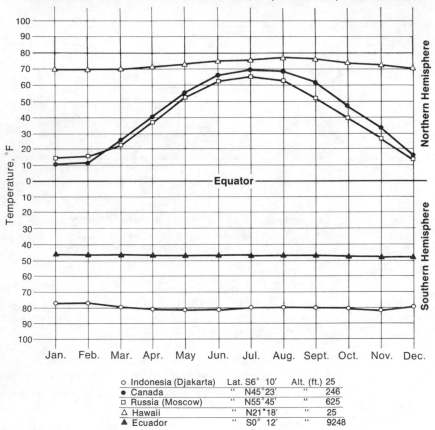

○ Indonesia (Djakarta)	Lat. S6° 10′	Alt. (ft.)	25
● Canada	" N45°23′	"	246
□ Russia (Moscow)	" N55°45′	"	625
△ Hawaii	" N21°18′	"	25
▲ Ecuador	" S0° 12′	"	9248

Fig. 11. Note how much information this line graph carries. Consider how long and detailed a purely verbal description of this data would be. (Data from *New Horizons World Guide*, 16th ed. New York: Pan American Airways, 1969.)

amount character. For example, in a graph reporting train delays, a line representing a railroad company might be followed across the graph as it dips during a time (with periods of time indicated by headings listed horizontally) of a few delays (with number of delays enumerated by vertically listed numbers) and rises during a time of many delays.

AREA GRAPHS Area graphs are employed to show relationships between two or three related totals. Because they employ area or surface to show comparison, they can easily be misinterpreted. The unaided eye is not a good judge of area. Artists frequently give a third dimensional effect to graphs of this type, but this feature may make the graphs less easily interpreted, especially by school-age children.

PICTORIAL GRAPHS In pictorial graphs, picture-like figures, or small silhouettes are substituted for bars, lines, and shaded areas. One might show the relative incomes of men and women in a particular trade by drawing male and female figures dressed in work clothes, with differences in height of the figures depending upon the differences, if any, in their incomes. Pictures represent an almost universal language in graphing, although they are not as exact as other graph types because there is a certain amount of estimation on quantity. Children like this type of graph, perhaps because it is "less abstract" to them than other forms of graphs.

All the above types of graphs serve the same purpose: that is, they tell a story easily and quickly. The type of graph selected for a specific purpose *depends, as has been shown, on the facts to be told and the age audience for which it is intended.*

DIAGRAMS AND SKETCHES

Diagrams employ lines to show relationships. Usually their use requires a certain amount of background and understanding by both teacher and students. For example, electrical circuit diagrams can be highly abstract.

Sketches, on the other hand, as used by most teachers, are simple, impromptu drawings. The industrial arts teacher may step to the chalkboard and sketch the difference between the teeth of the crosscut saw and those of the ripsaw. In elementary science the teacher may sketch the difference between claws of birds and those of animals. A sketch serves an immediate and specific purpose and is then erased. Of course, materials likely to be used repeatedly may be placed on large posters and kept for further use.

CARTOONS AND COMIC STRIPS

Cartoons and comic strips are grouped together here because they are similar. A *cartoon* is an interpretive picture which makes use of symbolism, often bold exaggeration, to present at a glance a message or point of view concerning news events, people, or situations. The *comic strip* is a serial or continuous comical pictorial story.

Cartoons

A cartoon employs many of the principles of caricature: grotesque and ludicrous exaggeration, or the distortion of parts of a whole to emphasize the part—for example, a nose, a chin, a style of haircut, or the length of a cigarette holder.

The educational value of the cartoon is generally accepted. Research suggests that thirteen is the earliest age at which children can be expected to make correct interpretations of exaggerated drawings. Before this age, meaningful reading of the captions is also a factor.

A study of 300 junior and senior high school teachers' use of cartoons showed these interesting findings: (1) all of the teachers indicated that they favor the use of cartoons for one reason or another, but not all were using cartoons in their classrooms at the time; (2) 97 percent of the students indicated that they like to have their teachers use cartoons; (3) the greatest use of cartoons was made by teachers of social studies, English, and mathematics; (4) the reasons given for use of cartoons were illustration, attention-getting, clarity, emphasis, and humor; (5) in most classrooms it is possible to find students who can help teachers prepare cartoons for classroom use: 89 percent of the students polled felt that there were students in the class who had cartoon ability, while 39 percent actually claimed that they had the talent; and (6) both students and teachers overwhelmingly approved of textbooks that employ cartoon illustrations.[1]

Cartoons do have drawbacks. Frequently they employ stereotypes which may have lost some of their original vitality. For example, the bulldog which represents England or English characterisitcs and the donkey and the elephant which symbolize American ,political parties have lost their original humor. Another disadvantage is that cartoons are often quite abstract and depend on a rather full background for correct interpretation.

Clearly, the effective use of these drawings depends directly on the nature of the teaching-learning situation. In journalism class, for example, the editorial cartoon may serve well, but in social studies the historial cartoon may have better application.

Cartoons are useful in the classroom in four ways: on the chalkboard, on the bulletin board, as "handouts," and as projections. All these techniques are time-consuming, so that the value of the material must be weighed against the time involved in preparation.

The transfer of cartoon to chalkboard can be accomplished effectively by techniques described in Chapter 6. Bulletin or display board use is similar to chalkboard use. It should be remembered that cartoons simply pinned on the board have little or no value. Frequently they are there as space fillers and fulfill no educational objectives other than the vague hope that they will motivate students in some mysterious way. If either chalkboard or bulletin board use is contemplated, teachers should encourage students to assist in the production of cartoons. Cartoons from newspapers, magazines, and the like can be easily copied on a stencil and mimeographed for general distribution to students, to be used as the teacher plans.

Another common technique for cartoon use is to project

1. Dean A. Leptich, "The Effective Use of Cartoons by the Secondary-School Teacher" (Unpublished Master's Thesis, San Diego State College, 1960).

the drawing so that the entire class can see it at one time. The opaque projector is ideal for this purpose because the cartoon needs no processing before use. With a little effort, it is possible to put cartoons into a form for use on the overhead projector or the 2″ × 2″ or 3¼″ × 4″ slide projector.

Some yardsticks help teachers decide when and where to use cartoons. A cartoon must be constructive, capture the interest of the students, directly relate to the subject under study, be within the maturity level of the students so that they can correctly interpret the implications, and be handled so that the students are able to evaluate the point of view pictured.

Comic Strips

Comic strips are a debatable educational tool. Some educators feel they are a form of infantilism, while others accept them because of their almost universal appeal, especially to younger children. Those who defend the comics say they are amusing, generally easy to read, exciting, and satisfying to a child's idea of art. Since comic strips are here to stay, probably the best advice about their use is to say: use them judiciously and as they fit but encourage better comics and a gradual switching to other forms of communication.

POSTERS

The poster, usually symbolic in nature, is designed to convey its message even more quickly and succinctly than other graphics. Usually, posters carry a single idea and make extensive use of slogans. They are characterized by boldness, strong color, large lettering, and, often, exaggeration.

Schools use posters for announcing events, promoting campaigns or issues, teaching ideas or processes, and as reminders. Poster-making and the employment of posters to communicate can begin in the primary grades, with the simple message of "Don't Run—Walk" and can continue throughout school with posters about fire safety, brotherhood, littering, and the like.

The fostering of curiosity and the development of classroom atmosphere are two objectives fostered by posters. Many teachers use posters to carry out these objectives as part of their readiness program in starting new units of work. The social studies teacher who begins a unit on Mexico, for example, can use travel posters advantageously at the start of the unit. Posters also serve in developmental work and in concluding activities.

GRAFFITI FENCE WRITING

Among the uses of graphics not always recognized as a curriculum activity is drawing or writing on a *graffiti fence*, or any easily accessible surface that has been prepared for the impromptu writing of students—walls, "fences," or other areas reachable at standing height. The technique is old and promotes unstructured, uninhibited communication by individuals of ideas, poems, fantasies, expressions, art, or what-have-you. Many people of almost any age seem to be stimulated by a fence or blank wall, plus some paint, charcoal, colored crayons, paper strips and a hand stapler, or other cheap materials. The high construction fence around a new building on almost any college campus is a commonplace example of the wide appeal of graffiti.

Some teachers may throw up their hands at the thought of any educational value to be derived from such a medium. Others, particularly those who work in urban areas, recognize the uncensored, uninhibited writings and drawings on fences, sidewalks, and walls as an avenue by which young people express themselves. For many alienated, or disturbed youth, graffiti work is a natural and creative way to relate to one's environment.

Questions come to mind in connection with graffiti. How much encouragement should teachers lend? Should teachers lay down rules? Structure the work? How much of the hip language of the street should be permitted? If the school condones graffiti, will the activity encourage or discourage defacement of public and private property? Will the "fence" become a public bulletin board for anti-this and anti-that sentiments? Will it stir up animosities and/or gang territoriality? As with so many media, the surrounding environment, including teacher encouragement and direction, will determine whether this medium will truly allow students to *express* themselves or simply to *assert* themselves.

MAPS AND GLOBES

Some consider maps and globes as graphics, others as flat pictures, and others place them in a separate category. They are discussed here under graphics because, like graphics, they delineate by symbols, words, and drawings, and they employ lines in their representation.

Maps and globes are designed to show relationship, to indicate what the earth, or part of the earth, looks like, and to locate land and ocean masses. Both are scaled: maps are two-dimensional, globes three-dimensional. In use, maps and globes complement and supplement each other. The reading of maps and globes must be learned because, in addition to the line representation, they employ many symbols, colors, shadings, stars, tiny circles, and legends. Because they are so drastically reduced in size (an inch, for example, represents hundreds or thousands of miles), they must omit details and condense much of the information they include.

Maps

Maps serve many purposes. They provide students with a knowledge of both relative and exact positions of political units, land masses, and water areas. They also furnish information about areas, distances, directions, shapes, sizes, and relationships. In addition, they add meaning to straight descriptive material. Finally, they stimulate interest in people, places, and geographical study. The map has an importance today which has seldom been matched. Each day's news spotlights areas around the world which citizens need to locate and to understand—Vietnam, Israel, Biafra, Bangladesh, and so on. The threats of war, the "buffer" nations, and the explosion of new political groups make geographical understanding imperative. The map can be a permanent learning tool. When well taught, it remains with an individual throughout life.

Fig. 12. Map study need not be an isolated unit. Here, elementary school students integrate it with social studies by connecting the native lands of immigrants to America with the U.S. towns in which they settled. (Photo, courtesy Pittsburgh Public Schools.)

Obviously, no one map can accomplish all of the above; hence there are a variety of maps for specialized purposes.

PHYSICAL-POLITICAL MAPS   The physical-political map, the most common classroom and textbook map, usually shows political boundaries, mountains, rivers, cities, deserts, and water forms. Usually it is in color, used to mark off boundaries and to represent elevations. The following international scheme of map coloring is generally used:

blue: *water*
green: *lowlands (less than 1,000 ft. above sea level)*
yellow: *1,000–2,000 ft. above sea level*

Fig. 13. An "Actionmap," designed for floor use and measuring 12½'
× 8', at an open house in Houston. (Photo, courtesy Dennoyer-
Geppert.)

tan: *2,000–5,000 ft.*
orange: *5,000–10,000 ft.*
brown (sometimes red): *10,000 ft. and above*

RELIEF MAPS   Relief maps show the earth's surface and
bring out elevations, irregularities, and other topographic
features.   Most classroom relief maps make use of coloring,
shading, contour lines, or photography of a simulated three-
dimensional type.   Patented processes are now available so
that a high-grade camera lens will show with a three-
dimensional effect the surface of the earth or moon.   Recent
satellite photographs are useful in this connection.   Actual
three-dimensional maps may be constructed by students or

Fig. 14. This lunar satellite photograph (taken from the spacecraft Lunar Orbiter, 28.4 miles above the moon's surface) yields geographic data useful in creating a relief map of the moon. NASA reports that this photo gave scientists the following information: "Mountains rising from the flat floor of the crater are 1,000 feet high with slopes up to 30 degrees . . . . Cliffs on the rim of the crater are 1,000 feet high . . . . From the horizon to the base of the photograph is about 150 miles. The horizontal distance across the part of the crater shown in this photograph is about 17 miles." (Photo, courtesy NASA.)

the teacher, with the contours scaled to an appropriate size for the classroom.

PICTORIAL-STATISTICS MAPS Among the specialized types of maps are those which make use of pictures, dots, "isotypes," or other symbols or drawings to show location of important data or relationships. A pictorial map need not be statistical. For example, students may be asked to tack samples of various products on it in order to fix general ideas, rather than amounts, to the areas represented.

ROAD AND AIRPLANE MAPS   Road maps are so common that they are taken for granted, but this does not mean that children, or adults for that matter, read them easily and comprehensively. They can be used effectively as a tool for teaching map-reading.

The airplane or polar air-age map is relatively new. It provides the reader with a visual concept of the land and sea as seen from either the North or South Pole. With increasing air travel, this map assumes great importance. People are beginning to understand that the shortest distance between two points on the globe is not a straight line but an arc or a great circle connecting the two points with the plane of the arc passing through the center of the globe. International air travel follows these great circles. Students can compare the route between Los Angeles and Copenhagen on an air-age map with that on a Mercator map, for example.

According to reports of teachers, polar maps are difficult for students to understand. Students experience difficulty because a polar map puts North in the center—not at the top—and South in any direction outward. In working with polar maps, it is essential to use globes, at least until the basic map-reading concepts are established.

OUTLINE MAPS   The outline map is simply a skeleton which gives little more than boundary markings. It is designed so that students place information on it, or adapt it as study dictates. Sometimes these are called work maps, and they are available in sizes ranging from the large wall type to the 8-½" X 11" size for individual work. The outline feature is also employed in some globes.

In addition to paper and cloth outline maps, teachers find the "write-on" map extremely useful. This map is printed on rubberized fabric and functions as a chalkboard. Teachers or students can chalk—or crayon—in names, trace routes, or outline areas as other students watch. Write-on maps, and globes as well, are available in colors much as are modern chalkboards. Maps of this type encourage active student participation.

Maps are presented to students in three forms—in desk or individual type, wall type, and as projected pictures. Desk maps can be purchased in printed form, or they can be reproduced by ditto or mimeograph stencils. Usually wall maps are paper or cloth and are displayed for group use. Maps can be shown as films, slides, filmstrips, opaque projections, and transparencies and overlays.

ATLASES   Most schools, at least most secondary schools, are equipped with atlases. An atlas is a collection of maps bound together. In addition to its graphic features, it is a gazetteer and guidebook.

Globes

The globe has been defined as "an artificial sphere on the surface of which are drawn maps of the land and water bodies of the earth or a representation of the heavens." Terrestial globes show the land and water bodies; celestial globes show the sky and heavenly bodies.

In most respects the globe is a better representation of places and distances than the map because it shows the entire earth's surface, but the globe is on such a small scale that students frequently have difficulty in interpretation. Globes are used to maximum advantage when they are correlated with flat maps.

Globes can be as small as three inches in diameter, but for school use, anything under eight inches is of doubtful value, and globes of twelve, sixteen, and twenty inches may be more appropriate depending upon specific instructional application and whether they are to be used by large groups, small groups, or individuals.

The value of the write-on globe has already been pointed out. Other special models of value are such recent innovations as deflatable rubber globes, plastic globes, and those made of pressed paper pulp. All are called "work" models.

Use of Maps and Globes in Teaching

Primary school students have almost no place-orientation ability. They find their way from place to place by habit rather than by place understanding. Teachers can introduce map ideas by beginning with the immediate environment and obvious locations. A drawn outline of the classroom, indicating doors, windows, and furniture placement, is a good starting place. The teacher should always stress the fact that the drawing is a representation which stands for something and is smaller than reality. Floor maps on which students can place models of homes, schools, churches, automobiles, and other familiar things help develop orientation and place meaning. Field trips and place understanding go hand in hand. A simple mapping of the schoolyard, a safe way to go to the market, or the location of a harbor with coastline, docks, ships, and related areas are all good approaches. By the end of the third grade, students should have acquired some understanding of basic map symbols for land and sea areas. The globe is extremely useful in the primary grades, and students should have both structural and instructional opportunities to handle and study it. They soon learn to note the poles, equator, and the land and water areas.

Understandings which can be developed about maps and globes in the intermediate grades and high school include: road map use, the idea of scale, computing and expressing directions (linear measurement), the meaning of area-size, the meaning of meridians and parallels, understanding map distortion, and practice in tracing great circle routes.

Although much of the teaching of these concepts falls to social studies teachers, the map is a cultural tool which all teachers should be able to teach.

SELECTION AND SOURCES Most beginning teachers will have little opportunity to assist in making map selections for district use, but they will need to select some for their classes. The teacher should concentrate on what is available from numerous sources, such as commercial map companies, government agencies, nonprofit agencies and societies, and other distributors of free and inexpensive materials.

CORRELATION WITH OTHER INSTRUCTIONAL MEDIA The optimum use of maps and globes is made in conjunction with other learning resources such as field trips, films, bulletin boards, television, and printed materials. Flat pictures can materially aid in the use of map understanding in the elementary grades. Motion pictures heighten and extend map knowledge. The use of slide, opaque, and overhead projections has the additional capacity to enhance student achievement by providing the abstract skill of map reading with multiple, less abstract, referents.

As an example, let us consider a high school teacher of German who uses a map to provide enrichment by showing the way of life of central European German-speaking peoples. She structures her map use as follows:

Basic Learning Objective:
Students will be able to cite orally, first in English, then in German, one example each of the influences of geography upon the social, political, cultural, and economic life of a country whose language they are studying.

Basic Teaching Strategy:
Austria, a good example of a mid-European German-speaking nation, is selected as the country around which this project is developed for this second-year class in German.

The Influence on Austria of Her Neighbors
Specific Learning Objectives:
In a test written in German and in English, students will be able to:
– locate Austria and her six neighbors, given a small outline map of Central Europe

– list the seven countries of Central Europe in order of area size

– list two influences of each country on Austria

– name the language spoken in each country

Specific Teaching Strategy:
A large map of central Europe is used for the study. Stress is placed on the general location of the country, its borders, size, topographical features, and the reasons for the language spoken. Members of the class are then divided into six groups—one each

for Austria's neighbors: Germany, Italy, Switzerland, Yugoslavia, Hungary, and Czechoslovakia. Each group then studies and discusses what possible influences its assigned country might have had on Austria. These influences are then listed on the board in German. Next, the group prints these influences on colored paper arrows and pins them to the map.

Topographical Influences on Austria
Specific Learning Objectives:
  Given a large wall map of Central Europe, students will be able, in German and in English, to:

  – trace the waterways and mountain ranges of the seven countries

  – describe three influences of the Danube River on Austria

  – locate Austria's major cities on the map and give a plausible geographical explanation as to why each developed.

Specific Teaching Strategy:
  Students now study the topography of the country and, as they do so, again pin names on mountains, passes, valleys, rivers, lakes, cities, and trade centers. The main highways of Austria will be heavily inked on the map, noting particularly border crossings by the use of arrows. Students will be encouraged to discuss crops, wine industry, forestry, and industry. At this point the map study will be supplemented with films.

Geographical Influences on Austria's Arts
Specific Learning Objectives:
  Students will be able to:

  – mark in German on a small map of Austria the location of highly developed forms of arts and crafts: art, music (folk and classical), dance, literature, textile design, and such home crafts as embroidery, wood and metal carving, and toy-tinkering

  – make a written, one-page German report on the Salzburg Music Festival

Specific Teaching Strategy:
  Students will be asked to research and point out the areas where folk music and art flourish. Essentially, these will be Salzburg, Graz, Innsbruck, and Vienna. Use will be made of recordings and collections of wood-carving, embroidery, petit-point, inlaid-wood work, and metal carving.

Contemporary Austria: A Product of Her Location
Specific Learning Objectives:
  Students will be able to:

  - show on the map why Vienna's location and geographical
    characteristics made it a key point in German, American,
    and Russian war and/or reconstruction efforts

  - debate forcefully with each other in German Austria's delicate
    position between East and West

  - locate on a large map of Europe at least two examples of
    small countries somewhat similar to Austria in geographical
    and cultural influences

  - write in German three major influences of geography on the
    Austrian population, well enough to receive a grade of at
    least 75 in syntax.

Specific Teaching Strategy:
  In this last step students will discuss the influences of the
  density of population, climate, the struggle of the nation to
  survive numerous wars, and the mixture of ethnic groups.
  The occupational zones after World War II will be discussed,
  as well as policies of the various occupational forces and
  Austria's present sympathies and antipathies. The rebuilding
  process has been hard for Austria because of her lack of raw
  materials and her long distance from great world markets.
  The map will hold the key to an understanding of the problems
  and resources of this small, German-speaking nation.[2]

CHARTS

A chart is a visual symbol which may employ other
graphics—diagrams, cartoons, pictures, graphs, drawings—and
even verbal materials for the purpose of providing a concise
visual summarization of ideas and concepts. (Diagrams are
frequently misclassified as charts but, as we have seen, diagrams employ *lines only*.) If we define a *chart* as a graphic
which gives information in tabular, graphic, or diagrammatic
form, we can see that it lends itself to a variety of uses by
anyone wishing to present data visually and concisely.

Charts can be created on paper, poster boards, chalkboards,
magnetic boards, flannel boards, or fabrics. (See Chapter 6

2. Reported by Anne-Marie Shed, San Diego City Schools.

for a detailed discussion of chalkboards, magnetic boards, and flannel boards.) Several chart designs are possible. One might incorporate progression, for example, by using a *strip chart*. As each step in the lesson is discussed, a paper strip attached to the appropriate section of the chart is removed and the new step illustrated. Progression which requires entirely new figures may be shown by using a *flip chart*. A flip chart is made by attaching together as many sheets of newsprint as are necessary to show the steps in the progression, in a way that facilitates simply "flipping" over each page of graphic material for each step. A flip chart may be mounted to an easel by rings or strips of metal or wood, for easier presentation.

More details on types of charts follow:

Experience Charts

Used by primary and intermediate school teachers, experience charts record visually stories, news, or experiences of the class. At other grade levels, they are used for directions and routine tasks.

Organization Charts

As their name suggests, organization charts show how parts are organized into a whole: as this organization varies, so do the types of organization charts:

FLOW CHARTS Flow charts show sequence and relationships: for example, United Nations structure, governmental branches, student government.

STREAM CHARTS Stream charts show how several events or items come together to form a larger event: for example, contributions to a campaign, income of a corporation, sources of county taxes.

TREE CHARTS Tree charts are the reverse of stream charts. For example, they can be used to show by-products from a given substance, such as petroleum; derivatives from a main channel; school program; and so on.

TABULAR CHARTS   Tabular charts depict tabular data: for example, profit and loss, balance sheets, export and import, time tables, and television program schedules.

PROCESS CHARTS   Process charts illustrate steps in making something, or succession of events: for example, making a silk screen print, developing a photographic print, causes of war, making an apron.

Time Charts

Sometimes called time lines, time charts show relationships of historical events, chronology, growth changes: for example, inventions of transportation, ages of mankind, American fictional writers in time sequence.

Other Charts

MAP CHARTS   Map charts include maps, dots, and other symbols to show comparisons and relationships: for example, television coverage of national networks, population by areas, grain production, national parks.

PICTORIAL CHARTS   Pictorial charts include conventional or symbolized pictures: for example, bags of grain, ships, size of armed forces, natural resources, industrial output, basic foods in a diet, wood finishes.

ISSUE CHARTS   Issue charts present side-by-side comparisons, contrasts, or points of view: for example, political party platforms, advantages and disadvantages of the Common Market, gold and silver money standard.

All the above types of charts appear commonly in books, magazines, newspapers, and other reading matter. Teachers should gain as much experience in constructing them as they can, because there is almost no limit to their usefulness. In addition to teacher- or teacher/student- prepared charts, there are many commercially prepared charts which school districts supply to teachers. Purchased chart materials usually are more complicated than those which can be produced by teachers, and in general are more permanent. Beautiful multicolored commercial charts are available in virtually any area the teacher wishes to explore.

LETTERING

No discussion of graphics would be complete without some mention of lettering, especially its value to clear communication and some of the more conventional devices used in good lettering composition. Legibility is the key to effective displays, chalkboard presentations, projected media, and other visual forms involving the use of words, numerals, or symbols.

Readability criteria for lettering include:

- appropriateness
- simplicity
- legibility
- spacing
- line separation
- capital letters for short titles
- capitals and lower-case letters for longer captions and phrases
- script letters for chalkboard and to a lesser degree for posters and displays

The most common use of handwriting learning materials (script or print) is probably at the chalkboard. At times teachers tend to employ the chalkboard as a routine device, and consequently presentations may become slipshod. Commonest errors lie in the size and strength of the lettering. Letters that are too small or too faint lessen or negate learning values. Classrooms may be twenty or thirty feet, or more, in length. For reading at thirty feet letters should be 2½ inches in height. They should be properly spaced and written in a bold readable style such as gothic. Some teachers have difficulty in keeping lines vertical so that the writing bends noticeably uphill or downhill. Such a fault can easily be corrected by using shorter lines or by using a dot at both starting and ending points of the line. An occasional stepping back from the board for an optical aiming is helpful.

Teachers who have had no special art training often feel at a disadvantage in lettering posters and display materials. Such need not be the case, because of the many lettering techniques and devices now available. Among these are:

Typewriter: a primary medium, supplies large boldface type with high legibility, especially suitable for titles and subtitles, clean keys and fresh ribbons a necessity.

Three-dimensional Lettering: allow use of wood, cardboard, cork, plastic, fabric, and other substances with or without pin backs; relatively inexpensive; excellent for titles and work to be photographed; usually reusable.

Paper Cutouts: easy to use; allow color variety; available inexpensively at stationers'; must be gummed or pinned to background.

Gummed-back Cutouts: good for titles and labels; easy to use and inexpensive; come in many styles and sizes.

Freehand Cutouts: require practice and skill, but are pleasingly artistic; can be any color; require only scissors and paper.

Dry-transfer Lettering: available in large sheets, many styles and sizes, and color or monochrome; applied by pressure; neat and professional in appearance; relatively inexpensive.

Freehand Lettering: done with felt pens (bevel-edged or sharp-tipped), small brushes, colored chalks, wax pencils, inks, or watercolors.

Stencils: purchased from stationers; come in many sizes and styles; made from materials of cardboard, plastic, wood, or metal.

Lettering Guides: require special pens, guide blocks, and templates; come in numerous styles and sizes; are sometimes expensive; necessitate practice and unhurried preparation; can be messy for the unskilled.

Stamped Lettering: involves pressure, or heat and pressure, or embossing; requires equipment; results are of professional quality.

Spraying and Shading: involves color spraying with an air brush or pressurized paint can; requires translucent color sheets with adhesive wax backing; has limited school use; recommended for professionals.

PROJECTION GRAPHICS

Some teachers will have occasion to produce graphic materials which will be used in slides, filmstrips, transparencies, motion pictures, and television. Others will have few occasions to prepare such materials. Because these are specialized visual forms, teachers should consult specialists in charge of film or television production. Most learning resources centers can provide such assistance.

A few general cautions and directions may be of value to all teachers. In the first place, careful pre-planning is essential. Graphics are an integral part of any production and must receive the same care and attention given to any part of the program. No small part of this planning is that of setting aside adequate time to do a satisfactory job. Another consideration is that of size. Letters, figures, and symbols must stand out for easy reading. The teacher planning to prepare projection or television visuals should consult supervisors or technicians for formulas governing size. The Eastman Kodak Company recommends the dimensions in Table 1.

Production authorities recommend that outlines or lists should be limited to four or five lines each containing no more than four or five words.

It must be borne in mind that the television format is in the ratio of 3:4. Graphic materials should be arranged in this proportion. There is also a loss of one-sixth the marginal area on each side when images are picked up on television receivers. At present most school television receivers are black and white; therefore, materials prepared in colors are transmitted as blacks, whites, and grays.

Graphics and visuals should be prepared on television illustration cardboard (sometimes referred to as French gray, with 14 ply recommended). If an $11'' \times 14''$ board is used, the working area is restricted to $6'' \times 8''$ in the center. For a $14'' \times 17''$ board the working area is $9'' \times 12''$ (note the

Table 1. Minimum Letter Sizes*

Medium	Maximum viewing distance	Ratio of letter height to height of art-work area	MINIMUM LETTER HEIGHT (LOWER-CASE LETTER M)	
			For area 6¾" X 9"	For area 9" X 12"
Slides, filmstrips, transparencies, motion pictures	6W[†]	1 to 50	0.13"	0.18"
Television	12W	1 to 25	0.27"	0.36"

Legibility Standards for Projected Materials, pamphlet S-4 (Eastman Kodak Company: n.d.); also, *Artwork Size Standards for Projected Visuals*; pamphlet S-12 (Eastman Kodak Company: n.d.).
[†]W-horizontal dimension of the picture on the screen.

ratio of 3:4). Lettering should be simple and bold, using an appropriate technique or device mentioned above. Teachers planning to use illustration boards should work closely with studio technicians, especially if they plan any complicated changing of titles or animation.

GRAPHIC ASSISTANCE FROM THE LEARNING RESOURCES CENTER

School districts with learning resources centers are usually able to provide substantial graphic assistance. These centers often maintain artists and craft specialists on their staffs who advise teachers about construction and use of graphic materials in their teaching. Most learning centers stock a variety of raw materials, which are available to teachers on request. In some instances, the learning resources staff will assist with the actual work. However, this is not likely to be the case unless the completed product is something with a wide application—that is, a product that can be used by several teachers or several buildings.

When graphic services have been decentralized, the teacher must become a do-it-himself producer. He can seek guidance from art teachers, industrial art teachers, the building audio-visual coordinator, and others, but in the end he must develop the necessary skills and do his own work.

IMPLICATIONS OF GRAPHICS FOR TEACHERS AND STUDENTS

This discussion of the use of graphic materials cannot be closed without highlighting some of the ideas already presented.

Remember these simple slogans: graphs show *relationships*, diagrams show *how*, cartoons *exaggerate for emphasis*, posters show *concepts*, maps show *where*, and charts show *how much*.

The graphics media described in this chapter provide concreteness, motivation, economy, and creativity in learning.

In our discussion of graphics and pictorial media, the importance of visual literacy has been stressed. If the student cannot adequately interpret what he or she sees on a graph, chart, map, diagram, or what-have-you, then much of the value of these media is certainly lost. This premise of student readiness, which goes hand in hand with those of teacher preparedness and wise selection of media, will once more be borne out in Chapter 5's focus on effective listening as a basis for use of audio media.

Chapter 5

Using Auditory Media

BEHAVIORAL OBJECTIVES

After studying this chapter, the reader will be able to:

1. Compare and contrast records and tapes, covering function, fidelity, operation, editing, cost, storage and handling, speeds, and maximum length of play.
2. Construct a lesson plan employing two of the following functions of recordings: musical effects, presentation of subject matter, and poetry study.
3. Identify four advantages of the cassette tape recorder for individualized instruction.
4. Design a remedial or make-up lesson utilizing a listening post for a subsection of a class.
5. Construct a lesson plan employing Telelecture, following the seven guidelines for media use set forth in Chapter 1.
6. Support, and then attack, the statement, "Radio is an obsolete medium."
7. Identify two considerations that ensure optimum utility of a public address system.

Like visual stimuli, the world of sound has great potential as an avenue of learning. Schools have always relied on the voice of the teacher as a major medium for the transmission of knowledge. But recent developments in the use of sound, both with and without pictures, are changing auditory communications as much as or more than the invention of printing did five centuries ago. Whereas it was difficult, in the early days of audiovisual development, for teachers to work audio into the mainstream of instruction, today's conception of the teacher's role has expanded to include the use of *better planned* sound. New emphases on learning objectives and rapid technological innovation, too, have helped bring better planned sound usage into wider and wider acceptability.

This chapter will discuss media that are primarily auditory: records, tapes, radio broadcasts, wireless microphones and listening stations, and various instructional systems based on sound.

EFFECTIVE LISTENING

Before exploring common auditory devices, we should note that their proper use depends upon good listening skills. Listening is an often overlooked communication skill, even though it clearly plays a significant role in learning. It is not planned for and taught as a skill, as are reading, writing, and speaking. The assumption has been that students can and do listen, if told to do so. Recently, however, a new view of this aspect of communication has emerged, especially in the elementary school.

Elementary school children spend from one-half to two-thirds of their school day listening: to instructions, to class discussions, to conversations, to reports, to readings, to teacher comments, to outside noises. The quality of a child's listening, we now realize, has a direct bearing on the learning achieved and the study habits formed—throughout that child's career in school. Thus listening, although it has no content area of its own, is very much a part of the curriculum. The ability to grasp meaning from auditory stimuli is as complex and as important as the ability to grasp meaning from visual stimuli.   Every teacher needs to consciously develop this ability in his students. Every class period, every assignment, every activity of the day's program demands that students listen, for one reason or another. These situations are natural opportunities for direct or indirect instruction in listening techniques.

Research evidence shows clearly that discriminative listening can be taught. The objectives and techniques in teaching listening to elementary and secondary school students are essentially the same: first, building a positive attitude toward listening, including a respect for the skill; and, second, providing practice in listening through planned opportunities to use auditory media, and through instruction in how to sort out fact from fiction, how to recognize major and minor points, and the like.

The National Education Association recommends to the attention of educators the following facts about listening:

Listening cannot be forced.

Listening cannot be measured with total precision.

Listening is a skill to be developed for the duration of a lifetime.

Listening is related to the pattern of courtesy.

Motivation is essential to listening.[1]

Listening experiences can be said to occur on three levels: appreciative, informative, and/or critical. Listening is *appreciative* when an emotional result is anticipated, *informative* when acquisition or recall of facts is important, and *critical* when judgment is involved. Even kindergartners listen on all three levels.

RECORDS AND TAPES

Recorded sound, on either disc records or magnetic tape, is a vibrant instructional material and is important in any dis-

1. "How To Teach Better Listening," *Elementary Instructional Service* (Washington, D.C.: National Education Association, 1962), p. 4.

cussion of instructional media. Recordings are easy to use and are completely under the teacher's control, unlike television, radio, and some aspects of films. Flexibility in timing, reuse, and availability of materials is a major advantage. A recording may be played through continuously to the end, stopped, started, replayed, or interlaced with other learning materials. Recordings are suitable for use with students of all ages and with groups of any size, as well as in programs of individual study.

With the growing fidelity (or accuracy of reproduction) of recorded sound, the volume and range of recordings have grown by leaps and bounds, stimulating ever new uses and a continuing improvement in playback equipment. Long-playing records and transcriptions free teachers from having to attend to the machine frequently, allowing more attention to utilization.

Disc recordings were originally grooved for 78 revolutions per minute, but newer developments have added the 15, $33\frac{1}{3}$, and the 16 rpm.

Possibly no electronic development has had more significance for education than the magnetic tape recorder. Not only is it capable of capturing and storing original sound, but it makes the recording available instantaneously without the use of any additional playback equipment. Like phonographs, magnetic tape recordings have versatility in playing speeds. School tape recorders now operate at two or three speeds, usually $1\frac{7}{8}$, $3\frac{3}{4}$, and $7\frac{1}{2}$ inches per second with a few systems at $\frac{15}{16}$ ips.

Cassette Tape Recorders

Miniaturization has entered the field of recording in the form of the *cassette tape*. The term *cassette* is used in tape systems to refer to a unit of two parts—a miniaturized tape and a housing or magazine which encloses the tape. A specially designed recorder and/or playback machine completes the system. The cassette magazine is a flat plastic case smaller than a deck of cards; together with its enclosed tape, it is also called a *cartridge*. There are two hubs in each cas-

sette, and the tape moves from one to the other. Cassettes
are usually sonically sealed, although a few can be opened.
The tape itself is $1/7''$ wide and runs through the machine at
$1 7/8$ ips.

The cassette tape recorder is exceedingly simple to operate.
The cassette is dropped into place without any threading or
touching of the tape itself, as in reel-to-reel tape systems.
The teacher need merely push buttons to play or record without any fussing about the loose tape ends, scratching, or
breaking. The cassette tape can be turned over, and a new
recording played in the opposite direction, much like the
"flip side" of a phonograph record. In this sense it is similar
to open-reel recorders, which track in two directions.

Other features add to the versatility of this system. The
cassette system has perfect mono-stereo compatability. Virtually all the machines have both "fast forward" and "rewind" capability, and can record on either track. Machines
are battery operated, though some also allow for open electric circuit operation. Most machines provide an automatic
level control for volume, so that sound variations at input are
equalized.

Molded into the back of each cassette are two small cavities
covered with plastic tabs. If these tabs are removed, the
recorder is locked out of the "record" position so that the
cassette is usable only for playback. This ingenious device
prevents erasure of a tape designed for permanent use. Commercially recorded cassettes (permanent programs) have the
tabs removed before they leave the factory. It should be
noted that the holes left when the plastic tabs are removed
can be plugged or taped over so that the cassette again becomes a "record" unit.

Aside from being popular for school use, cassette recorders
are used in data-recording installations, telephone answering
services, and virtually anywhere one might wish either to record or play back. The unit's portability makes it suitable
for traveling (most cars use a cartridge system), home, office,
and many other uses. It is a reliable instrument for recording
radio programs, conversations, interviews, and, depending

upon the quality of the recording capability, music. Industry reports indicate that cassette sales exceed reel-to-reel.

Cassettes are available either as blanks or prerecorded units. Their running time ranges from 30 to 120 minutes. Their compactness has eased handling, storage, and transportation problems.

Teachers are enthusiastic about the ease of use and the adaptability of the cassette recorder. It serves equally well for individual use, small groups, or an entire class. It can safely be placed in the hands of even small children for recording or playing back, especially playing back if the "record tabs" have been removed from the cassettes. A cassette tape recorder can be purchased for under twenty-five dollars and, in any price range, is always less expensive than reel-to-reel machines. Some educators have felt that too much money was being spent on tape recorders in the past, especially reel-to-reel, when they were used primarily for playback only. The small machine is ideal for this latter purpose.

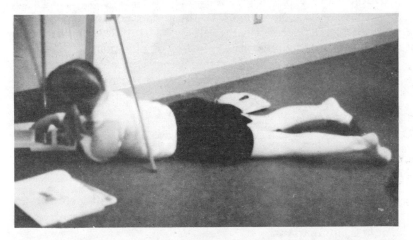

Fig. 15.   Learning needn't be straitjacketed. This student enjoys kicking her shoes off and working with the cassette tape recorder *under* the table. (Photo, courtesy of Penfield, New York, Central Schools, Department of Educational Media.)

Unquestionably, greater student use of the cassette recorder is developing with younger children as well as older students. Teachers and librarians are using the cassette more and more in storytelling, writing and reading poetry, or narrating experiences, recording field trips, recording and analyzing debates or discussions, conducting interviews, practicing skill development in foreign language and music, carrying out routine drills, and recording radio and television sound, to name only a few uses. Integration with such other media as visual symbols will be facilitated. The device also seems ideal for check-out for home study or for student purchase in some cases in lieu of a text.

It seems unlikely that endless-loop recording will replace open-loop recording. At the moment the fidelity of the former is below that of the latter, but future developments will improve fidelity. Great strides are being made in providing a backlog of educational prerecorded materials on tape. The National Tape Library at the University of Colorado now has all of its materials on both standard and cassette tapes.

Duplication of recorded materials, in all tape sizes, is a simple operation. No longer is the reel-to-reel one-at-a-time duplication a necessity. High-speed duplicating machines make multiple copies in a matter of seconds. Four-track tapes may be duplicated at one time separately or simultaneously. Duplication may involve reel-to-reel, cassette-to-cassette, reel-to-cassette, or cassette-to-reel. The growth, inexpensiveness, and adaptability of the cassette in the tape recording family has been likened to the emergence of the paperback book in printing.

Records and Tapes Compared

Although records and tapes have been treated together here because of their similarities, they are noticeably different, as Table 2 summarizes.

Another important difference between the two media, of course, is that the battery-operated cassette tape recorder can be used in a much greater variety of settings than the more cumbersome, electrically operated phonograph.

TABLE 2. Comparison of Tapes and Records

	Records	*Tapes*
advantages	provide a large selection of material on most subjects are permanent, non-erasable are widely available and accepted	lend themselves to teacher-student preparation have great flexibility allow two-way communication
weaknesses	are easily scratched, breakable allow only one-way communication require commercial production almost exclusively	are easily erased accidentally have not been in use long enough to provide a large selection of material
fidelity	satisfactory to excellent	satisfactory to excellent, depending on equipment and recording conditions
ease of operation	simple; can be operated by students	simple; can be operated by students
editing	not possible	simple
cost of equipment	$40 and up	as low as $25 for cassette recorders
cost of new material	prerecorded: $1 and up raw stock: 50¢ and up	prerecorded: $5 and up raw stock: less than $1/2$ ¢ per foot
storage and handling	fairly compact, but care required to prevent warping, scratching, or breakage	compact easy to store
speeds	16, 33, 45, 78 rpm	$^{15}/_{16}$, $1^7/_8$, $3^3/_4$, $7^1/_2$, 15 ips
maximum length of play	30 minutes	varies with recording equipment and tape

Effective Uses of Records and Tapes

There are few teachers for whom recorded sound is not valuable. Foreign language teachers without tape recorders and prerecorded tapes are unquestionably handicapped. (See Chapter 7.) Even in subject areas where use may be limited, illustration or enrichment value undoubtedly will be found. A truly comprehensive listing of use for records and tapes would be voluminous and never complete, because new ones are devised every day. A few examples of typical uses, from primary through secondary schools, will suggest many more.

FOR MUSICAL EFFECTS   Recordings are of special value to kindergarten and primary-grade teachers, who use them for rhythm development, storytelling, and playing games. Nearly all the classic children's stories and songs have been recorded, and much recorded classical music can be used creatively with children. In teaching a unit on fairy stories, for instance, the teacher may use recordings alone or in conjunction with the oral reading of the stories and the showing of flat pictures and projected slides. The music of Tchaikovsky's *Nutcracker Suites*, Nos. 1 and 2, for example, is widely successful with children, as it abounds in fancy, with various toys and the ancient nutcracker playing roles. Its divertissements such as "Dance of the Sugarplum Fairy," "Waltz of the Snowflakes," and "Waltz of the Flowers" create a fanciful, fairy story atmosphere which enchants children and sets their imaginations stirring.

It is important with young children—as, indeed, with any student—to ensure that recordings are appropriate to the listener's vocabulary development. It is also important, as with all instructional media, to introduce the material properly. The teacher might introduce the *Nutcracker Suite* by talking about Tchaikovsky's intent and summarizing the story. He might point out, "In this record you will hear several exciting dances. One is called "Dance of the Sugarplum Fairy." Try to pick it out and later tell me what the Sugarplum Fairy was like. See if you can tell what musical instruments are used. Now listen to . . . ." Discussion can follow the playing, and the record can be replayed once or several times, depending on one's learning objectives.

Rhythms can also be taught with the use of recordings. Children can be instructed to listen to the music and then to clap the rhythm. The clapping rhythm may then be extended to dancing. A third-grade teacher explained her use of records in this way:

> In the beginning I used the tom-tom for simple rhythm. After the children had acquired a fair degree of competency in walking, hopping, skipping, and running to the rhythmic pattern of the tom-tom, I introduced the toe-heel, canoe, and step-hop patterns used in authentic Indian dances.
>
> The first use of the record was a listening activity, and later the children clapped the rhythm. Because of the limited classroom space, and to allow each pupil to observe and participate, the class was divided into small groups. As one group was dancing, the other groups watched and sometimes clapped to help their classmates. The children were encouraged to use the steps they knew and to develop any other movements which they felt were more suitable or expressive to them. Eventually, a pattern for a complete dance evolved.[2]

Recordings provide a rich source of examples of types, textures, and rhythms of music—as well as demonstrating historical developments of musical forms and giving students practice in music appreciation skills.

FOR PRESENTING SUBJECT MATTER Elementary school teachers, especially, have recorded materials available in almost every area of their work. Some emphasize correct pronunciation of different letter sounds. Others assist in teaching vowel and consonant sounds. Still others sharpen, illustrate, and analyze basic reading, writing, and listening problems.

Social studies teachers, elementary and secondary, find that recordings help break time-space barriers. Through recordings, students can hear contemporary or historical, social,

2. Reported by Margaret Ward, San Diego City Schools.

economic, and political ideas. Records allow students everywhere to have a front-row seat in Congress, state legislatures,
and the United Nations. Many good quality records presenting a historical period, event, or figure are available, as are
records devoted to the cultures of other lands.

Recordings for the high-school level, too, are legion.
Records are available today which allow students to hear
Orson Welles and Judith Anderson read Shakespearian plays,
Charles Laughton and Ronald Coleman interpret prose,
Robert Frost and Carl Sandburg read their verse, John Stein-
beck and William Faulkner read and discuss the art of the
novel, and Cornelia Otis Skinner and Vincent Price interpret
contemporary drama.

Recordings can help students realize that American literature is a record of social, political, and moral issues in our
country. Recordings such as the above can effectively be
woven into multimedia teaching along with films, textual
materials, study prints, and art materials. Most recordings
useful in American literature have supplementary values for
American history, and vice versa. A record of music from
the Pilgrim period, for example, gives students the mood and
tone of the *Bay Psalm Book*. Showing the Pilgrims' desire to
fit the meaning of the Psalms to hymn tunes, it helps the student detect what was lost in rhythm and in beauty of phrase
of the *King James Bible*. Similarly, a recording of the Colonial and Revolutionary period can underscore the problems
of the Continental Congress; the work of such leaders as
Washington, Franklin, and Jefferson; the writing of the
Declaration of Independence; and the writing of *The Crisis*
and the *Book of Common Sense* by Tom Paine.

FOR HELP WITH POETRY   Teachers often find it difficult
to put vitality into the teaching of poetry. And students can
regard poetic imagery, with its unfamiliar combinations of
words, as a tedious business. If they are between the ages of
ten and sixteen, they may be near rebellion when poetry is
taught! Poetry is frequently read poorly by the teacher, or
students are asked to read a verse and then tell what it means
"in your own words." Of this procedure Edgar Dale cau-

tions, "You cannot say precisely what the poet says if you use different words. The whole value of the poem consists in the poet's own words and their specific order."[3]

Records can often add depth and understanding to poems. The flight of the bumblebee, and the dashing waves on a lonely coast, the life of a bustling city, or the sparkle of spring are a few examples of recordings which integrate with selected poems. Although some poems are made up mainly of abstractions, most are noticeably concrete—studded with imagery, figurative speech, symbols, rhyme, tone, and other poetic characteristics. Audio-visual imagery is widely used by poets: "a noiseless patient spider," "the whirring pheasant springs," "he feels the fiery wound," "the highwayman came riding," "two roads diverged in a yellow wood." Teachers should build on the poet's concrete images for student understanding and motivation.

Poets feel that poetic word arrangements express their thoughts more succinctly than the lengthy prose forms. Tennyson's verse essay, "The Eagle," is a good example:

> He clasps the crag with crooked hands;
> Close to the sun in lonely lands,
> Ring'd with the azure world, he stands.
>
> The wrinkled sea beneath him crawls;
> He watches from his mountain walls,
> And like a thunderbolt he falls.

Recordings of poetry read by trained voices help the bare lines of print tell what the poet wishes to say. Good reading adds connotation to denotation. Alliteration, rhyme, onomatopoeia, and cacophony are frequent poem patterns; and only by hearing a poem read aloud does one get the full import of the poet. Even more exciting is hearing the poet read his own composition, because he can put into the accents and tones the feelings and nuances which were in his mind when

3. Edgar Dale, *Audiovisual Methods in Teaching*, 3rd ed. (New York: Dryden, 1969), p. 558.

he wrote the poem. Anyone who has heard a record of Robert Frost reading his own poems feels intensely the swinging from birches, the mending of a stone fence wall, or a lazy ride in a horsedrawn carriage with soft snow sifting down. Robert Frost's voice had the flavor of New England.

SPECIAL ADVANTAGES OF TAPES   The tape recorder has an almost endless variety of uses in nearly every classroom. Students like to hear their own voices in reading or relating an incident.   Ingenious teachers have made good use of tape recorders to supplement or relieve them of routine dictation in spelling, arithmetic, and various drill activities, so that they can assist individual students as the lesson develops. Often questions arise which the teacher is reluctant to take up because they break the continuity of the lesson or the attention of the other students.   After an exercise is taped, it can be kept for later use with students who were absent when the exercise was first used. Such use assures uniformity of example and presentation.

Recorders are also used to teach phonics and for listening, remediation, reporting, and numerous other uses.

One teacher of an urban fourth grade class had much success with the tape recorder by instituting a tape exchange with a rural school in another state halfway across the nation. Students in both schools described on tape their schoolwork, their home schedules, their recreational activities, and some of their aspirations.   Similar projects involving overseas exchange have also had great success.

The tape recorder has proved effective for a wide variety of objectives, ranging from rather mechanical exercises which free the teacher from having to read material aloud to creative work such as dramatization and student "compositions" on tape in conjunction with workbooks, outlines, and tests.

A simple use is in connection with tests of visual discrimination, given at intervals throughout the year for the purpose of determining progress in vocabulary. The lesson is taped in advance and is presented in connection with a worksheet, as shown in Figure 16. The plan is described to the class, and

come	which	looks	funny
came	what	looked	fun
can	where	look	for
eat	have	here	where
at	here	the	which
are	has	there	what
when	and	said	can
then	said	saw	came
there	see	see	come
that	here	and	one
there	there	said	on
them	where	see	no

Fig. 16. A visual discrimination worksheet to accompany a taped presentation.

then the tape is played. The tape might sound something like this:

> Look at each block of words on the worksheet carefully. I will say one word from each block. Find the word which you think I have said and draw a circle around it. Circle only one word in each block. Even if you cannot decide on a word, move on to the next block when I tell you to. Later I will go through the words a second time, and you will have a chance to catch up on anything you missed. As you work, I will move quietly around the room to help those who need help, but I will not tell you any of the answers. This is a test to see how much you know about some words. We are now ready to begin. Do your own work. Now look at the words in the first block. Circle the word *come*. Move to the next block. Read the words carefully and circle the word *where*.

The same procedure is followed until all blocks have been completed, after which the tape continues and quickly reads the words again.

Correcting students' work can be facilitated by the tape recorder, as the following report by a teacher indicates:

> Instead of relying solely on the red pencil to try to bring about improvement in book reports and other written work of my stu-

Fig. 17.   Young students view a filmstrip and hear a coordinated recording. (Photo, courtesy Pittsburgh Public Schools.)

dents, I have been recording my observations and comments on the tape recorder in a series of short, personal messages to each individual student.   In this way, I share the positive gains in each paper with the student, give approval and encouragement, and point out those features wherein improvement is needed.   Students, one by one, are given time to go to the tape recorder, which is in one corner of the classroom.   With headset in place and composition in hand, the student listens privately to my evaluation of his paper.   The tape then tells the student how to leave the recorder for the next student.   How do students like this method of evaluation of their work?   They have accepted it wholeheartedly.   They feel that I am working with them personally.[4]

Some teachers allow students to check out tape recorders and/or cassettes for home use. Students have recorded per-

4. Reported by Jack E. Krill, San Diego City Schools.

sonal problems which they wished to bring to the attention of a teacher or counselor but not face-to-face. In such instances students feel somewhat freer and more relaxed in discussing problems.

Another use of student taping can be seen in the following report:

> One of my most successful uses of the tape recorder came up this past year in my senior English class. Four boys in the class had read *The Ugly American* by Burdick and Lederer. Instead of just reporting on it in class, they wished to bring some "realism" into the report. They turned to the tape recorder. One of the boys announced a "CBS Special Radio Report." The announcer then said, "Now we switch to —— in South Sarkhan, Southeast Asia." The tape consisted of the boys taking the parts of the four main characters in the book—the American ambassador, the Russian ambassador, a priest, and an American Air Force officer. Each correspondent made a rather complex analysis of his segment of the book. Interest was high and the discussion which followed was among the best I ever had on a student report.[5]

Another English teacher developed a kit for teaching Shakespeare's *Julius Caesar*. She used a Shakespearean record album, a tape made from a television broadcast, and a tape clip made from the verbal section of the funeral oration by Mark Antony as given by Leo Genn in the film version of *Julius Caesar*. She prepared her tape as follows:

> The section of the telecast which I taped makes an ideal introduction to Shakespeare, since it weaves together in a unified pattern the man, his times, and his work. In introducing Shakespeare to tenth graders, background material holds the potential of becoming a swampy bog. To begin with a dramatization of one of the most colorful characters who lives through the inspiration of Shakespeare's genius is smart, and that is just where the tape begins—Sir John Falstaff in a scene from *The Merry Wives of Windsor*. It moves on through other plays and events as indicated by the guide which follows. Upon completion of the tape the listener feels he has touched a time, a man, and several great ideas.

5. Reported by Pauline Forman, San Diego City Schools.

Tape Footage	Scenes
0–26	Windsor Castle and Sir John Falstaff
27–35	Henry IV and young Prince Hal cavorting with Falstaff
36–61	The death scene; Hal becomes Henry V, wiser than father thought
62–74	Shakespeare's homes; the death of his son; the Lord Chamberlain's men; the Globe; the chorus as a device; explanation of settings
75–108	Harry at Agincourt
(109–119)	(Erased Commercial)
120–154	The death of Elizabeth; the plague; James I becomes King; the playwright is honored with *Macbeth*
155–171	Scenes from *Macbeth*
172–193	The church at Suffolk whose windows portray the seven ages of man; dramatization of same
194–214	The Tower of London, a scene between Duke of Gloucester and Henry VI
215–225	The death of Richard III; the Earl of Richmond's marriage, and Elizabeth; end of the War of the Roses
226–250	Hampton Court built by Cardinal Wolsey, presented to Henry VIII, son of Richmond; the Cardinal's "Farewell to Greatness" speech
(251–275)	(Erased Commercial)
276–300	Newplace; Shakespeare's death
301–328	The Royal Shakespeare Theatre keeps works fresh; Johnson's tribute—"not for an Age, but for all time."[6]

Through taping excerpts from several sources, the teacher added richness and variety to her unit which would not have been possible had she confined her media use to the record.

Listening Posts

The term *listening post* designates an area, such as a booth, room, or section of a room, devoted to quiet student listening. The post is equipped with a disc, and/or tape recorder, a

---

6. Reported by Dannelle Barton, Grossmont (California) School District.

Fig. 18. Even in a crowded classroom the creative teacher can help meet individual student needs with audiovisual tools such as the record player, tape recorder, and a listening post. (Photo, courtesy Long Beach, California, Unified School District.)

plug-box, and several sets of earphones. Most listening posts are nothing more than this equipment placed on a table in the rear of a classroom. Pupils go there to listen to stories, music, foreign languages, short plays, or exercises in spelling or other skills. Usually the equipment is planned for groups of about eight. Some listening posts are equipped with facilities so that students can tape as well as listen. An example of a teacher's script for a listening lesson follows:

Tape speed: 3³/₄ ips
Tape time: 11 min.
Reading text: We Are Neighbors[7]

7. David H. Russell and Odille Ousley, *We Are Neighbors*, rev. ed., Ginn Basic Reading Series (Boston: Ginn, 1961).

Story: *Mike Mulligan and His Steam Shovel*[8]

Sequence	Narration
greeting	Hello, boys and girls! Do you have your headsets adjusted correctly? How do I sound . . . too loud? . . . or too soft? Will the group leader adjust my voice to a level that is comfortable? Good! How's that?
materials needed: 2 pencils, worksheet	We always want to be ready before we start a listening lesson, so let's check and see if you have all the materials you'll need. Do you have two pencils? You'll need an extra if your first one breaks. Do you have a worksheet for the story you just finished reading in *We Are Neighbors*, pages 224– 233? If so, we can begin.
listening standards established	Remember, today while you are listening, to keep in mind that the other boys and girls are working quietly and you'll have to do all your work at the Listening Post with your ears. So remember: seal those lips, sit up straight, and *listen*.
sound effects and review of story	Now, *listen* . . . (pause: insert sounds of steam shovels) . . . What does that sound remind you of? Listen again . . . (pause: insert sounds of steam shovels) . . . If you thought it was a steam shovel, you were right. Those sounds might have been the same ones "Mary Ann" made in the story about *Mike Mulligan and His Steam Shovel* that you just finished.
reading of the story	Do you remember? . . . (The teacher tells the story) . . .
worksheet directions and exercise from the	Now that the story is fresh in our minds again, let's turn to the worksheets. Pick up your pencils and listen. Are you ready? . . .

8. Virginia Lee Burton, *Mike Mulligan and His Steam Shovel* (Boston: Houghton Mifflin).

Teacher's Manual, p. 420[9]	Fine. At the top of the paper, fill in your name, I'll wait ... (pause) .... There, that should do it. After number 1, you'll notice a list of words found in the story. Put a circle around the words as I give you a clue and write the number I say by the word.... Understand? ... (repeat instructions).... Look and listen. Pencils ready! "Mulligan," "cellar," "hall," "men," "farmer," "furnace," "sit." (1) tells what can be used to heat a house (write the numeral 1) (2) is a man's name (write the numeral 2) (The teacher's voice continues through all questions on the worksheet.) There. Did you circle and number them correctly? Oh, I hope so. Now let's check them. I will say the correct numbers straight across your papers starting with "Mulligan" and ending the first line with "men," second line starting with "farmer" and ending with "sit." Ready? Pencils ready! (The teacher supplies the answers, in order.) 4, ... 1, ... 6. Did some get lost? If you did, I'll repeat ... (pause). Ready, first line 2 ... 3 ... 7 ... 5 ... second line 4 ... 1 ... 6. Pencils down and let's listen again.
seat work and directions	I want you to fold your papers in half and on one side write all the words that have the *hard c* sound, and on the other side write all the words that have the *soft c* sound and be ready to read them to the group when you meet next time.
closing: standards established	Now, on the signal of the steam shovel noise, I will ask you quietly to remove your headsets, push in your chairs, quietly return to

9. Adapted from the lesson plan by David H. Russell and Odille Ousley in the *Manual for Teaching Second Reader-1*, to accompany *We Are Neighbors*, rev. ed., Ginn Basic Reading Series (Boston: Ginn, 1961), pp. 420–25.

	your seats, and write the words in the correct group.
correcting work	If you finish early, check your words and be sure you did not omit one. Check again to make sure you have each word at the correct place.
extra art activity	If you finish you might make a picture with crayons of Mike and "Mary Ann" trying to dig the cellar in one day.
closing sound effects	All right! Are you listening? Are you ready? (Insert steam shovel noise.)[10]

As with all instruction, group use of tape recorders, such as in the listening post example above, must be planned with individual student readiness clearly in mind. Because the tape requires all students in the group to work at pretty much the same pace, students who sit at the listening post together must be similar in level of understanding and rate of work.   (The listening post can, of course, be modified for individual instruction if sufficient equipment is available.) Teachers should be aware that this technique does not allow for immediate feedback between teacher and students, so that some interaction with students is desirable as soon after the listening post experience as possible.

RADIO

When television catapulted to importance in the 1950s, many people relegated radio to a minor role and some predicted its demise. Yet radio has acquired a new life today because it has certain unique characteristics which have enabled it to coexist with television, films, and pictorial magazines.   Almost every family in the United States has one radio, and many have two, three, or more, including car radios and portable transistors. Unlike television, radio does not demand the entire attention of the receiver. Because it is completely auditory, recipients can drive a car, work about

10. Reported by Rose Warren, San Diego City Schools.

the house, or carry on other activities not requiring full concentration.

Schools have taken advantage of the fact that copies can be made of broadcasts by magnetic tape recordings, which can be stored like books and replayed at any time. In this way, schools build up libraries of vocal and instrumental music, speeches, workshop proceedings, interviews, literary readings, and other auditory communications. In most schools, radio is currently employed as a supplement to television: its chief functions are to transmit music and news. In addition to these, it is widely used in the schools of Los Angeles, St. Louis, Atlanta, Chicago, Cleveland, New York City, Detroit, and other large cities for supplementary educational experiences. Some states, such as New York, Ohio, Indiana, Wisconsin, and Texas, have regional or statewide school networks broadcasting carefully designed curriculum-coordinated programs.

Radio's Advantages and Disadvantages

Because too many teachers are still prone to assume that radio cannot compete with television in the classroom, it is well to look, in Table 3, at the medium's strengths and weaknesses as objectively as possible.

Effective School Use

Where its full potential has been explored, radio has been found to be a valuable instructional aid for most students. It has been used effectively by teachers of most subjects, for enrichment experiences, for appreciation, for understanding techniques and skills, and for keeping abreast of new ideas, opinions, and research.

Student-produced radio programs offer a practical means of learning through production and performance activities. Student-prepared programs benefit those who prepare them even more than those who "consume" them. Motivation is high and the learning value is significant. Radio productions are on a simple scale, are less costly, and are less a "show" than television productions. Consequently less time is

TABLE 3. Strengths and Weaknesses of Radio

Advantages	Disadvantages
provides a convenient, economical way to hear experts and specialists	provides too few curriculum-correlated broadcasts
allows easy recording of programs for reuse at any time	contains disruptive advertising on commercial stations
especially valuable for remote localities	often pitched to a low cultural denominator
allows editing of programs as desired	seems to take second place to TV among many teachers and students
allows for auditioning of programs if they are taped for delayed use	solely an audio medium
good for both in-school and out-of-school listening	provides one-way communication only
one of the best media available for current history, special events, and spot news	
the ideal medium for music broadcasting	
an excellent medium for transmission of student-prepared programs	
unparalleled for conveying naturalistic and impressionistic sounds	
available practically everywhere	
inexpensive	
provides ease of tuning and use	

needed, and in many cases they are just as valuable instructionally.

Two types of program origin have been alluded to: commercially sponsored programs and school-produced programs. The former, despite advertising, bring to the classroom specialists and authorities and a feeling of universality. These programs may be for either in-school or out-of-school listening. School districts which have their own broadcast facilities or which use state or regional educational networks (mostly

FM) usually work with curriculum-oriented programs in science, music, literature, history of art, and health.

Radio has provided unparalleled service for isolated areas of the world. American educators might well emulate the notable example of the Australian outback country, where radio has for many years performed outstanding service to children so remote from organized schools that their education is confined to home study. Equally notable is the famed "flying doctor" service it provides to the same area.

The growth of FM broadcasting, especially, has caused radio to become more specialized in recent years. FM broadcasting in stereo has increased Americans' enjoyment of good music in much the same way that the British Broadcasting Corporation has for years provided national school broadcasts.

Although general principles of media use were set forth in Chapter 1, the following reminders are especially important for instructional uses of radio.

Objectives are as necessary in radio lessons as they are in any other type. The programs must fulfill specific student needs. The teacher must prepare himself by getting all the information he can from manuals, handbooks, teacher's guides, and bulletins in advance of the broadcast. School districts which have their own educational radio stations usually have programs planned by teachers and studio specialists.

Students, too, must be prepared for the broadcast. They should understand why the broadcast is used, what to listen for, and what uses will be made of it. For example, the preparation for a broadcast on the United Nations or on labor problems in the United States may call for extensive research and reading, while one on music or foreign language will require less preparation. No matter what the content, however, good listening skills are essential. Programs should be listened to, in the regular classroom, under the best possible listening conditions. Equipment should be in good working order and should be correctly tuned. The receiving set should be turned on and allowed to warm up slightly before the program comes on the air. Disturbances can be minimized by placing a sign outside the classroom door to prevent interruptions.   Pencil sharpening and window-shade adjustments should be done before the broadcast begins!   Additionally, follow-up and evaluation are as important to radio use as they are to all other media.

OTHER AUDIO DEVICES AND SOUND SYSTEMS

In addition to records, tapes, and radio, modern technology has provided other types of auditory equipment, some of them "systems," which can assist in the classroom.   Among the latter are the dial-access and audio-tutorial systems, which properly belong to our discussion of "media systems" and, accordingly, will be treated in Chapter 8.

Telephone Sound Systems

Educators working with the Bell System telephone company have developed a device known variously as "The Spokesman," "The Speakerphone," "Telelecture," or merely "the classroom telephone."   It is usually a portable installation which can be carried into any classroom or conference room that is equipped with a telephone jack.   The equipment—a telephone, an amplifier, and a microphone—is plugged in to make a call.   Amplification is such that both sides of the telephone call can be heard easily in any classroom, possibly by an audience in a small auditorium.

The purpose of the classroom telephone is to allow students to use a wide range of resource persons without leaving the classroom.   The technique might be likened to a vicarious audio field trip.   Students in almost any grade or any subject can use the device profitably, inasmuch as every community has a number of splendid resources.   For example, a foreign language class may telephone an airline official, a foreign consul or ambassador, or the captain of a vessel that has docked in a port city.

Arrangements for telephone interviews should be made a a few days in advance.   The person to be called must be briefed by the teacher or some other school official as to the object of the call and the types of questions students are likely to ask.   Students, meanwhile, should talk over the questions they would like to ask, who or how many will do the talking, and the like. When the call is put through, the teacher usually introduces the class and the interviewee. The interview is then turned over to the class. Most interviews last from fifteen to thirty minutes. After the interview, students discuss it, write reports, make evaluations, or suggest future interviews.

Reports from both students and interviewees are valuable. Specialists relish the idea of sharing their knowledge with students, and most of them prefer this method to actual field visits because of the time involved. On a grander scale, the telephone interview can go to distant places, even overseas.

Several colleges are using this technique to have student groups interview national figures. Students in Omaha, for example, have talked to persons in New York and Washington for costs of from $100 to $150. If the same persons had come to their classrooms or campus, the cost would have been from $1,500 to $2,000.

New uses for this equipment arise constantly. It can bring specialists to teachers' conferences, workshops, and PTA meetings. An adaptation of the device is now being tried out in one city so that a teacher-supervisor contacts a number of homebound children at one time for actual teaching purposes.

Topeka, Kansas, has experimented with the Telelecture system simultaneously in three high schools for a year, in a project involving 225 students and six teachers in science, social studies, and foreign language. Telelecture was used by "master teachers" to supplement the work of regular classroom teachers. The telephone facilities provided two-way contact for speaker and students in all three schools at one time. The audio discussion was augmented by the use of a tele*writing* device so that the students had a visual link. Talks were supplemented with written notes, outlines, formulas, and drawings as needed. These visual symbols were projected on a large screen in each classroom. Results were highly satisfactory, and the project, with some modifications, was made a part of regular instructional procedures.[11]

11. "Teaching by Telephone," *Audiovisual Instruction*, 12 (September, 1967): 683–85.

Another interesting use of Telelecture was at the University of California at Los Angeles, where an extension course was taught by this medium. Enrollees for the course met on campus for the first class session, and thereafter all meetings were entirely via the two-way telephone system with computer assistance. Each class discussion was taped. If a student missed a session, he could simply call in and have the tape replayed to him.

Wireless Listening Stations

It is possible today to transform any classroom into an electronic classroom by use of a wireless long-wave audio system. Large and small listening areas are possible with broadcast sound from a phonograph, tape recorder, radio, television set, motion picture projector, live speech, or any sound source. The classroom is outfitted with a built-in antenna loop to which sound output is fed. The loop in turn radiates a short distance as a magnetic wave. Small individual

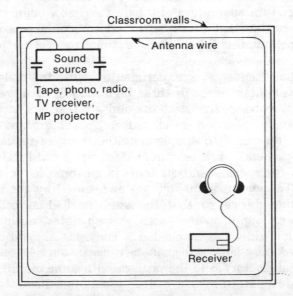

Fig. 19.   A classroom equipped with a wireless listening station.

receivers (the size of a deck of cards) are fitted with earphones to pick up the magnetic waves. The receivers are battery powered and can be operated anywhere without an electrical connection. Cost of installation is remarkably inexpensive—antenna wire and inexpensive headphone sets only. Any electrician can install the wire in a classroom. More sophisticated units are equipped to carry three programs controlled by the student through the use of a three-way switch and volume control devices on his receiver.

Wireless loop transmissions are not only economical but provide unusual flexibility for listening areas. The variety of applications of the equipment is practically endless. The room is free of loose cords and ambient noise is eliminated.

Wireless Microphones

An important new electronic development now eliminates the use of cords in broadcast microphones of the lavaliere type (microphones worn around the neck). The system is complicated, owing to the fact that a radio transmission channel is needed. Furthermore, the microphones are designed with outputs to match various amplification systems, which often cause problems. Schools using these microphones will need to be licensed for FM frequency bands such as those allocated for industrial communication. The microphone activates a loudspeaker, a portable AM/FM radio, or other sound outlet, so that the tangle of speaker cord, as well as the frustration of limited cord footage, is eliminated.

Speakers using wireless microphones find a new freedom of movement around the speaking area. Both hands are free, and attention can be focused completely on the message. Only limited use has been made of this development to date; however, its possibilities are manifold for large group instruction, as in physical education (field or gymnasium), dance centers, rehearsal of marching bands, and large science and industrial arts laboratory sessions. Teaching in auditoriums, as team teaching, for example, will be facilitated by this device, as will teachers or demonstrators who use numerous displays or multiple pieces of audiovisual equipment.

Public Address or Central Sound Systems

Public address systems serve three general purposes: administrative, instructional, and recreational. In the first instance, the system makes possible building-wide announcements and amplifies sound for large gatherings. Instructionally, the system can be used to distribute radio programs, programs prepared by students, and other speech and music programs to various parts of the building. Recreational uses include music, reports of athletic events, and drama. Coordinated visual material can be provided if the school has a closed-circuit television system.

Most modern schools have permanently installed public address systems. These are often supplemented by portable systems so that sound can be carried to or picked up from areas outside the building—for example, on playgrounds and athletic fields.

In many school buildings the system and its use have become a routine affair, and its value subsequently diminished. So many announcements are made over the system which affect only limited groups of students that the majority tend to "tune out" all broadcasts. Optimum effectiveness of the equipment could be achieved by a school-wide study of its use, after which its operation could be placed in the hands of an interested and capable teacher assisted by well-chosen student personnel. This recommendation, of course, may well be made for coordinating the use of all auditory devices in a school.

Chapter 6

Standard Instructional Materials

BEHAVIORAL OBJECTIVES

After studying this chapter, the reader will be able to:

1. Plan a chalkboard lesson in terms of the guidelines for effective media use set forth in Chapter 1.
2. Compare and contrast feltboards, magnetic boards, hook-and-loop boards, electric boards, and multipurpose boards.
3. Given a learning objective, describe a lesson in which three-dimensional materials or displays are used to accomplish the objective.
4. Given five learning situations, select the most appropriate dramatic technique (including role-playing and puppetry) for each and support the choices.
5. Name six functions the bulletin board can serve, and offer a practical suggestion for implementing each function.
6. Given a specific community and specific learning objective, identify three resources in the community which can fulfill the objective, and explain how each can be utilized most effectively.

This text, like any textbook on instructional media, presents a number of significant new developments in the field. Teachers wish to know about the latest innovations in media, particularly if the devices have been properly tested and researched. But teachers are also interested in more effective use of older, less expensive, less mechanized materials and tools which have been the backbone of instructional procedures for many years.

This chapter will consider such media under four headings: special boards and displays, three-dimensional materials and displays, dramatizations, and community resources as learning materials. These materials and devices are for the most part concrete, as they parallel first-hand experience. Some are commercially produced; others are so easily constructed that they can be readily produced by teachers and students.

SPECIAL BOARDS AND DISPLAYS

Seven types of instructional boards or display spaces are commonly used in the classroom: chalkboards, feltboards, magnetic boards, electric boards, special or multipurpose boards, bulletin boards, and hook-and-loop boards. Although their purposes vary, from demonstration to drill work to display, their common feature is a surface on which to manipulate figures or moving parts, thereby giving the teacher or student a great deal of flexibility in the structuring of materials.

Chalkboards

Although the chalkboard is possibly the most widely used of all teaching tools, it is often badly used. To be a truly effective instructional communication device it requires planned use. In practice, however, it is often no more than a convenient place for a type of doodling only slightly related to the instruction being given. Effective chalkboard techniques need practice. The chalkboard is not likely to make a poor teacher a good teacher, but its appropriate use can make both poor teachers and good teachers better teachers.

Formerly, chalkboards were always black and were usually

made of slate, and, of course, were called blackboards. Today, the chalkboard comes in a variety of pastel-colored nonglare surfaces—green, blue, coral, brown, and, of course, black. Although slate is still sometimes used, materials are more likely to be pressed wood, wood fiber, cement-asbestos, mossy-surfaced glass, plastic, or vitreous-coated steel boards. Iron in the material makes it possible to use it as a magnetic board as well as a marking board.

Usually chalkboards are a permanent part of the classroom. If the space devoted to chalkboards is not generous enough, portable chalkboards can easily be made by the teacher or a school custodian. Such boards may be no more elaborate than a piece of masonite painted with chalkboard paint.

A newer kind of nonpermanent chalkboard has been perfected which is totally different from slate, porcelain enamel, or composition. It is a thin, flexible, lightweight roll, not unlike wallpaper, and will adhere to almost any surface. It can be cut with scissors, contains a pressure-sensitive backing, and can be mounted in minutes. This development should be a boon to classrooms with temporary partitions, freestanding panels, glass dividers, or folding walls.

BEST USES OF CHALKBOARDS   All teachers at all grade levels and in all subject areas use chalkboards in all sorts of capacities.

One hundred and twenty-five years ago, Horace Mann is reported to have said, "Indeed, in no state or country have I ever seen a good school without a blackboard or a successful teacher who did not use it frequently." While the philosophy of modern education makes the above statement seem quaint, the general soundness of it remains.

Uses for the chalkboard are numbered in the hundreds because of its extreme flexibility. The chalkboard is an important supplement to instruction, facilitating the illustration of points in a lesson and the clarification of obscure or complex ideas by visualizing them. Equally significant is its usefulness in outlining procedures where precise directions are needed. Further, the chalkboard can be of immense help in reinforcing the spoken word and eliciting new ideas, events, or facts.

Some of the following suggestions for improving chalkboard use are relatively new; others have proved their value for years.

- Uses of the chalkboard should be planned as carefully as should use of all instructional materials. Ask yourself: What parts of the lesson are important enough to be placed on the board? What aspects of the lesson are likely to be unclear to some members of the class? What diagrams or drawings can I use to explain difficult points? How can I capitalize on the immediate feedback from the board? How can I involve the students in active participation? Will using the chalkboard consume too much time? Should work be placed on the board before the class assembles or when the group is present? Would it be better for me to use some sort of paper duplicating device, an overhead projector, or a chart instead of the chalkboard?
- While working at the board, face the class at an angle so that you can glance at the class frequently. Speak to the class, not to the board. Move about occasionally so that all the students can see the work.
- Erase and clean with an eraser or a sponge. Don't use your fingers, even though the excuse is to save time.
- Use colored chalk to stress or pinpoint an issue, not to "dress up" the board.
- Never "hurry" the use of the board. Its use should be adjusted to the best instructional speed for the class.
- Use a pointer to direct the attention of the class to specific items.
- Be careful not to expand your bulletin board area at the expense of the chalkboard. Each has its own proper function.
- Letters or symbols placed on the board should be large enough to be seen by every member of the class. A viewing distance of 32 feet requires that letters be at least 2½ inches high. A simple letter style is preferable

to a fancy one. (See Chapter 4 for a more detailed discussion of lettering.)

- See that the chalkboard space is clean when you leave the classroom, especially if another teacher is to occupy the room. Naturally, you may wish sometimes to make arrangements with other teachers to leave certain materials on the board.

- The students should not use the chalkboard en masse.

- If you want to place an entire visual presentation of a lesson, test, or outline on the board in advance, the work can be covered by wrapping paper or window shades.

- Use mechanical chalkboard drawing aids—rulers, blackboard stencils, colored chalk, and templates (patterns)— to save time and give accuracy to drawings. Most teachers prepare templates when certain shapes or forms are to be used repeatedly. Templates are usually teacher-made from plywood, pressed board, or some other lightweight material. Drawer knobs or empty spools mounted on templates facilitate their use. Many teachers find stick-figure drawings easy-to-make and effective communication devices.

- Check lighting to be sure that there is no glare on the board.

- Draw semipermanent lines with soft chalk soaked in a sugar solution. These lines will be visible for a long time unless wiped off with a damp cloth. Semipermanent lines are useful in some map work, music lines, or graph lines in mathematics or social studies.

- For enlarging materials use a pantograph, or a system of *proportional squares.* This method is sometimes called the *grid method.* The material to be transferred to the board is ruled into squares and then the chalkboard is marked off into similar but larger squares. By following the original drawing, the chalkboard enlargement is made square by square.

- Use an opaque projector to transfer complex drawings from books or small pictures to the chalkboard.

- You might use the *pattern* or *pounce* method in transferring material to the chalkboard. Holes are punched into a sheet of paper or fabric to follow the outline of a design or picture. A dusty chalk eraser is then patted over the perforated pattern as it is held against the board. The chalk dots are connected freehand. Patterns may be stored for reuse.

- Ask students who are artistic to assist in making chalkboard drawings.

- Make certain that a map and chart rail is provided along the top of the chalkboard, for most advantageous use of space.

Although the overhead and other projection equipment tend to replace the chalkboard for many uses, chalkboards will continue to be important and effective communication devices.

Bulletin Boards

The bulletin board, usually set aside from the chalkboard by a narrow, wooden frame, is designed specifically for visually displaying students' work, pictures, clippings, posters, small objects, or other creative learning materials. The surface of the board is of cork, linoleum, burlap, or a similar substance. Pegboard surfaces are used occasionally because this type of board lends itself to the display of small objects and specimens. Pegboards are made of soft composition material punched with small holes about one inch apart.

Most of the principles of bulletin board use have been presented in the chapter on graphics. Bulletin board spaces are found in most classrooms and in other places around school buildings, such as halls, cafeterias, and offices. The bulletin boards of most concern for teachers are those found in the classrooms, or those in the halls just outside the classrooms and assigned to particular rooms. Usually bulletin boards can be the responsibility of both teacher and students. Supervisors and visitors to a classroom—let alone one's students—get their first impression of the teacher from the appearance of the room. The bulletin board reflects something of the philosophy of learning which prevails in the room.

BEST USES OF BULLETIN BOARDS   Regardless of subject or grade taught, practically all teachers find bulletin boards useful. They can be used to provide a stimulating room atmosphere and make a cheerful and interesting classroom; create a readiness for the study of new units of work; serve as an outlet for students' talents; provide a suitable place for the posting of announcements, assignments, honor rolls, committees, and the like; allow the whole class to see material of which only one copy exists; and serve as a focus for summaries and reviews.

As with all instructional materials, good planning insures that the bulletin board will serve specific purposes, will be integrated with the general instruction, will facilitate student participation, and will be conducive to helpful follow-up activities. Other important pointers follow:

- Keep a file of photographs, pictures from periodicals, students' work, and notes about the quick location of other materials.
- Experiment with varied techniques for using the board. One of these is the hidden board, which is prepared in advance and kept covered until the proper time arrives. Among the other attention-getting techniques are colored papers, string and yarn, arrows, colored tacks and pins, turntables, and gimmicks of many kinds.
- Designate a student editor for the bulletin board, a position which rotates frequently. Student committees serve the same purpose and provide for greater participation.
- Keep in mind the aesthetics of bulletin boards. Obviously, displays should not be left posted for long periods of time. Up-to-dateness is imperative. The material must be varied from time to time or the lack of novelty will hamper the board's effectiveness. It must be neat and clean and, like a poster, it must be terse. Captivating headlines or captions employing slogans, popular phrases, or pointed statements get and hold attention. In

general, the board should be organized simply and informally.

SELECTED EXAMPLES OF BULLETIN BOARD USE Bulletin board use can enliven the teaching of subjects which at first glance might not appear to lend themselves to the medium. A typing teacher, for example, wanted to help her high school class build up typing speed. She used the following technique:

Learning Objective:
Students will be able to type at least 50 wpm at a level of accuracy sufficient to pass the typing test.

Teaching Strategy:
A bulletin board was made by covering a display area with a large map of the United States obtained from a local service station. A route from Michigan to Florida was outlined with a felt pen. Members of the typing class would travel along this route each day at the rate of 100 miles for each correct-word-per-minute of typing beyond the speed attained at the time the project was started. For example, a student whose typing rate increased from 35 to 60 wpm made a net increase of 25 words which when multiplied by 100 gave him a distance of 2,500 miles on the map. Map tacks and colored labels indicated each student's progress on the trip. The labels were moved each day in accordance with the student's speed of improvement. The contest lasted twelve weeks.[1]

ADDING BULLETIN BOARD SPACE Additional bulletin board space is relatively easy to supply. Sometimes it is simply a matter of covering unused chalkboard space, or it may be temporary conversion of space between windows, backs of doors, or wall space at various places in the room. Corrugated paper, burlap, monk's cloth, or flannel are excellent coverings. If these coverings are not available, ordinary construction paper will do. Portable panels made by covering old shipping cartons can be set in chalkrails or on top of tables. Easels can be converted to the same purpose. Room

1. Reported by Lois Carole Zimmerle, Britton (Michigan) Public Schools.

dividers used to separate work areas in a classroom may very well add more display space. Tightly stretched wires along a wall will provide extra display space on which flat picture materials may be hung with paper clips. If placed somewhat farther away from the walls, the wires may suspend three-dimensional materials such as models.

For both permanent and temporary bulletin board space, some attention should be given to proper lighting, because the board must be seen and read quickly. The light may be natural or artificial. Floodlights or spotlights will set off almost any display.

Feltboards

Although chalkboards are valuable for their immediacy and ease of handling, among other things, felt or flannel boards have an additional feature which can save a great deal of time: movable parts which eliminate the task of redrawing for each step in a demonstration or the telling of a story, or other such activities.

A feltboard captures the attention of students of almost all ages. The device is so flexible that it can be used in almost every subject. It is generally known that long- or coarse-fibered materials tend to adhere to each other with sufficient strength so that they can be used on display boards. Chief among these materials are felt, flannel, suede, duvetyn, and fuzzy-surfaced paper. A sheet of thin plywood or heavy cardboard can be covered, and a remarkably versatile demonstration or display board results. Cutouts for use on the board may be prepared from any of the same materials, or from paper or lightweight cardboard backed with strips of sandpaper, felt, or any of a variety of flocculent (covered with woolly material) substances. Lightweight three-dimensional objects can also be backed and used on the board.

Primary teachers have found feltboards exceedingly valuable in number work, color discrimination, vocabulary development, and developing rudimentary ideas of size and proportion. Elementary teachers use them for dramatizing

Fig. 20. Learning can follow many channels. While receiving individualized instruction in mathematics from a tape recording, this fifth-grade student manipulates objects on a flannelboard to "concretize" the concepts. (Photo, courtesy Pittsburgh Public Schools.)

or highlighting storytelling, developing concepts, drilling in fractions, presenting historical facts, teaching note reading in music, diagramming, charting and graphing, and in dozens of other ways. High school teachers find them useful in driver education, science, language structure, economics, manufacturing processes, and a great variety of subjects and situations in which some concrete imagery is needed. Students do not make use of feltboards to any considerable extent except as they work with display materials furnished by teachers. They could, however, prepare cutouts and make greater use of the boards.

Magnetic Boards

The magnetic board is like the feltboard except that magnetism rather than friction is the adhering force. The magnetic board is specialized in use, as we shall see.

Since magnets adhere to any iron base surface, chalkboards can be overlaid on an iron base and become dual purpose boards. With small magnets attached to them, many kinds of flat or small three-dimensional instructional materials can be displayed on this type of board without tacking or taping. When the materials are removed, the board is not marked or defaced in any way, nor are the papers torn or smeared. Portable magnetic boards are also available.

Because the movable pieces can be attached and detached so easily and quickly, physical education teachers frequently make use of magnetic boards to mark the boundaries of playing-field models and to indicate the position of players in plays. For much the same reason, home economics teachers can use magnetic boards in the discussion of furniture placement, step-saving remodeling, and table and place settings. Business education teachers can use similar techniques in studying display styles and designs. Journalism teachers can make effective use of a magnetic board of newspaper size to discuss layout, placement of headlines, lead articles, advertising blocks, and so on. In anatomy, paper cutouts of bone parts of the skull can be put together in jigsaw fashion to emphasize name, location, and relative size.

Electric Boards

Electric boards are usually teacher-made, but are meant more specifically for individual student use than bulletin boards—and for more direct feedback to students than felt-boards. The principle of the board is to match up cues or questions with answers so that selection of the correct answer will make an electrical contact and ring a buzzer or light a small bulb. Electric boards are usually quite simple and arranged so that pairs of matched items fit together, but they may also be constructed so that three, four, five, or more bits of information must be correctly put together before a circuit is completed. The more elaborate the board, the more flexible it is.

In effect, electric boards are programmed learning devices. The teacher builds into the board understandings he wishes the students to learn. The students then test their knowledge or association of ideas against the program.

To operate a board, the student holds a prober (a handle containing a wire ending) in each hand. He then reads the question and touches the end of the wire on the left with the contact point at the question or picture. The other end of the wire is brought into contact with an answer. If the student makes the right choice, a bulb lights or a bell rings. If he is wrong, nothing happens, and he knows that he must search further.

The clues or data on an electric board should be changed from time to time. Even the wiring of the device may be changed periodically to forestall memorization.

BEST USES OF ELECTRIC BOARDS   The novelty of electric boards captures attention, especially at the beginning of a unit. Later in the unit, the board can serve as a drill or testing device. When review material is programmed on an electric board, repetitive practice is made interesting to students: it is not unusual for them to spend a great deal of time going over the cues and answers. Since students find the device intriguing, it provides an opportunity for self-exploratory work. With correct answers built right into the board, an immediate feedback is given to students about their performance. The following topics for electric-board questions, by subject area, illustrate the diversity of uses of the electric board:

Science: *characteristics, history, specific symbols and formulas*

Foreign Languages: *vocabulary, grammar, simple translations*

History: *dates, locations, leaders, epochs, movements*

Mathematics: *computational combinations, terms, deductions*

Commercial Subjects: *shorthand symbols, letter writing, typewriter keyboard data*

Language Arts: *vocabulary, pronunciation, story plots and characters*

In teaching reading and the language arts in the first grade, for example: the teacher might program the electric board so that students can match letters and sounds, recognize correctly placed accent marks, correlate a word with its pictorial representation, match colors with their names, capitalize and punctuate properly, link things that go together (e.g., hammer-nail), match words with their opposites, or list the sequence of events in a story.

Special or Multipurpose Boards

Several manufacturers have developed multipurpose boards which improve on the single-purpose unit.   These new models, labeled by one producer as "visual aid panels," are either wall-mounted or are mobile units provided with casters.

The new boards use not chalk but large watercolor marking pencils, since the writing surface is a smooth plastic.   These pencils, available with either easily removed or semipermanent dyes, serve like chalk but are somewhat neater with more exact, dust-free markings.   The new panel boards have been so impregnated that they also serve as magnetic boards. Since the boards are white in color, they add to room visibility and can be used for a third function, that of nonglare projection surfaces for films.

Fig. 21. A hook-and-loop board like the one on this classroom wall can support these heavy musical instruments and auto parts via tiny loops, woven into the board's nylon fabric, which interlock with hooks to which the objects are attached. (Photo, courtesy Charles Meyer Studios, Inc., Akron, Ohio.)

Hook-and-Loop Boards

Similar in purpose to the bulletin board, but actually an extension of the feltboard, is the hook-and-loop board. This board is built much like the feltboard except for the fabric covering and the way in which materials are attached to it. When first marketed, the boards came in black only, but now a variety of colors is available.

Display materials are outfitted with hooked tape, which interlocks with tiny nylon loops on the surface of the board, resulting in unusually strong gripping power. This adherence is stronger than that of the feltboard, eliminating slippage of attached objects. As an advantage over the bulletin board, it has been reckoned that the holding power of the hook and loop is five to ten pounds per square inch, making it capable of supporting three-dimensional objects of considerable weight such as toys, tools, boxes, cartons, books, and similar items.

THREE-DIMENSIONAL MATERIALS AND DISPLAYS

Three-dimensional materials provide depth-experiencing and a more complete understanding of real things because they involve more of the senses than other instructional aids. Students like to experience the texture, size, shape, and "substance" of things. Coinage around the world, for example, can be discussed verbally or with pictures, but a collection of real coins will result in richer learning and greater enthusiasm.

Three-dimensional learning materials are usually made to be handled by students, so that manipulation is a key factor in the use of three-dimensional materials. The only exceptions are those materials which are too large, too fragile, too costly, or too rare. As a class, three-dimensional materials are inexpensive, and many are free except for the expenses of collecting and storing. Students bring these materials to their teachers as a matter of course, and a teacher's request for certain items for classroom use usually results in an extensive collection. Some commercially produced models, mock-ups (to be defined further in this chapter), or other three-dimensional devices, on the other hand, are expensive.

Objects, Specimens, Samples, and Artifacts

As with all instructional materials, three-dimensional materials should be closely related to the class's studies. They can be unique objects, such as a small collection of bones from prehistoric animals or artifacts from the excavations of Aztec ruins. A wooden mask from Africa, a vina from India, or a pair of sabots from some of the European countries cannot help but stimulate students' curiosities about these areas.

Classrooms almost everywhere have collections of rocks, coal, shells, soil samples, leaves, cross-sectioned samples of wood or tree growth, insects, and scores of other items. Such collections should be catalogued so that such facts as source, time of acquisition, and possibly a thumbnail description are given. When specimens are gathered on field trips and brought back to the classroom, they should be catalogued or given some kind of organization.

Models and Mock-Ups

Models are scaled representations, which may be equal in size, smaller, or larger than the original. Mock-ups are less accurate in the sense of being precisely like the original; they depend for their impact on contrived or simulated representations of things. They are in some respects imitations which draw freely on the imagination of the learner who will use and understand them. Models are more common than mock-ups. They can be so simple—for example, cones, pyramids, and the like in mathematics classes—that students make them from cardboard. A great variety of other materials can be used in model construction: paper, papier-mâché, clay, wood, plaster of paris, metals, plastics, string, and so on. Commercial firms produce and sell a great variety of models. It is also possible to purchase a great many ready-cut models, such as miniature airplanes, which can be assembled by students. Commercial sets of building blocks, such as Tinker Toys, Fiddlesticks, and Lincoln Logs, add to the variety of possible student-generated models.

Models are generally classified into four main types. The first, *solid models*, are used chiefly for recognition or external features. These include such items as puppets, cars, engines, housing, and transportation models. A second type shows an internal structure and is called a *cross-section* or *cutaway model*. Engines and machines, animal anatomy, an oil well, or a coal mine are good examples. *Construction models*, which can be put together part by part, are also useful. Construction models of the human torso, insect bodies, geometric forms, machines, and instruments are important teaching aids of this type. *Working models*, which demonstrate the operation of the thing represented, are also effective. Working models of machinery, water purification plants, canal locks, or the slide rule might be constructed.

Fig. 22. Making models of volcanoes reinforces earth science concepts in this British primary school. (Photo, courtesy Drs. Clarence Calder and Vincent Rogers of the University of Cincinnati. Reprinted through the courtesy of *Phi Delta Kappan*.)

PRINCIPLES OF USE   Models are easy to use in demonstrations for generating student interest and for challenging thought, but they have limitations. They are, after all, only representations, and oversimplification is a danger. The student must remember that the model of the eye shows the organ separate from the complex and complicated body of which it is a part, and that it functions with many other body organs and processes. Nothing can substitute for a trip to Chicago's stockyards or to the United Nations, even though models or mock-ups of these places may be good learning devices.

The use of models can be more effective if, in addition to the major principles for all media use, some of the following principles are observed:

- Use models in as interesting a manner as possible. Anecdotes and interesting historical sidelights may add to the effectiveness.
- Place the model in a convenient location so that it is visible to every student. Closer examination or individual study may follow. As mentioned before, every possible opportunity should be given students to handle and manipulate the model.
- Encourage students to examine the model, ask questions, and make generalizations. Attention should be given to the elimination of erroneous concepts about size, complexity, and the like.
- Put unrelated objects, specimens, or models out of sight so that they do not confuse the students or divide their attention. Good storage facilities permit materials to be kept hidden until the time for actual use. After the model has been used, it should be put away for future use.
- Utilize models to add interest and meaning to exhibits and displays.
- Encourage students to produce models to illustrate concepts, objects, or principles with which they work. How much of this will warrant the time spent will vary with different individuals and groups. The teacher will have to set the time limits.

Dioramas

The *Dictionary of Education* defines a diorama as "a three-dimensional representation composed of various symbolic and real materials, such as pictures and specimens; it frequently utilizes both transmitted and reflected light to produce a natural scenic effect." The diorama may be considered a model placed in a dramatic setting.

Because professionally made dioramas are quite expensive, they are not widely used. Some school systems, through their audiovisual centers, produce a limited number, which can be rotated among the schools when certain units are studied. Units in history, safety, nature, play production, science, home economics, literature, and industry are most amenable to the use of dioramas.

Students at all grade levels can make dioramas. The setting may be a shoebox, a lettuce crate, a cardboard box, or some similar container. Sketches showing what the diorama will look like are prepared. The front and top of the box are removed, and the next step is to paint the background and make a realistic bottom. Figures, buildings, plants, and miniature toys complete the construction. The "depth" and perspective desired are achieved by using different-sized objects, exaggerated angles, and foreshortening of the sides. Bold colors add realism and interest. Most dioramas are lighted from the top, either naturally or with bulbs.

The diorama, in a sense, is another version of the old-fashioned sand table since both are simulations of real-life settings. Both, too, are usually constructed to scale; however, dioramas employed by museums are often quite large, even life-size. Amateur school models are usually small, and, along with the sand table, they employ chiefly a variety of scrap materials in construction. The degree of sophistication and skill in a diorama may range from a simple grocery store made by first-graders to an Elizabethan stage or a Roman galley made by high school students.

Exhibits and Displays

Exhibits and displays are terms used more or less interchangeably to signify something placed in public view for a competition, a demonstration, or a show. Usually "display" connotes an arrangement of flat or two-dimensional materials, while "exhibit" connotes three-dimensional materials. There is no real division, however, and most arrangements may, and usually do, combine both types of materials. Whether a classroom arrangement of objects and artifacts from India is called a display or an exhibit does not matter: the purposes of both are the same—to inform, to influence, to interest, and to stimulate. Those who view the table can gather accurate ideas about costumes, art objects, musical instruments, architecture, or any of a hundred bits of information about India.

Simple exhibit-displays are found in classrooms, science rooms, shops, laboratories, and school corridors. More pretentious exhibit-displays are the rule for hobby shows, parents' nights, holidays, celebrations, and planned visitations. What is an "open house" without an exhibit-display?

Although teachers are concerned mainly with student exhibit-displays, commercial displays are also available. Usually these are concerned with materials that are not readily accessible to students. Some of the commercial exhibit-displays are useful, but often they are designed for effect rather than for fostering learning.

BEST USES OF EXHIBITS AND DISPLAYS The guidelines for media use outlined in Chapter 1 apply, of course, to exhibits and displays. For example, exhibits should be well-integrated with other media, such as bulletin boards, for specific educational purposes. Especially important for exhibits and displays are the following principles:

- Have a central theme. Then arrange materials, colors, lettering, and design to carry out the theme. Set down plans on paper much like an outline for a theme or a scenario for shooting a motion picture to ensure unity and coherence.
- Build drama into the exhibit. Color, lettering, spacing of objects, lighting, and location in the room all contribute to this quality.
- Make it a working exhibit rather than a static one. Stu-

dents working in the exhibit add interest and vitality. Numerous activities can be planned to accompany exhibits: for example, painting, craft making, charting and graphing, sewing, clay modeling, and wood or metal crafting.

– Involve as many students as possible. If the exhibit shows work done by a class, all members should be represented in some way, unless the exhibit is a "show" designed by one group for the rest of the class.

– Dismantle the exhibit before it becomes shopworn or overly familiar.

Kits or Loan Boxes

Schools commonly collect and supply kits of instructional materials for teachers. School kits are analogous to the tool boxes of repairmen, carpenters, and garage mechanics. In school use, however, they become educational materials, providing varied materials for demonstration purposes and productions by teachers and students. Kits insure better production because the teachers are provided with better and more specialized tools than they would ordinarily have. They are convenient for check-out, lessen duplication in school purchasing, and may be circulated from teacher to teacher and school to school. Kits probably are most easily collected for the sciences, health, art, home economics, and industrial arts, but the other subject areas offer possibilities also. In physics, for example, kits can be compiled so that when sound is taught, the teacher has the devices and equipment he needs to introduce and develop the unit.

The learning resources center in the San Diego schools, for example, has a variety of kits which it calls "loan boxes." A box for the social studies unit on colonial life contains many interesting objects, such as hand-woven fabric, wooden bowl and spoon, gourd dipper, wool carders, candle molds and candles, Indian corn, a miniature spinning wheel, some flax, cotton, and a doll dressed in colonial costume.

Science and mathematics teachers have found the kits not only valuable for class demonstration, but useful for individual learning when they are loaned to students for home use. Many experiments ordinarily done in school can safely be performed at home with a great saving in time both for teacher and student. Also, some studies have shown that students who have kits of materials get more out of their reading: for example, a kit on rockets can add depth to reading a textbook account on that subject.

Brevard Junior College (Florida) has been experimenting with a "shoe box" kit for use in the Department of Nursing. The box contains medical equipment and supplies and is accompanied by a prerecorded set of instructions on a cassette tape. Cassette players, with headsets, are mounted in carrels in the nursing laboratory for students' use.

Several corporations such as railroad, telephone, and petroleum companies prepare kits for long-term loan to schools, usually through the learning resources center. Some minor problems occur in connection with kits either for school use or home check-out, and the kits must be returned to the audiovisual center or some home base periodically for replacement of missing or broken parts. Losses, however, are usually very light and the overall costs are insignificant.

DRAMATIC TECHNIQUES

Another commonly used instructional medium, which might be considered to have deeper student involvement than such media as exhibits and displays, is dramatization. Students are the prime teaching tools in dramatization, which, if properly conceived and conducted, adds interest and zest to classwork. It promotes unity and cooperation, and students of all ages enjoy it, either as participants or as members of the audience.

Extemporaneous Dramatization

Preschool and early school-age children naturally engage in imaginative play. Train rides, automobile trips, telephoning, weddings, or building are common games. Such activities will undoubtedly help students create vivid sensory images to associate with the scene, story, or incident interpreted.

Dramatization allows students to discover new behavior patterns and teachers to gain new insights about their students. As children mature there is less make-believe in their play, and more attention is given to details, facts, and authenticity. Psychologists believe that all these activities are wholesome and should be encouraged.

The Pantomime

The pantomime is a nonverbal expressive form which has much value in education. Often even shy students will take part in pantomiming and lose their timidity by gesturing with hands, face, and body. Pantomiming does not require rehearsals, costuming, or staging. It can be utilized in almost any classroom and in many learning situations. A suggestion from the teacher that students act out such activities as finding a seat in a theater, eating dinner, answering the telephone, or accepting a dance invitation will provide a springboard for a variety of lessons.

Tableaux

The tableau is formal and stylized. Here students, either as individuals or as groups, try to represent some scene, such as the signing of the Declaration of Independence or the landing of the first man on the moon, by a silent, motionless posing. Tableaux by themselves are infrequently used in school work, but the tableau may be a useful part of some other dramatic activity.

Pageants

This semiformal display involving drama, costumes, and music is best-suited to the work of older students. It can be correlated easily with numerous school studies such as history, geography, literature, the arts, and home economics. Pageants call for such broad participation that they are more suitable for entire school projects than for the small class. But they involve a good deal of time and usually some money and may noticeably interfere with the school program.

Role-Playing

Role-playing is usually informal and extemporaneous, yet it can be planned and even rehearsed. The person taking a role creates it as he sees it, and his actions are characterized, of course, by the attitudes, interpretations, and knowledge he attributes to the character he plays. There is no memorization of lines. Role-playing a scene in the United Nations to censure a member nation, for example, may involve planning, but it will also reflect the knowledge and attitudes of the participants.

BEST USES OF ROLE-PLAYING Incidents suitable for role-playing which do not involve psychological or psychiatric training on the part of the teacher vary widely, ranging from those based on subject content, such as an historical episode, to personal behavior, such as courtesy, etiquette, and issues in interpersonal relations. These incidents can be illustrated by the following examples:

- Members of a senior history class assume the roles of members of President McKinley's cabinet. They hold a meeting the morning after receiving the news of the sinking of the *Maine*.
- Four state officials hold a meeting with three executives of a large corporation guilty of dumping waste and pollution into the principal river and lake of the state.
- A third grade child is habitually tardy for school.
- Carol Adams invites one of her junior high classmates, Bill Green, to the Adams home for dinner.

Role-playing can be a sophisticated activity: its successful use requires considerable skill on the part of teachers, since many situations involve highly projective techniques—techniques, that is, in which the past attitudes and experiences of the participants are all important. Interpreting the outcomes of a performance meaningfully also calls for maturity. Many pitfalls must be guarded against, such as labeling students, "making problems," poking fun, and exploiting or violating personal propriety, and care must be taken in casting roles.

As with all other media, general principles for proper selection, use, and follow-up should be kept in mind in role-playing. Additionally, the following rules are particularly important:

- "Set up" situations with care. The problems or incidents to be portrayed should be discussed by the entire group. The discussion should put the group in a receptive mood for the portrayal.
- Select roles carefully. Members of the group should usually be selected by the teacher. Students selected should be able to project themselves into roles or parts and be verbal enough to present a good case for the role. The ability to pretend is important.
- Give the actors time to think through their roles. Though most role-playing is spontaneous, the actors must understand the roles thoroughly, have a reasonable time to think their roles through, and plan their actions.
- Cue the audience about what the actors are trying to accomplish.
- Encourage students to develop the parts as they see them. The leader and members of the "cast" should be allowed to be as spontaneous as possible. If the action slows down or goes astray, the teacher should stop the procedure. Performances should be short and should explore only one point at a time.
- Discuss the performance with the class. The discussion can be held by the entire class or by subgroups. Both strengths and weaknesses of the performance should be brought out in free discussion.

Simulation Games

Within recent years exciting developments occurred in the area of simulation games. An extension of principles basic to extemporaneous play, dramatization, role-playing, and other play forms used by teachers for years, the simulation game is utilized in management training, military strategy, education of diplomatic corps members, and the training of educational administrators as well as in schools.

The simulations considered here provide both a method and a motivation.

Bock gives the following definition of simulation and gaming:

> ... [A] game is any contest (play) among adversaries (players) operating under constraints (rules) for an objective (winning, victory, or payoff). Games can be typed according to four basic standards: (1) the relationship between the player and the subject matter (reality, historical, hypothetical and fantasy games); (2) the degree of control which the players collectively exercise over the outcome of the game (skill vs. chance); (3) the degree to which the outcome depends on interaction among players (showdown vs. strategy); (4) and the degree to which the set of actions which a player may take is constrained by the rule structure of the game (completely free role-play vs. a rigidly structured situation.)[2]

Simulation games may be either purchased commercially or devised in the school. They should not be considered merely extemporaneous free play. The old-time favorite game of Monopoly, for example, has rules to be followed and materials to be manipulated. A new simulation such as Napoli, Crisis, or Market is no less structured. In most instances, teachers' manuals, student guidelines, possibly workbooks, and evaluation devices are available.

BEST USES OF SIMULATION GAMES   In a way these simulations are sophisticated role-playing. Students role-play situations that are impractical to experience and understand otherwise. In most of these situations, many things happen at once. The setting may be hypothetical, historical, or based on current events.

Most of the so-called games are basically "reality" games which have been found exceptionally valuable in social studies, guidance, vocational opportunities, and community

2. Barbara Bock, "Role Playing Reality," *Educator's Guide to Media and Methods*, 2 (March 1969): 45.

study. Teachers in the past have often found it difficult to motivate students in these areas, even though they involve life problems or activities which, outside the classroom, have much meaning for students. Thus students find games helpful in understanding the workings of Congress, the stock market, national politics, consumer buying, international money, mercantilism, revolution, dictatorship, propaganda, and other complex concepts. Although games are also employed in three-dimensional devices as trainers, mock-ups, and models, the simulations seem to make their greatest contribution to the area of *idea-manipulation*. They offer challenges to students of varying abilities.

A great many simulation games are of the strategy type, in which the course of action of players is much influenced by the action of others. Intelligent decisions cannot be memorized: they must be rationally derived through analysis, synthesis, and evaluation. Some simulation games quite naturally lean more heavily on factual background, others on interactions of people. At times the action hinges on long-range planning.

Through simulation games, many passive, shy, or indifferent students can become active participants in learning activities. Simulation games have been welcomed enthusiastically by teachers of inner city students, but they seem to have equal appeal for suburban and rural students. Many courses are enriched by simulation games with a more concrete set of experiences; social studies, for example, is a field which can be open to laboratory situations analogous to those of physics, chemistry, and industrial arts. But, as in most instances, educational games and simulations are not a final answer to all learning problems. Some educators believe that simulations have not been fully researched and their values should, as in all instructional situations, be tentatively accepted. Activities must be selected which have the greatest potential of allowing students to reach previously articulated instructional objectives.

Puppetry

Puppetry is a specialized form of dramatization which employs doll-like figures of human or animal forms. The puppets are operated by students who either speak memorized lines or ad lib. Action is the most important element in puppetry.

Puppetry has two main props: *puppets* and *marionettes*. Puppets, which are simpler to make and operate, are held and moved by the hands of the operator. Marionettes are manipulated by strings, wires, or rods from above. They have jointed legs and arms which, along with the head and body, are movable. The operator controls movements with strings attached to a crossbar, commonly in an H shape, which he moves or wiggles. Marionette performances are usually presented on some sort of stage, whereas puppets can be used anywhere. Puppets and marionettes can be utilized for a number of educational purposes, in many curriculum areas and at all levels. Students may develop new interests in reading and oral and written expression, and shy students in particular have an opportunity to develop some poise. Also, special talents can be discovered and developed, since creativity and imagination are stimulated as color, design, craftsmanship, storytelling, and dramatization are brought into play. In most cases puppet work calls for group endeavor and cooperation, and since there are many facets to puppetry, students with varied abilities can make a contribution to the project. Finally, of course, puppetry entertains and gives students practice in meaningful and orderly audience listening and participation.

Several kinds of puppets can be made. Stick puppets are exceedingly simple, and consist of a figure, such as an animal or a human being, cut out and stapled to a stick. Hand puppets range from those made of simple paper bags to carved wooden or papier-mâché ones. Paper bags may have faces painted on them with crayons, or openings for eyes, nose, and ears may be cut out and yarn or string hair used. The bag is placed over the hand for operation with a rubber band at the wrist to hold the puppet in place. Gloves also can be adapted as puppets. Making puppets of papier-mâché or with carved wooden heads or bodies requires skill and time.

Masks made by primary school children can also be classified as a type of puppet. The main use of masks is as an accompaniment to fairy stories, folk tales, and other forms of storytelling.

Demonstrations

The demonstration may be classified as an audiovisual technique because it employs instructional materials to enrich learning on the experience level. Demonstrations are important for teaching skills, showing processes, defining a problem in concrete terms, and conveying information. The technique may be used to introduce a new topic or a unit of work, to provide additional information or understanding after a topic has been studied, or to help in summarizing a unit. Effective demonstrations help students understand a problem, learn methods of attacking or solving the problem, become aware of fundamental relationships, and draw conclusions.

Although most demonstrations involve materials and equipment, the verbal model in foreign language instruction is truly a demonstration. If, for example, the Spanish teacher is not satisfied with students' pronunciation of *veinte*, he can demonstrate the correct form by saying it in the context of a make-believe situation and by showing how the voice mechanism should be adjusted. Demonstrations may employ simple materials or complicated equipment.

EFFECTIVE DEMONSTRATIONS   The principles underlying effective demonstrations are basically the same as those for any good lesson and for all media use. As detailed in the major principles set forth in Chapter 1, preparation, presentation, evaluation, and follow-up are the hallmarks of an effective demonstration.

Demonstrations vary in their concreteness. In general, the age and background of the students will control the degree of concreteness-abstraction involved.

COMMUNITY RESOURCES AND LEARNING MATERIALS

A great variety of learning materials and activities exist in every community. Even the so-called impoverished community has many resources if teachers are energetic and imaginative enough to find them. Community learning opportunities involve people, places, things, and ideas, and thus add vitality and relevancy to learning.

Schools which use community resources find them a two-way street: the school goes to the community for ideas and learning materials, and the community brings the school its problems, solutions, and understanding. This interaction can provide excellent motivation. Ideas are not locked into watertight compartments of history, science, shop, agriculture, and other school subjects. Housing, for example, is more than graphs and tables of economics; it is a broad human problem.

Unfortunately, few of these ideas are ever put into practice. Reports of successes and failures are scarce; hence, it is not surprising to find federal funds funneled into community-action school programs. Among these programs are Headstart, Follow Through, Vista, PCP, Job Corps, Neighborhood Youth Corps[3], and others. Funding for government programs is often insecure because they are subject to political expediency. Most of the above programs draw heavily on community resources and local personnel. Headstart, for example, relies solidly on the assistance of paraprofessional aides (parents and young people from the community, chiefly volunteers). The active cooperation of representatives of outside civic and social organizations such as youth agencies, churches, police, welfare agencies, and the Urban League, are brought into the educational framework. Thus in actual practice much of the school curriculum is taken directly from the community. The community does indeed become a learning laboratory.

In the past, most often the schools were ready to recognize and use historical locations, high-class cultural agencies and institutions, and well-accepted commercial enterprises. Only recently have educators realized the potential their local com-

3. Headstart—federal assistance for preschool children; Follow Through —continuation for children who started in Headstart; Vista—Volunteers in Service to America; PCP—Personalized Curriculum Project; Job Corps—youth in vocational training; Neighborhood Youth Corps— youth assisting in community improvement.

munity holds for their classrooms and the potential their classrooms hold for the community. The entire community, teachers, students, parents, and nonparents need to participate in decision-making affecting the educational opportunities available both inside and outside of the school building. Although each community possesses unique possibilities, many resources are common to almost all communities as follows:

Resource Persons

Non-teaching knowledgeable individuals who live in the community and are willing to come to the school to share their knowledge and skills with the students are called resource persons. They can be invaluable in discussing local cultural influences, occupations, industry, government, home and family living, community agencies, and countless other subjects. Resource people often convey new and vital understandings to students.

The resource person should be unbiased and able to present his topic clearly. Some guidance about what is expected should be given him. The class should have some background on the topic of the talk. Intelligent questions can be preplanned and there may be subsequent discussions, interviews, and related activities. A "thank you" letter from the class is always in order.

Field Trips

The term *field trip* embraces short trips in the immediate vicinity, usually referred to as the *walking trip*, and the longer trip, involving travel by bus or automobile, usually called the *field study*, *excursion*, *journey*, or just the *field trip*. The *extended field trip*, which covers several days or even several weeks, may have unusual values for special student groups.

Five important steps, which follow the format and inherent planning of the principles for all media use, should be followed in planning and executing a successful field trip:

Teacher preparation: The teacher selects a meaningful and possible trip, contacts area authorities, obtains the approval of school authorities, arranges for transportation, checks safety and other details, contacts parents, and alerts other teachers who may be affected.

Class preparation: Teacher and students discuss the reason for the trip, plan and discuss such details as finances, safety, appropriate dress, and necessary committees, and plan for documentation of the trip by note-taking, pictures, sound recording, sketching, interviewing, and so on.

The trip: The group shows courtesy and interest, arrives promptly, does not disrupt the work of employees, and takes samples of specimens only with the approval of the host.

Follow-up: The teacher and students discuss objectives of the trip, listen to committee reports, explore the benefits derived from the trip, write "thank you" letters, and display pictures taken or specimens gathered.

Evaluation: Teacher and students answer the questions, "Was the trip worthwhile?"; "Should this trip be recommended to others?"

The *extended field trip* requires all of the above planning and more. For example, a Spanish class that plans to spend a week in Mazatlan, Mexico, has a full-scale planning problem on its hands. But if problems are multiplied, the understandings and results may also be multiplied.

Free and Inexpensive Learning Materials

Free or low-cost learning materials of many kinds are abundant. Hundreds of American and foreign firms make and distribute free pamphlets, samples, models, charts, graphs, filmstrips, and many other kinds of supplies and materials available to schools. Some of this material is valuable, but some is merely advertising. Schools or teachers who use these free materials must develop a policy of "looking a gift horse in the mouth." Many school districts have a policy governing the use of such materials. Others leave the use to the discretion of the teachers. Several professional organizations have drawn up standards to govern the selection of sponsored materials.

Foreign Exchange Students and Teachers

Exchanges between countries of students and teachers are becoming numerous, and the firsthand knowledge of another culture they afford is very valuable. Often foreign students live in the homes of American students, attend classes with their new friends, go to sporting events, and participate in many of the activities of the host school. They also act as resource people, speaking to classes and answering questions about their home countries.

Schools which have foreign exchange students should not overlook the fact that they have on their doorstep resource persons of great value. Authentic speech accents and knowledge of certain subject matters most relevant to other students should not only be used "live" with peer groups, but should be recorded for reuse as occasion warrants.

Telephone Interviews

With the improvement of telephone communications, the use of the telephone interview in the classroom has expanded and developed. These developments are discussed in Chapter 5 under "Telephone Sound Systems."

Camping Activities

In some sections of the country, limited camping activities are part of the school program. These programs are woven into the regular curriculum of both elementary and secondary schools. The school camp (the school need not own a camp to have an outdoor or camping program) is an activity for all students, and may feature a summer or a winter program.

School camping uses the talents of teachers, counselors, and a trained camp staff. Usually student activities have three main divisions: (1) Study—reading, discussion, writing, and listening to resource persons; (2) Recreation—athletics, dramatics, hiking, and crafts; and (3) Work—making beds, washing dishes, making fires, and personal hygiene.

Almost every child enjoys camping, and a school camping program can fulfill a worthwhile educational function.

As Conant says, "The community and school are inseparable." The farsighted school attempts to capitalize on community learning opportunities. This concept of community importance to education is not new. It was noted by Aristotle and has been observed and emphasized down through the years by educators.

But overemphasis and overenthusiasm for community resources *can* become a professional fetish which may backfire. Schools should use the community as one of many important learning resources. At some times reading a book, listening to a lecture, experimenting in a laboratory, or practicing and creating in a studio are apt; at other times these can be stereotyped and meaningless, and greater value will come from community visitation, study, and analysis. The proper balance between these two environments calls for professional and social understanding.

As mentioned earlier at the outset of this chapter, the standard learning materials and techniques continue to be widely used, and improvements on them are constantly evolving. Keeping in mind the important role in the classroom of these basic aids, we shall turn now to some of the more complex concepts of instructional media.

Chapter 7

Mediated Instructional Procedures

BEHAVIORAL OBJECTIVES

After studying this chapter, the reader will be able to:

1. Define the terms *mediated instructional procedures, multimedia, multi-image,* and *synergy* with reference to the systems approach to instruction.
2. Compare and contrast broadcast and closed-circuit television and explain how Samoan ETV, MPATI, and satellite broadcasting exemplify educational use of television.
3. Given a specific learning situation, justify the use or non-use of color television instead of black-and-white television in that situation.
4. Summarize two provocative findings of evaluative research about ETV and, for each, suggest any other factors which should probably be considered before drawing any conclusions from the research.
5. List four characteristics of VTR and of EVR.
6. Summarize the development, components, and advantages of the learning laboratory, and list three ways to ensure its effective utilization.
7. List five distinguishing features of programmed instruction, citing why each can be advantageous to students.
8. Distinguish between DAIRS and CAI, and identify two ways in which each acts as the student's "memory bank."

Earlier chapters have dealt with the simpler and more conventional media and their use. This chapter will discuss what are now referred to in educational literature as *mediated instructional procedures*. This simply means single- or multichannels of communication (usually the latter) phased together so as to form a system. This new approach may involve a teacher performing alone or working in conjunction with other teachers and paraprofessionals as a team.

Whether automated learning involving many self-instructional and mass learning devices will prove a renaissance for education is debatable. Such talk frightens those who mistakenly believe that mediated instruction renders the teacher obsolete. In spite of the objections raised, however, electronic and manual technology continue to advance steadily in school use. Educational commissions continue to find positive learning results in technological experimentations, and continue to recommend further implementation. But this is only part of the story. Strong efforts are also being made to modernize the school at the "human" level. Some say the teaching process is a century behind the times in this respect.

Laymen and educators have no doubt realized by now the naivety of branding anything technological as "anti-human" or "mechanistic." Although instructional media involving electronic components *may* depersonalize instruction if hardware and software have not been properly designed, we have seen in earlier chapters that teaching and learning through media can significantly increase students' interest and mastery.

Some modern equipment makes it possible to instruct effectively a great number of students simultaneously, whereas other innovations provide tailored instruction for the individual. Most prominent among mediated systems today are "Telemation," or automated classrooms; educational television, including videotape; language laboratories, now finding their way into other subject areas, where they are becoming known as "learning laboratories"; various forms of programmed instruction; dial-access information retrieval systems; and computer-assisted instruction. Each will be examined in this chapter.

All of these systems are *mediated*, and some are characterized as *multimedia*. The latter utilize a variety of audiovisual media and experiences, often integrated with other learning materials, in order to foster learning. It is important to distinguish between multimedia and *multi-image*, at the outset. Multi-image may involve two images from a single projector or from two projectors, or from motion pictures, slides, filmstrips, or other projections. Multimedia, on the other hand, implies presentation employing more than one medium, not necessarily an image. Thus, two or more media might be integrated to convey or reinforce a single message, or the media might be used consecutively. The question of how many media or what types seems to be of no particular consequence. What matters is whether the media are focused on a single goal. A multiplicity of multimedia do not in and of themselves make an effective presentation. As we have emphasized throughout this book, they should be carefully selected and their use planned in terms of the objectives sought.

When multiple media such as books, workbooks, newspapers, models, specimens, tapes, slides, and films are used to accomplish a designated objective, the whole becomes greater than the sum of its parts—it is a *synergy*. Applications have been nearly legion in the sciences, foreign languages, health education, and other fields. So-called teaching kits are examples of multimedia materials in elementary schools. On a more advanced level we find the production of a whole series of film lessons in physics and chemistry. Someone has said the development has been "from kits to systems."

A still more advanced application of synergistic principles as now employed in several universities utilizes several electronic media for a large group instructional program and is referred to as *multimedia*, *multi-image*, or *multi-screen* instruction. This technological advance brings together commercially and/or locally produced and organized materials into a clearly designed system or subsystem all working toward one end.

One manufacturer of automated classroom equipment provides a machine which combines many types of equipment controlled either automatically (by an electronic pulsed tape) or manually (by the instructor) so that one medium after another glides smoothly into operation. The machine stops for work assignments or instructor's explanations, then starts up again, and registers student responses to questions and problems. In some respects a computer is a multimedia system.

TELEMATION AND RELATED MULTIMEDIA SYSTEMS

Telemation is a new term which means about the same as *automated classroom*. A number of experimental centers have set aside specially equipped classrooms that provide the teacher with multiple viewing screens and several sound outlets. Motion pictures, still projections, and television images may occupy the screens simultaneously or in rapid succession. A console with a teleprompter allows the teacher to lecture while, using electronic cuing devices on the script, making pictures and sound appear mysteriously from nowhere. All equipment is out of sight. Some of the installations have built-in student response systems at each seat.

Telemation and similar multimedia approaches fit neatly into the *systems* approach to instruction. They interrelate various instructional materials, objectives, methods, and evaluations so that an orderly "systematic" approach to learning is promoted. Finn characterized the systems concept in education with the statement: "It is, I believe, safe to say that this move toward organization and system in the instructional materials field is one of the most solid trends of the technological revolution in education. Its implications for the role of the teacher of the future are, of course, tremendous."[1]

EDUCATIONAL TELEVISION

Among the new instructional media, television may have the greatest potential for reaching large audiences simulta-

1. James D. Finn, "The Emerging Technology of Education," in *Instructional Process and Media Innovation*, ed. Robert A. Weisgerber (Chicago: Rand McNally and Company, 1968), pp. 303–4.

Fig. 23. Recent television programming for children such as "The Electric Company" (above) or the popular "Sesame Street" mix humor, fast action, and animated cartoons in an attempt to present early educational concepts through a mass medium. (Frames, courtesy The Children's Television Workshop.)

neously. Evidence has indicated that educational television can improve the caliber of some types of instruction and provide a stimulus to learning at many age levels and subject areas.

Television can bring to the classroom an enriched content ranging from unique or remote industrial processes to cultural experiences. Class size is no longer a problem. Much of this chapter will be devoted to the specific effects of television on formal school education.

Television programs can be divided into two broad categories: *broadcast television* and *closed-circuit television*. (A third category, *narrowcast television*, is less prominent.) Broadcast or open-circuit television is the more common type

Fig. 24. A closed-circuit television system provides educational agencies with their own television network for classroom instruction and communication, as well as giving students practical experience in production techniques. (Photo, courtesy Long Beach, California, Unified School District.)

and consists of programs broadcast on licensed commercial or educational channels on a regular schedule. Although broadcasts are either commercial or educational, educational programs are usually special broadcasts. *Educational television* (ETV) stations broadcast programs of both specific and broad cultural orientation, while *instructional television* (ITV) stations broadcast programs of a more limited or specific nature. Neither type of station carries advertising but is supported by taxation, public subscription, and/or grants from foundations and industry. ITV uses are usually more closely related to the classroom instructional program than are ETV programs.

Closed-circuit television reaches only receivers which are connected to the transmitter. Such broadcasting requires no licensing. It is used widely in schools, colleges, and universities for programs of specific interest to one or more groups. It can and is being used by some districts to connect every building in the district. Closed-circuit relies mainly on cable connections between camera and receiver; microwave broadcast, however, is also used for longer distribution. Two extensive uses of closed-circuit television to reach numerous buildings in a district are found in the Anaheim Elementary School District in California and the Washington County Schools, Hagerstown, Maryland. The success of the medium in both of these districts has received wide publicity. South Carolina is an example of the use of closed-circuit TV at the state level. At last report the state system was serving 213 schools, five universities and colleges, thirteen hospitals, six technical schools, three private schools, and three other state institutions. The state's closed-circuit system is also supplemented with open-circuit broadcasting.

Although *coaxial cable* ETV is widely used, some schools prefer to own and operate a so-called 2500-mHz (megaHertz) station. This system is an FCC-controlled transmission system in which signals are radiated by the use of repeaters and microwave to reach all buildings in a district. The 2500 mHz is a frequency band much higher than UHF (890 mHz) and is a band reserved solely for education. This is known as "line-of-sight short distance" (about 25 miles) broadcast, and suffers from attendant problems of possible repeater stations, and still other problems of reception. Nevertheless, considerable experimentation with it goes on, and future years may find this type of transmission cheaper and generally more acceptable.

Educational television utilization has become so important today that scarcely a school building is erected which does not have installations for TV, either for current or later use.

Since 1952, the Federal Communications Commission has reserved over six hundred television channels for educational purposes. Some of these are in the *very high frequency* (VHF) band and some in the *ultra high frequency* (UHF) band. Heretofore the UHF bands have not been considered of prime quality, but technology is changing this situation. Presently a move is afoot to extend the number of reserved channels for education to approximately one thousand. At the moment, some one hundred VHF and seventy-five UHF channels are in operation or will be in operation shortly. Many others are in the planning stage. Some cities—Pittsburgh, for instance—are operating two stations. All this has happened only two decades after KHUT (the University of Houston, Texas) went on the air as the first noncommercial television station.

The growth of ETV has, in fact, been so pronounced that only two or three states are without a station. Except for the Rocky Mountain area, all states have two or more facilities. In addition, states have formed regional networks to facilitate cooperation and the exchange of programs. These systems are the Western Educational Network, Rocky Mountain Network, Midwest ETV Network, Central Educational Network, Eastern Educational Network, and Southern Educational Communications Association.

At various times the federal government has given financial assistance in outright gifts or matching funds for the establishment of stations in cities and states. In 1967 Congress passed and the president signed the Public Broadcasting Act, attesting to the government's belief in the importance of television and radio for educational purposes. At this writing, unfortunately, not much has come of this act, but the legislation is on the books.

Sixteen large cities—Baltimore, Boston, Buffalo, Chicago, Cleveland, Detroit, Los Angeles, Memphis, Milwaukee, New York, Philadelphia, Pittsburgh, St. Louis, San Diego, San Francisco, and Washington, D.C.—have organized a Research Council of the Great Cities Program for School Improvement, one important goal of which is intercity cooperation. These cities enroll 10 percent of the nation's school population. One section of the council's project focuses on ETV. The cities in this group use all three kinds of transmission—closed-circuit, open-circuit, and the so-called narrowcasting (Instructional Fixed Service and the 2500 mHz).

SAMOAN ETV Interestingly enough, the nearest approach to total teaching by television in America is to be found on the island of American Samoa, 2,300 miles west of Hawaii. The island represents a long-neglected territory which has few resources—economic or cultural. A complete open-broadcast facility of three channels was built especially for school use. Since its inception in 1961, the program in its entirety has been a complete new design in education in matters of curriculum, methods, coverage, and teacher acceptance and utilization.

Every day a major part of the instructional program, including every subject and every grade from primary to high school, is beamed to every school building on the island. The daily broadcasts are reinforced with professional preparation for teachers—manuals, guides, lesson plans, and so forth. The teachers are enthusiastic about the medium.

Students sit on the floor at very low desks and watch the television receivers. But the watching is far from passive. Pauses and cues in the telecast bring viewers into active participation. Hands are raised and answers or opinions are voiced, or in some instances the group answers in unison. The principal of one building, who was from Maryland, and a native vice principal conveyed to the author their approval of the program and their faith in the planning, methods followed, and overall effectiveness. A visit to the broadcasting studio (later to the transmission station atop a mountain) reveals a group of dedicated teachers (both mainland and native), most of whom have had collegiate and professional education on the mainland followed by workshops, conferences, and classroom experience. Both English and native language is used. The Samoan program is a fine example of classroom teachers, studio teachers, and administration working as a team with close liasion and constant feedback.

THE MPATI PROGRAM One of the boldest experiments with educational television was started in 1960 with the Midwest Program of Airborne Television Instruction. As the name implies, telecasts of videotaped lessons were radiated over UHF channels from a "flying classroom" five miles above earth on fixed courses. This form of broadcast provided tremendous coverage, so that signals were received in classrooms in all or parts of six states.

Although costly, the initial experiment was considered a success. It has now moved into a new and less spectacular phase of operation. The experiment did much to dramatize ETV. It showed the feasibility of reaching several million students at one time with high-quality learning materials. The similarity of this experiment to satellite broadcasting, described next, is worthy of mention.

SATELLITE BROADCASTING Classrooms of tomorrow will in all probability use domestic and international satellite broadcasting. To date, experiments have shown complete feasibility in this field. Costs are, of course, high but government and business have shared the expensive developmental work. Satellite coverage was launched as early as 1965 with telecasts to and from Europe. Nearly everyone in the United States has seen the pictures broadcast from Telstar and Early Bird, as well as President Nixon's visits to China and Moscow, and the Olympic Games in Munich. Great strides have been made in harnessing solar light power, in providing two-way communication, in stabilizing video transmission, and in achieving color fidelity. Still more encouraging is the fact that weather is no problem in satellite beaming.

Some of the developing countries have very special needs for this sort of communication: Indonesia, for example, with its vast population scattered over 3,000 far-flung islands, and India with an even greater population again extending over a large geographical area, and with staggering problems of illiteracy and multiple languages. India now has only one TV station. Instead of trying to expand ground TV piecemeal, space TV would be less expensive, be accomplished more quickly, and have greater potential. Because of the size of the country, per unit costs could be quite small.

Domestic transmission using point-to-point distribution is naturally simpler than hemispheric distribution. Hawaii uses this form of broadcasting for its instantaneous television from the mainland. Once a satellite is in orbit its path can be fixed (controlling its coverage), and it is possible to arrange channels to carry such specialized materials as news, entertainment, sports, and politics simultaneously, or to employ a separate language on each channel.

A great many problems must still be ironed out before satellite broadcasting becomes a commonly used medium. Costs, of course, cannot be overlooked. Other problems are political, involving frequency allocations, beam limitations, interference with already established ground systems, and a crowding of the radio spectrum. Furthermore, scientists envision competition for long telecasts from new transistorized cables, so-called millimeter pipes or wave guides, and even laser beamed messages. Can space broadcasts be integrated with ground broadcasts? If expanded, will one seriously limit the other? Will some nations, or states, object? As Wilbur Schramm has remarked:

> What we most need now, therefore, is not more and better satellites so much as better plans for using them. . . . Satellites will—in all probability be very important in future communication systems, but they will not be alone, and the entire future of educational, scientific, and cultural communication will not rest with them.[2]

The Classroom Teacher and Television

Using television requires the same procedure involving student and teacher preparation, use, follow-up, and evaluation, as any other instructional material.

Generally, teacher preparation for television use is established by the school district or by the school's media specialist, who states a philosophy and the objectives to be achieved. Districts which encourage or include television as part of the school program orient their teachers so that those who are selected to appear on camera are given specific preparation for this task. Most teachers do not broadcast but use broadcast lessons in their classrooms. These teachers need to understand the value of the medium and to learn how best to utilize it.

2. Schramm, Wilbur, *Communication Satellites for Education, Science, and Culture* (Paris: UNESCO, 1968), p. 7.

Study guides for classroom use of television are available, providing pertinent information on background, reception, and follow-up of programs.

The classroom teacher's role has been modified by television. He has less responsibility for content and more for managing learning situations. This new role should enable him to give more time to counseling individuals and groups. He can now arrange additional learning activities which involve extra study, investigation, or possibly field trips, motion pictures, and other devices.

Teachers who use television must realize that responsibility for instruction no longer belongs *only* to the classroom teacher; it is also the responsibility of the teacher who is before the camera. Usually, individuals who have a thorough knowledge of the subject matter, instructional techniques, imagination, and an awareness of the psychology of learning assist the studio teacher.

A Ford Foundation report has summarized the separate roles of the classroom and the studio in a section called "Team Teaching in Television Classes."

1. The studio teacher, classroom teachers, and the curriculum experts cooperatively plan the course in advance and prepare teacher guides.
2. The studio teacher presents, explains, and demonstrates the major points of the lesson, raises questions, and stimulates student interest.
3. The classroom teacher prepares students for the telecast part of the lesson, answers questions, clarifies points, leads discussion, makes assignments, gives individual help, and supervises testing.
4. The studio teacher and classroom teachers confer regularly to evaluate the lessons and make improvements.[3]

The fear that cameramen and TV directors will determine what students will see and learn is unjustified. No student

3. The Ford Foundation and The Fund for the Advancement of Education, *Teaching by Television*, 2nd ed. (New York: The Foundation, 1961), p. 12. (Out of print.)

receives all of his instruction on television even in districts which make the greatest use of the medium. Indeed, typically only a minor part of the instructional time is spent watching the television monitor. While certain complete courses may be given by television, the main part of the instructional schedule will be carried on by conventional methods.

Color for Educational Broadcasts

Color television has now become a way of life for the over 30 percent of Americans who own color television sets. Industry spokesmen claim a higher figure, from 50 to 60 percent. Whatever the exact figures are, a preference for color broadcasting is evident.

Definitive studies and replicated findings as to the instructional value of color television are not available, although some data exist on the instructional value of color motion pictures. Chu and Schramm[4] summarized the researches up to 1968 under a grant from the U.S. Office of Education. Most of the studies hinged on the value of color vs. black and white in flat pictures or instructional films, and their results bear only obliquely on television. Chiefly, these studies add up to no significant differences in the instructional value of the two media. Some researchers did state that the perfect representation of realism must include color, but the values, in the main, relate to feelings evoked rather than actual learning. Color is more satisfying and in most cases, students *prefer* it, but a positive bearing on acquisition and retention has not been fully established except in those learning tasks where discriminations must be made on the basis of color.

Bowman's survey[5] of 170 educational television stations indicated that 79.7 percent of the persons polled were favorable to color in ETV. Only 2 percent were unfavorable, with 12 percent undecided and 5.6 percent not responding.

4. Godwin D. Chu and Wilbur Schramm, *Learning from Television: What the Research Says* (Stanford: Stanford University Press, 1968, U.S. Office of Education Contract OEC 4-7-0071123-4203).
5. Marvin L. Bowman, "The Spectrum of Colorcasting," *Educational/ Instructional Broadcasting*, 2 (September 1969): 20-23.

The survey also revealed that full color capability is a reality, and that practically all new stations are completely equipped for color (with VTR, film chain, and live cameras). Furthermore, older black-and-white transmitters can be outfitted to handle color signals at a reasonable cost.

Interviews of educators on the merits of colorcasting produce mixed replies. Most would welcome color but question the advisability of such a move on grounds of cost, but recent convention displays of NAEB and DAVI indicate a dramatic reduction in costs of film chains, cameras, transmitters, and videotape equipment. Some educational stations, such as those at Miami-Dade Junior College and the Roanoke Public School System, are now broadcasting entirely in color.[6]

Evaluating ETV

Research investigations of the effects of educational television are less encouraging than one might expect on the basis of the enthusiasm of schools that have employed this medium. Although questions can be raised about the design of the studies carried out so far, it is nevertheless a fact that most research to date shows no significant differences between the learning of students taught via television and those taught by conventional methods. Approximately three-quarters of the studies conducted yielded this finding. In the remaining quarter of all studies, approximately two-thirds learned more with television, whereas the other third learned less. These results apparently apply to retention of information, critical thinking, and problem-solving performance.

In cases where televised teaching is more efficient than conventional teaching, of course, ETV offers an advantage simply because it can yield the same results with greater efficiency. But the educational community undoubtedly needs to look more closely at the effect of television, and at the ways in which its effectiveness is measured. A closer look at the research conducted to date may provide some useful insights.

6. Janet Rosen, "Color Increases Attention, Impact, Recall for WBRA-TV," in *Planning Educational Television Stations* (Camden, N.J.: RCA, n.d.), pp. 19–26.

Most, if not all, of the research has been based upon conventional teaching and assumes that this instruction was appropriate and "right." This may not be the case: McLuhan, for one, has raised the possibility that instructional television is merely an extension of the conventional lecture method (not necessarily accepted as an appropriate method). If they *are* so closely related, then it is only natural that ETV would do no better than conventional teaching methods in research studies comparing them. The research, although quite accurate, has doubtful validity in an era when we are trying to identify new learning *activities* capable of better fulfilling individual student needs rather than to apply new *techniques* to do the same old activities. Furthermore, it cannot be assumed that all students can view a group-paced presentation and learn at the same rate. Although they were not intended to do so, these research findings tend to make TV look more like a panacea than perhaps they should.

Generally speaking, television teaching seems to work better in elementary school than in high school and college. Although practically every subject offered in the curriculum has at some time been taught over television, by their nature mathematics, science, and the social studies seem to lend themselves better to ETV than do such subjects in the humanities as literature.

Attitudes of teachers toward educational television vary. Teachers tend to be suspicious of television at the beginning, but suspicion diminishes with experience. The advantages of television that the teachers see are: equal involvement by students in all parts of the classroom (no "front-row" seats), better-planned lessons, greater use of resources, and more encouragement of students to better their study habits and use the library more extensively.

Nearly three-quarters of elementary school students polled showed no dislike for televised teaching. In general they felt that more subject matter was covered, more resources and visual aids were used, and the lessons were more interesting. College students were less favorably inclined, and high school students fell between the two groups. Three disadvantages were noted: difficulty in taking notes, no opportunity to raise a question at the time a point is made, and technical difficulties leading to loss of sound or picture.

There is an often mentioned "gap between potential and performance." *Newsweek* magazine (February 26, 1968) commented, "From the promise of great oaks, only little acorns have grown in the field of public television." And back on January 13, 1962, *The Saturday Review* asked the question, "Can educational television turn the corner?" Most educators and communication specialists not only answer "yes," but say it has done more. Successes like "Sesame Street" and "Misterogers" provide proof. Numerous educators have gone so far as to call ITV the "A-V Synthesis." It is difficult to predict what the status of television in the classroom will be a decade from now. Perhaps the above findings will be substantially the same, or techniques of organization and presentation will improve. The major function of ETV may be furnishing basic instruction, providing enrichment, furnishing a much-needed type of stimulation, offering a practical solution to large-group instruction, or the achievement of all of these objectives.

Videotape Recording (VTR)

Among the burgeoning developments in television, none is more spectacular than the use of the videotape recorder and playback. VTR in educational television helps teachers achieve what has been their goal for years: to enable a student to see his or her own performance. This innovation greatly facilitates self-evaluation and remedial work by making it possible to record simply and at low cost any performance of teacher or student and to witness an immediate or delayed playback. *Showing* and discussing with the student his good points and errors is considerably more effective than simply *telling* him about them. Videotape has had a charismatic aura about it since the time it was introduced in 1946 for commercial broadcasting. At that time costs for the equipment were in the neighborhood of $50,000 or more, and most stations leased instead of buying. Since then, modifications and development, as well as imports,

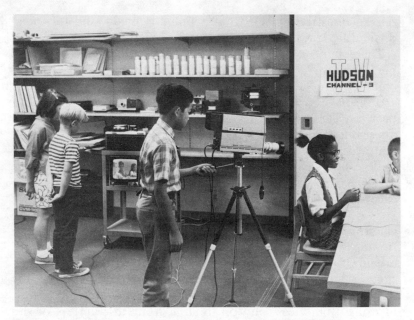

Fig. 25. The classroom videotape recorder encourages students at all levels to develop language skills. (Photo, courtesy Long Beach, California, Unified School District.)

have brought the price down to somewhere around $500. Videotaping for educational purposes began about 1964.

The design of the equipment has become less bulky and simpler to operate as it has developed. At one time a truck or trailer was needed to transport it; today it is portable and combines with a hand-held TV camera. For most educational purposes, videotaping or playback is a one-man operation, whereas in earlier days a crew of three or more was necessary.

A videotape system basically consists of a video camera, microphone, and a videotape recorder/playback. The recorder is arranged so that it can be carried over the shoulder and the camera with mounted microphone and view-finder is hand-held much like an 8-mm motion picture camera. Recorders use ¼″ or ½″ magnetic videotape on 5″ or 7″ reels. The entire unit weighs fifteen or twenty pounds. Many are battery powered and all are simple to operate with no cables or cords except a short one from camera to recorder. Larger units, less portable but with greater precision of picture and sound reproduction, are also available.

The following characteristics of videotapes make them particularly useful. They can be previewed before use, a condition not possible in "live" TV. They can be shared with other teachers, schools, or networks. They can be easily catalogued and stored. They are capable of being played back in a single classroom or fed into the TV distribution system. They are easily duplicated (or converted to 8- or 16-mm films, since film projectors are generally more available), and they can be erased, reused as needed, and edited as desired (splicing—joining pieces of film or tape— can be done by hand or preferably electronically). Videotapes, available in both black and white and color, can be shown at regular speeds, slow speeds, "stops," or "holds." With extra audio tracks, they are valuable for cuing information, for teaching foreign languages, and for other multiple-sound instruction.

The above characteristics make the following manifold uses of videotape available to teachers:

- Recording student performance for immediate analysis, evaluation, and discussion. Students watch their performance and observe their reactions and techniques.

- Recording preservice and in-service teacher performance— techniques, strategies, gestures, facial expressions, posture, idiosyncrasies. This type of use is frequently referred to as *microteaching*.

- Recording performance in athletics in the gymnasium or on the playing field.

- Recording performance in dealing with people—counseling, test administration, salesmanship, teacher-student interplay, student seminars.

- Recording performance for later use to determine levels of improvement.

- Recording lessons in any subject, but especially the performing arts—drama, debate, speech, music, dance.

- Recording demonstrations, laboratory experiments, skill developments, good lectures.

- Recording for retrieval storage. VTR may be placed in libraries or resource banks for later use.
- Recording for independent study in classroom or library carrels.
- Recording, for use in simulation games, either information for presentation or responses for later discussion.

It should be mentioned that videotape utilization can be "overdone" in supervision and remedial work. It has been found in some training aids programs, for example, that the subjects may feel too much pressure and excessive anxiety. Should this occur, self-evaluation may then become "self-confrontation."

VTR is not the only video system available. The Columbia Broadcasting System is currently marketing a system called electronic video recording (EVR). EVR is designed to convert conventional television sets into cartridge-loading video playback units. The equipment consists of a special thin-base tape which is dual-tracked and carries its sound in parallel lines on a magnetic track along with two rows of visual frames. The material is about 3/8″ in width and without sprocket holes. A circular cartridge encloses the film. A special player is attached by handclips to the antenna terminals of a TV set. The TV set is turned on to a channel that is not broadcasting and the EVR player with cartridge in place is started. The program is then reproduced on the TV set's screen.

The legal aspects of electronic copying of programs or parts of programs have not been fully explored as yet, but as a general statement the copyright law prohibits such copying without formal permission and attendant financial arrangements. Stations, even ITV stations, are very hesitant about such copying except for very short sequences and then only for strict educational use.

Microteaching

Microteaching—a method rather than a medium—relies so heavily on VTR that it deserves mention here. Lawrence has defined microteaching as "... a teaching encounter scaled down in time and in the number of students addressed by an instructor."[7] This is an instance in which a medium provides the foundation for method, means, evaluation, and research.

In general, procedures involve students in *pre-student teaching*, for example, preparing a three-to-ten-minute teaching segment which is done before a TV camera. Normally and naturally, discussion of the episode follows. The people who post-view the episode vary—the performing student alone, student and instructor, or student and classmates. Microteaching episodes may be repeated when necessary and convenient.

Some instructors prepare, or have the class prepare, a check and/or evaluation sheet. This sheet serves as a set of guidelines for better performance. The performing teacher presents the "pretended" lesson to peer students who role-play students of a given grade and subject. The lesson may involve a single teaching method or several methods with multimedia learning materials. The "pretended" lesson is videotaped. Microteaching supplements and extends other techniques for both preservice and in-service training of teachers. It is an admirable substitute for actual classroom observation of other teachers, and a means of observing oneself in action.

Additionally, microteaching can be just as useful in upgrading in-service performance. Classroom teachers may prefer to try the technique alone in their classrooms without supervisors, in which case equipment arrangements are set up prior to the lesson. Most portable VTR systems do not require additional personnel in the classroom at the time of the lesson. Teachers simply turn on the recorder at the beginning of the lesson and turn it off at the end. In these instances, teachers can evaluate themselves, and also observe their students' reaction to each other and to the teacher.

Microteaching is used mostly in education methods courses and student teaching. Application with elementary and high school students as a part of the learning process in perfecting

7. George L. Lawrence, "Resource Television in Teacher Education," *Audiovisual Instruction*, 13 (November 1968): 997.

motor skills and analyzing peer behavior has also been noted.
Experience shows positive results in improving teaching skills
via microteaching for students, practice teachers, or pre-prac-
tice teachers, who can see convincingly whether their performance was the kind of which they approve. They not only
observe their methodology and personal idiosyncrasies, but
they can observe in detached fashion the reaction of their
students. Change, as a result of self-analysis, is ordinarily
easier to bring about. Follow-up is a very important part of
the procedure. Some schools make it possible for teachers to
check out the equipment for personal use on their own time.

Equipment for microteaching consists of a camera (with or
without tripod), microphone, a videotape recorder, and a
monitor. These are all very simple to operate, and inexpensive after initial purchase. Both equipment and utilization
can become quite sophisticated and complex. They need not
be. Tapes may or may not be erased as the teacher sees fit.
If kept they may be edited, excerpted, or refined with post-
recorded narrative or dialogue over the pictures. It is possible
to build up a VTR library of well-rated teaching performances which might be observed or studied much as other
reference materials. This activity has been labeled "Resource
Television Teaching."

In general, students like the microteaching experience. The
experience can ease or circumvent extreme anxiety and
trauma. Anxiety about reception and effectiveness is nearly
always present in the mind of the dedicated teacher as he
approaches his profession, and even experienced teachers feel
much the same as they begin a new year or approach a new
class. Of course there have been abuses, such as unprofes-
sional viewing, unjustified inferential judgments, and inept-
ness in evaluation. In the first time around, some students
may shrug off a poor performance with "It's only practice
anyway," "The time was too short," "It was not a normal
situation." Overall, however, students not only accept it,
but welcome the opportunity it gives for improvement.

LEARNING LABORATORIES

Originally known as the *language laboratory*, this installation is now known as the *electronic classroom*, the *electronic*

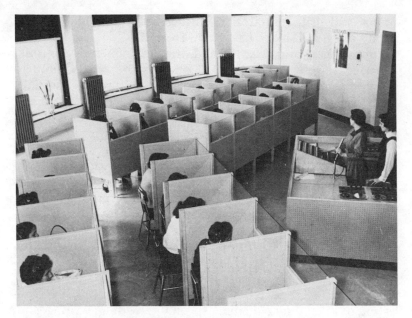

Fig. 26. In the language laboratory at Schenley High School, teachers at consoles instruct students in carrels. (Photo, courtesy Pittsburgh Public Schools.)

learning classroom, or perhaps, most appropriately, the *learning laboratory*. The *language laboratory* label persists because of the heavy utilization by foreign language departments. Nevertheless, other departments with a heavy emphasis on communication, such as English, English as a second language, stenography, and speech, can and do use audio laboratory facilities.

Language laboratories had their introduction in the early 1950s and, through federal funding, grew rapidly. Over 10,000 of these units exist today in the schools of the United States.

World War II created a need for men and women who could speak various languages. The need was so urgent that intensive courses were instituted by the government, resulting in the so-called Army method of language instruction. The courses consisted of intensive work, chiefly audiolingual, with up-to-date audio and visual equipment, special classrooms and drill laboratories, tailored learning materials, and highly skilled teachers, native and foreign.

Following World War II and the launching of Sputnik, Americans were convinced that schools should do more to help students acquire the language skills required to exchange ideas with the peoples of the world. Accelerated travel and an increasing number of world conferences increased this need. Foreign language teachers had long pointed out the low state of language teaching in this country, where most students received little or no exposure to languages, and even foreign-service personnel were so lacking in language skills that they were the butt of many jokes in international circles.

A massive effort was thus made to improve foreign language teaching in the schools. Federal assistance which began with the National Defense Education Act of 1958 was an important factor in the program. Recently, the national emphasis on required language instruction has been tapering off.

The usual method today is the audiolingual approach, consisting of aural understanding, speaking, reading, writing, and, lastly, grammar. Grammar used to come first and was frequently the sole approach to a language. Now, speaking and hearing are emphasized.

The language laboratory was a logical development of the audiolingual approach. It has gone through a metamorphosis of wild acceptance, disenchantment, re-study, refinement, and intelligent acceptance. The cycle is rather typical of most innovative teaching tools. A report from a committee of the Foreign Language Leadership Institute states:

> The question of whether language laboratories can improve the quality of language learning has been resolved. Most secondary schools possess some form of a language lab, and studies including the use of control groups show that their *proper* use markedly improves pronunciation, intonation, and the listening and speaking skills in general. As long as these skills remain high on our priority list, language labs or their equivalent will be indispensable to a foreign language program.[8]

8. Lester W. McKim, ed., "Designing and Using Language Laboratories" (A report of the committee prepared at a conference at Central Washington State College in the summer of 1967), *Audiovisual Instruction*, 13 (May 1968): 454.

Equipment and Materials for the Laboratory

Learning laboratory equipment ranges all the way from table model listening posts up to sophisticated electronic classrooms. The very heart of a good learning laboratory, as far as the teacher is concerned, is the *console*, a device by which the teacher can switch sound channels, talk to individual students or to a group, and audit practice without interrupting. He is in control of all the activities, and yet he can stay in the background. The learning laboratory teacher is truly a "director." Not unlike a symphony conductor, he is in complete charge at all times of all the action, hears and sees everything, and selectively directs his attention to individuals or groups as needed. The console distributes and controls all programs and consists of such components as record players, microphones, playback decks, and monitoring units.

Student reception stations include carrels or booths, microphones, record and/or tape players, and headphones. The more advanced installations provide carrels with such additional equipment as slide and filmstrip viewers, 8- and 16-mm projectors, TV monitors, and dial access information retrieval (discussed later in this chapter) so that sight and sound may be channeled directly to the carrel. Some labs also supply students and teachers with "language masters"—a unit which combines print or pictures and magnetic tape on cards.

In Chapter 5 the "wireless loop transmission" technique was described. This audio system has been adapted to the learning laboratory with good effect, and many of the costly wire installations of the conventional language lab are eliminated.

The "software" or learning materials are chiefly magnetic tape recordings, or possibly videotape recordings. Effective learning materials are the key to the value of the laboratory, but the production of sound and challenging instructional materials continues to be a stubborn problem. Schools need to recognize that materials have true value only if they meet set objectives. Some of the commercially published materials meet school objectives, and some do not. Schools have been reluctant to give teachers released time to prepare materials, a job that calls for team effort in the main. The suggestion has been made that sometime in the future, state and national

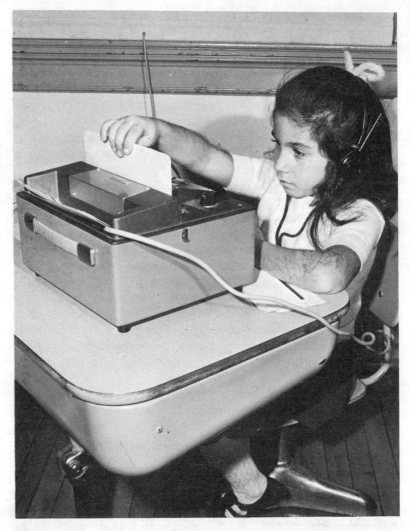

Fig. 27. Using a language master (with magnetic tape), this student sees, then hears, new vocabulary. The device thus promotes spelling and pronunciation. (Photo, courtesy Pittsburgh Public Schools.)

(possibly international) libraries be built up and shared through a system of storage and retrieval.

Advantages of the Learning Laboratory

In the learning laboratory each student is isolated from other members of the class and in effect works individually with the teacher or with a master tape. He listens alternately to his voice and that of the teacher or speaker on the tape. Since he is able to hear the difference between his response and the correct one, his errors can be corrected at once, not hours or days later. He has, in effect, a private tutor and can work at his own pace. The versatility of the laboratory allows teachers to work with students either individually or in groups.

The actual speaking practice given each student increases his speaking facility. In language study, students listening through headsets hear the language clearly and correctly. In order to *speak* correctly, one must *hear* clearly and correctly. The absence of all extraneous noises, moreover, sharpens attention. Learning labs can take the student over the same material again and again much as a private tutor might do. Teachers need not do this repetitive drill; the laboratory equipment can handle drill better than a teacher since it can "teach" many students at a time, but as individuals.

Students can have the advantage of the knowledge and skills of many teachers. Proper learning lab use is shared teaching and may, in addition to the classroom teacher, involve a coordinator, technicians and assistants, audiovisual consultants and administrative backing.

Learning materials can and should be more interesting than textbook lessons alone. Lessons may be live or recorded. Recorded materials are usually carefully prepared either by teachers or commercial concerns, many of whom employ nationally recognized professional assistance. Recorded materials may be used over and over as needed. Creditable libraries of materials are being built up for classroom teachers.

Difficulties of the Learning Laboratory

Few deny that the learning laboratory extends the effectiveness of the teacher. Labs are not, however, and can never be, substitutes for good teachers. But, if some of the snags and hurdles can be removed from their use, they can give valuable instructional assistance.

The present difficulties of the learning laboratory are the following:

- Methods of laboratory and equipment use need improvement.

- Teacher preparation for this type of teaching is unsatisfactory. A great many beginning teachers (foreign language in particular) come to their teaching assignments without prior experience with learning labs. This condition is being corrected. Several universities, Minnesota, for example, have found that VTR plus experience in the laboratory gives their teachers more confidence and expertise in handling modern learning problems. And, it is never too late for the in-service teacher to pick up the necessary skills.

- The laboratory phase of language teaching should not be treated as a sideshow. It is an integral part of the program.

- Curriculum materials with interest and motivation must be prepared, and in great quantity. It takes an incredible amount of new materials to keep a dynamic program going.

- Learning materials (language or otherwise) need to be coordinated with other media—ETV, VTR, CAI (discussed later in this chapter), motion pictures, and the like.

- Technicians and specialists must be brought in to round out a successful program. Electronic equipment is complicated, and one should remember Murphy's law, "Anything that can go wrong will."

- Equipment needs improvement; it should be less expensive and capable of more fidelity and flexibility.

– Time spent in the lab should be increased, in most cases. Research has shown the minimum to be two thirty-minute periods per week.

Future Possibilities

The learning laboratory has established itself as a basic technique in language teaching. In many ways this laboratory is a specialized type of "programmed learning" employing specialized "teaching machines."

The role of the laboratory and mediated instruction is increasing, and along with it, systems for dial-access and random retrieval are growing. Recordings may now be heard by students at such decentralized places as the library, learning resources center, dormitory, and even in the homes of students. Random-access systems use telephone lines, closed-circuit television, and computer-controlled monitoring to provide the availability of hundreds of prepared tapes to student reception stations. Costs, not technology, are the main factor in the slow growth of such systems. On the campus, the so-called electronic classroom transmits recorded material by wire to audio-active headsets, or a wireless transmission with antenna encircling the classroom (Chapter 5). Elton Hocking provides a comprehensive summary of the status of the lab and its future in this quotation:

> . . . research tells us that the language lab and its variations can indeed be effective instruments for learning; that the student's activities are in part determined by the nature of the equipment; and that the amount and distribution of time devoted to recorded materials is positively correlated with achievement. Nevertheless, the teacher's skill in the use of equipment, his general attitude toward recorded materials and the related media, and also the excellence of the materials themselves will continue to be more important than the media themselves, no matter how elaborate they may become.[9]

9. Elton Hocking, "Technology in Foreign Language Teaching: Recent Research and Developments," *Research Papers*, Purdue University, mimeographed (April 29, 1969): 4.

The learning laboratory may be extended so that small units are installed in any classroom, laboratory, shop, or other learning area. Units of this type may appropriately be called "audio-tutorial." They consist of booths or carrels with magnetic tape players/recorders mounted horizontally (desktop flush) or vertically (wall flush). These carrels become individual listening/learning stations. A student may hear a tape to its end, or he may stop it as directed (or desired) and perform experiments, examine materials, outline, classify, or do a host of learning tasks. Teachers, given the time, of course, prepare the tape lessons, tests, reviews, and other activities. Within bounds this type of tutorial work is rewarding, yet if it is carried too far and for long periods of time it may become monotonous.

PROGRAMMED LEARNING

Programmed learning refers to the teaching-learning technique which involves carefully written *programmed learning materials*. (Throughout this text, the term *programmed* is spelled with two *m*'s. Some writers use only one.) In this discussion, programmed learning will serve as the umbrella for *teaching machines, self-instructional devices, autoinstructional devices, scrambled books, tutor texts*, and related developments. Although programmed instruction bears heavily on individual learning, it is not confined to one person; it touches mass instruction as well. Many people think of the technology of instruction as connoting some sort of a machine, a so-called teaching machine. This is a misnomer, because individuals do not learn from machines, but rather from instructional materials placed in the machines. The machines are merely "holders" of instructional materials. By and large, the term *teaching machine* has been unfortunate, because it has tarnished the image of teaching. Teachers immediately think of being supplanted by a mechanical device, and the public feels that the personal benefits of student contact with an educated person are lost. The latter feel, mistakenly, to be sure, that teachers would rather relate to machines than students.

B. F. Skinner, one of the pioneer researchers in the field of individual learning techniques, has said:

> Teaching is the expediting of learning. Students learn without teaching, but the teacher arranges conditions under which they learn more rapidly and effectively.... An important contribution has been the so-called "programming" of knowledge and skills—the construction of carefully arranged sequences of contingencies leading to the terminal performances which are the object of education. The teacher begins with whatever behavior the student brings to the instructional situation; by selective reinforcement, he changes that behavior so that a given terminal performance is more and more closely approximated.[10]

We have seen that learning takes place because the student does something, not because the teacher does something. Programmed instruction is built on this hypothesis. It is actually a process of changing the student behavior by a systematizing of instruction with close attention to objectives, procedures, the nature of the learners, mastery of learning materials, and evaluations of the changes.

Essentially, the advantages of programmed instruction are as follows:

- Learning units are carefully developed and presented in logical sequence, involving small pieces of information one at a time, and generally lead the learner from simple ideas, concepts, and skills to increasingly advanced work.

- Learners must give sustained attention to the tasks at hand.

- Learning units are prepared so that they are self-sufficient, in that they state behavioral objectives, cause the learner to behave according to these objectives, and reward the learner for doing so.

- The learner is allowed to react to each question or bit of

10. B. F. Skinner, "Reflections on a Decade of Teaching Machines," in *Instructional Process and Media Innovation*, ed. Robert A. Weisgerber (Chicago: Rand McNally, 1968), pp. 405-6.

information by writing his answers, punching his selection on a keyboard, speaking into a tape-connected microphone, pressing a lever, making some other overt response, or even by responding covertly.

- The learner is informed of the correctness of his response at every step. The feedback is immediate.
- Reinforcement of responses is built into the process.
- The learner proceeds at his own pace.

Some educators trace (possibly *force* would be a better word) the idea of programmed learning back to Socrates, whose dialectical method led learners forward sequentially, bit by bit, until a deduction could be made or a concept developed.   Although teaching machines as such are quite new, mechanical aids to learning were built in the nineteenth century.   In 1912 Dr. Edward L. Thorndike foresaw what contemporary psychologists would devise for programmed learning when he wrote:

> If by a miracle of mechanical ingenuity, a book could be so arranged that only to him who had done what was directed on page one would page two become visible, and so on, much that now requires personal instruction could be managed by print. Books to be given out in loose sheets, a page or so at a time, and books arranged so that the student only suffers if he misuses them, should be worked out in many subjects. . . .
> Great economies are possible by printed aids, and personal comment and questions should be saved to do what only it can do. A human being should not be wasted in doing what forty sheets of paper or two phonographs can do.[11]

In the 1920s Dr. Sydney L. Pressey of Ohio State University experimented with mechanical devices in the presentation of information and in testing.   He viewed his devices not as basic instructional tools, but as supplements to regular classroom teaching.   In the 1950s Professor B. F. Skinner of Harvard and others formulated some new theories of learning

11. Edward L. Thorndike, *Education* (New York: Macmillan, 1912), pp. 165–67.

as a result of laboratory experiments with animals. They implemented their theories by different arrangements of the learning materials and developed mechanical devices for the presentation of the materials to the learner.

Types of Programmed Materials and Equipment

The term programmed materials refers to the unit of instructional material that the student handles himself. The unit can be in such mediated form as print, tape, film, and other varieties. These materials, as noted in Chapter 1, are commonly designated as "software"—the meat of the program. No program, regardless of how well it is conveyed, will be better than the materials of instruction. Among the formats for printed programmed materials which have been devised are the *programmed textbook*, the *scrambled book*, the *cut-back page booklet*, and the *tab-type page*. The first two of these types are important.

The programmed textbook has an information-presentation mechanism and a response mechanism. The information-question part of the "frame," or learning step, is a horizontal panel or band from the top of the page to the middle of the page, and the response part of the "frame" is a horizontal panel directly below the information-question panel. The learner moves through the pages in succession to the end of the book or section and then returns to Page 1 for the second band. This is continued until the book is completed.

The "scrambled book" is arranged so that the pages are not read consecutively. The first page, for example, asks a question or makes a statement, and the reader selects an answer from those provided which then directs him to a page somewhere in the book. On this particular page, the reader finds that he has responded correctly or incorrectly as the case may be. He is then directed to another page, or he may be asked to return to the original page and to begin all over, depending upon the correctness of the previous response.

Between books and machines are a variety of devices which simulate machines. Most of these devices are of the pencil-and-paper sort. They consist of punchboards, pull-tabs, pluck cards, sliding masks, paper scanners, and chemical cards. All are inexpensive and expendable. They are suitable for individual testing and drill of workbook type.

Teaching machines fall into three categories: (1) simple, manually operated devices; (2) complex, automated devices; and (3) highly complex electronic devices. The programmed materials for most machines are paper—cards, rolls, and packs or sheets. Slides, reels, and tape are used in some of the more complex equipment. Machines vary in size from those which resemble a portable typewriter to mammoth cabinets resembling a telephone switchboard.

The operations of all three types of teaching machine are basically the same. A program is fed into a machine. By operating a button, a lever, or a dial, the student moves the programmed matter one step at a time into a small window in the machine. Each step is called a "frame." The student reacts to the material seen in the window. His response is put on paper or punched into a keyboard. After he has recorded his response, the student moves a lever and exposes the correct response, which he compares with the response he has made. If he is correct, he moves to the next frame. If he is incorrect, he is given other clues and a chance to try again. In some machines the incorrect response is automatically "marked" and the question will appear again.

Programmed instruction follows two main patterns. One is known as *linear* or "straight line" and the other *branching* or "adaptive." The former pattern is fixed and uniform. All students do the same work and follow the steps in order. In the branching pattern the arrangement is modified, though the essentials are given much as they are in the linear pattern. In the second pattern provision is made for branches or bypaths off the main stem, allowing the program writer to clarify concepts, to permit students to attempt generalizations, and to follow up errors with remedial work. Branching programs attempt to provide for individual differences. For example, bright students make use of only a limited number of the bypaths because they can select more appropriate answers and stay on the "main line." Less able students use all or nearly all of the branches because they need the additional information and practice.

Best Uses of Programmed Materials

An unusual amount of experimental study has been given to this new form of instruction. Many people have been intrigued by the idea that a human can learn from a machine. Across the country many schools are testing the effectiveness of automatic learning. Many questions remain unanswered, however. Will programmed learning destroy creativity? Will learning be dictated by a machine? Will learning which is broken into small fragments fail to come together into generalizations and integrated systems of information? Will programs of this type promote a rigid "caste" system in education, whereby students are automatically shunted into a single "track"? One also might ask if this type of learning can provide long-term sustained challenges to the students and if it contributes anything to the handling of the problem of individual differences. The problems of cost and integration of programmed learning into the basic school curriculum are also significant.

According to a goodly number of research findings, programmed learning is the equal of or better than conventional instruction. Schramm is emphatic about the effectiveness of students' learning from programmed materials. He states:

> The research leaves us in no doubt of this. They do, indeed, learn. They learn from linear programs, from branching programs built on the Skinnerian model, from scrambled books of the Crowder type, from Pressey review tests with immediate knowledge of results, from programs on machines or programs in texts.[12]

Studies, however, tend to follow conventional patterns of comparison, not a very satisfactory way of evaluating programmed learning's worth because of the complexity of teaching-learning problems.

On the other hand, Lindgren, speaking from an educational

12. Wilbur Schramm, *The Research on Programmed Instruction* (Washington, D.C.: Office of Education, 1964, #34034, Bulletin No. 35), p. 3.

psychology point of view, is critical of programmed materials:

> Although the past years have seen the development of a rich variety of programmed materials, research studies have not been able to show conclusively that Skinner's approach to programmed learning has any advantage over Pressey's. Shirley Curran Lublin (1965), for example, tried various ways of reinforcing learning in a programmed course and found that *no* reinforcement gave the best results. Students with strong needs to engage in independent thinking did very poorly, which led the researcher to wonder whether error-free programs, such as Skinner's, are actually too easy to be very interesting.[13]

As we have noted, it is most unlikely that programmed instruction will replace either teacher or textbook, but it just may make both of them more effective in their roles in instruction. The use of teaching machines and programmed learning is not an all-or-none proposition. Where they are being used, students take turns working with the machines. Teachers need give only a minimum of supervision to the students working the machines, and they devote less time to testing and evaluation because this is a built-in feature of programmed materials. Teachers are not expected to write the materials of instruction. This is left to experts. The teacher is more a selector of programs than a writer. Nevertheless, he retains full responsibility for planning the quality and sequencing of the instructional experiences his students undergo.

It should be pointed out that the quick rash of production a decade ago has subsided. Today, only the better researched and designed models survive, but new and more sophisticated ones are constantly being devised. Some of the machines employ slides, filmstrips, magnetic tapes, and 8- and 16-mm films. It is entirely logical to think of most of the "hardware" being developed for learning laboratories as programmed. Individuals or large groups may be drilled or

13. Henry C. Lindgren, *Educational Psychology in the Classroom*, 3rd ed. (New York: John Wiley, 1967), p. 259; similar comment p. 338.

taught. No teacher need be present—thus, a form of mediated teaching is evident.

DIAL-ACCESS INFORMATION-RETRIEVAL SYSTEMS

As programmed instruction becomes more diversified, distribution methods and problems become more complex. *Dial-access information-retrieval systems* provide an up-to-date way to make this instruction readily accessible to students. With DAIRS, working in special carrels or other "headquarters" students may dial many types of programs (audio and video, with response mechanisms) for study, review, testing, aesthetic interest, or other purposes. Carrels are usually found in libraries, instructional materials centers, student work rooms, study laboratories, or even in dormitories. As soon as a student dials a particular lesson, an electronic switching device activates responding devices which make available the needed stored information. Several universities now have elaborate installations of such equipment.

Dial-access information-retrieval systems evolved from the language laboratory. In the primitive audio laboratory, recordings, like library books, are manually checked out to students who take them to study booths for playback. Such an arrangement is grossly limited in the number of students it can serve and the scope of lessons available, and at the same time it involves a large number of man-hours of labor.

More recently developments have produced electronic marvels which make it possible automatically or semi-automatically to provide hundreds of programs to hundreds of students on a self-service basis. Present audio equipment enables a student to utilize any of three function-levels, (a) audio-passive (listening only), (b) audio-active (listening and responding), and (c) audio-active-compare (listening-responding-recording). Full-track recorders are supplemented by two-track and four-track, reel-to-reel equipment, and by cartridge and cassette components. A tape library of thirty reels using four-track equipment would thus store 120 programs. This outlay could be multiplied as many times as desired. Certain problems, however, are inherent in this sort of programming.   Although costs are reduced when more than one program is placed on a tape, running times of programs may differ and difficulties in retrieval and confusion in cataloging may occur.

A student seated in a booth or study station containing a small access station or console dials one, two, or three digits as per an index of recorded lessons. The electronic switching system is activated and a tape is played. This tape will repeat following rapid rewind until the user "hangs up." Certain features of the equipment enable any number of students to dial into any program whether or not it is in use, or the system can be so modified that after the initial dialing, students may get a "busy" signal. Still another feature allows a student to block out any attempts to dial into a program once he has it activated. With some equipment a student may dial an attendant at the audio center for a tape which is not at

Fig. 28. Input: data are relayed from a transmitter at a remote computer terminal, via programming language. Information reaches the central processing unit via the auxiliary data phone at the right. (Photo, courtesy Miami-Dade Junior College.)

Fig. 29. Output: an operator at a computer terminal remote from the main computer room codes in a query to elicit information from the data storage bank which appears on the screen. (Photo, courtesy Miami-Dade Junior College.)

that time mounted on the control-switching panel. "Live" programs may also be distributed from origination points to classrooms and laboratories. Programs are heard on headsets in the carrels and on public address speakers in lecture halls, classrooms, and auditoriums. Soundproofing of carrels has not been completely satisfactory to date, and therefore the use of earphones is necessary. If carrels are located in libraries and in the rear of classrooms, for example, even muted noise can be disturbing.

Most of the existing dial-access installations are audio systems only; however, video is also possible. High costs have held down installations of the latter systems, but it is quite possible to dial and retrieve all sorts of video materials— films, videotapes, television programs, and other video-lectures and supplementary materials such as charts and diagrams.

Future refinements in all the audio-video dial-access information-retrieval hardware is a certainty. It is hoped that costs will be lowered with extensive use and production. Classroom uses will also be extended so that most departments in a school can be benefited. Educators also look forward to broader based storage banks so that schools may dial beyond their campuses to various regional sources.

COMPUTER-ASSISTED INSTRUCTION

Computers may be tied into the above installations, but they can also go beyond the mere information retrieval function. With its elaborate memory bank, the computer can work so directly with a student that it not only tells the student if he is right or wrong but gives him new tasks or questions. If the task is a test, for example, the computer can score the test and even furnish an analysis of errors made. It can also provide the student with comparisons with former performances or performances of other students.

The materials of electronic computers vary from key-punched cards or paper tapes to coded and documented magnetic tapes, drums, and discs that can record, organize, sort, store, retrieve, and transmit information of almost any sort. The effectiveness of the machine depends on how it is used and what material is put into it. Computers are highly sophisticated, expensive, and demand exceptional skills for operation and maintenance.

Computer-assisted instruction (CAI) depends upon skillful programming. Into computers data can be fed that describe complete work/study programs and units of instruction. The student may obtain feedback regarding his progress at daily, weekly, or other intervals. Such a print-out can tell both student and teacher what has been done and what needs to be done. In such fashion the computer is a boon to individualized instruction. In order to use this equipment efficiently teachers need a new kind of imagination and skill. With this skill, programming can be so thorough that none of the behavioral objectives—cognitive, affective, or psychomotor— are lost from sight.

In addition to the instructional functions just cited, computers can do yeoman service in test construction, administration, and analysis. Researchers find computers a most valuable tool in their trade. Administrative, secretarial, and library functions are served in similar manner. Data storage and retrieval in library administration is only in the incipient stages, yet the potential is there. Someday students and teachers will need only to push buttons in order to locate source and resource data on any subject. With proper computerization, for example, a science teacher might call upon the library for assistance on a given topic and receive in reply a list of books, films, filmstrips, videotapes, and other resources.

Presently, there are many limitations to CAI. Costs, either for lease or purchase of equipment, are high. Suitable program materials are not available and their future is cloudy. Gentile says:

> It is ridiculous to ask classroom teachers to program their courses. Even if programming were as easy as writing a book, it would be out of the question to expect classroom teachers to have the time or capability of writing a good program. How many teachers write books? Program writing will ultimately be left to professional programers and their subject-matter consultants.[14]

14. J. Ronald Gentile, "The First Generation of Computer-Assisted Instructional Systems: An Evaluative Review," *AV Communication Review*, 15 (Spring 1967): 31.

Costs, though high, can be reduced somewhat by round-the-clock use of the equipment. During school hours it can serve various instructional and research purposes, and in after-school hours such administrative purposes as payrolls, attendance recording, cost accounting, and growth studies. Another angle to reducing costs lies in cooperative time-sharing arrangements between school districts, universities, colleges, and possibly nearby industrial and commercial firms.

The computer seems the ideal teaching machine with its capabilities (dependent upon programming) for great information storage, immediate feedback, response analysis, and tutorial capabilities. No teacher could possibly dispense knowledge with such dimensions.

This chapter has stressed electronic media and systems which place more emphasis on technological developments than do the optical-photographic and conventional audio-visual materials discussed earlier. Many educators feel that the "tools" for quality education are now available and that it behooves theorists, researchers, and teachers to evolve proper methods of utilization. From the arsenal of electronic educational aids, one writer singles out eight as contemporary "musts":

1. Centralized tape libraries from which local systems could select, for example, an entire course of instruction, or specialized lectures prepared by the greatest teachers in special fields
2. Closed-circuit TV systems for a school system or region and individual videotape players—the see and hear devices—to enable each classroom to utilize the course materials that can be made available to every school
3. Electronic teaching machines that have been particularly successful in language instruction
4. Programmed learning systems for detailed, repetitive instruction
5. Scanning devices in each classroom that would be linked to the library and records office to free teachers from many routine functions
6. Computer centers for grading examinations for a school, or an entire school district, relieving teachers of a time-consuming chore

7. Computers for cataloguing and retrieving information
8. A flexible open-circuit educational TV network to bring a variety of current-events type of instruction to classrooms.[15]

Again it must be stressed that no matter how comprehensively a system is developed it must be supplemented by wise selection, proper preparation, and intelligent use in order to function successfully.

15. John L. Burns, "Our Era of Opportunity," *Saturday Review*, 50 (January 14, 1967): 38–39.

Chapter 8

Creating a Learning Environment

BEHAVIORAL OBJECTIVES

After studying this chapter, the reader will be able to:

1. Given a specific classroom, rate its suitability for media use, specifying the criteria used.
2. Given a specific classroom, specify four ways in which media can be used to improve the psychological environment.
3. List three structural features of a modern junior high school which were not present in past junior high schools.
4. Given a specific learning material, indicate its suitability for local production according to six criteria, specifying the criteria used.
5. Identify six methods of reproducing instructional materials.
6. Discuss four aspects of the legality issue surrounding the reproduction of commercially produced instructional materials.

Educators have long recognized that the surroundings, conditions, and influences that make up the environment in which students live and work affect their behavior. Laboratory tests have shown the effects of environment on various animals and on man. We know that man reacts to his surroundings.

Environment encompasses buildings, furnishings, patterns, arrangements, temperature, color, texture, and articles of all kinds. Winston Churchill once said, "We shape our dwellings and afterwards our dwellings shape us." Commercial institutions strive to create a particular environment. The wise proprietor of a store or restaurant hopes that the environment he creates helps to sell goods, to produce satisfied customers, to create an image. Teachers, believing that students learn best in a pleasant atmosphere, try to arrange the class environment. In drab and unattractive surroundings, tensions build up and sullen or antisocial behavior is much more likely to occur. Poor lighting and high noise levels lower morale. Even the teacher's voice can be shown to have an effect on student behavior.

In this chapter, we shall see how a learning environment can be enhanced by sensible building design and creative classroom decoration. We will see, too, that a learning environment is not complete unless effective learning materials are readily *available*. Later in this chapter we will explore how teachers and students can arrange to make such materials available through their own handiwork.

SCHOOL PLANT DESIGN, INSIDE AND OUT

School plant design, curriculum, media use, and instructional methods are interrelated. Only recently has there been an awareness of this relationship. In colonial days we built square or rectangular log buildings. This was entirely reasonable. As villages grew, the square one-room building was divided into two rooms, then four, and eight, and when we stacked one or two floors above the ground floor, we repeated the pattern. Thus, we crystallized an eggcrate-shaped school pattern. In these buildings, flexibility was nil. Generation after generation of teachers, many innovation-minded, have been frustrated with their environment. Most frequently seats in straight rows were bolted to floors. Teachers' desks, cupboards (if any), windows, and blackboards were always in the same spots. Even paint colors were standardized to the point of boredom.

Neither media nor students function well in straitjacketed classrooms. Room darkening, poor acoustics, inability to hold conversations, lack of ventilation, scarce electrical outlets, and similar problems have been the bane of many teachers. School plants have been and are still being built without any thought to media use. For example, let us consider a junior high school built in the 1950s. A splendid building to all appearances, it was designed by a leading local architectural firm. But, inside a classroom, a teacher and her students

Fig. 30. This light, open, and airy school library at Eugene, Oregon's, Lane Community College shows good design. Note the individual study desks and carrels, carpeted floor, comfortable upholstered chairs, and open shelving on the mezzanine. (Photo, courtesy the Oregon Board of Education.)

use six-foot-high stepladders to paste butcher paper over high windows in order to show a motion picture. Besides all the bother involved, the safety hazards merit changes in the building, but they haven't been made. Once nailed together, a school building tends to stay that way.

Small cracks are appearing, however, in the old stereotyped designs. Study halls slowly disappeared from building plans. Libraries are no longer just two classrooms with the partition removed. Main reading rooms are augmented with collateral workrooms and storage areas, small group study or committee rooms are appearing, and individual carrels are not uncommon. Audio "live" libraries are undergoing transformations with carpeted floors (as a subterfuge, sometimes referred to as acoustic floor coverings), acoustical plastering, draperies for windows and walls, and even climate control (air conditioning).

Most of the other special rooms of the school remain generally unchanged from decade to decade. More concern is shown for appearance than function in auditorium planning. In the minds of many educators, auditoriums are sacred white elephants which score about 10 percent on utilization.

Fig. 31. This auditorium at Miami-Dade Junior College is one of several lecture halls specially equipped for large-group instruction. (Photo, courtesy Miami-Dade Junior College.)

Modular spacing and movable walls have had some effect on functional patterns. Whether called classrooms or special rooms, space is needed for individual study, small group seminars, and mass instruction (large groups). Teachers need not only lounges, but conference rooms and rooms where they can interact with students individually or in small groups. New instructional and organizational methods such as team teaching, flexible scheduling, nongraded rooms, honors classes, dial-access, and computer-equipped space need to be taken into consideration. Planned spaces are needed for groups of 1, 10, 25, or 150 students at a time, but any such grouping may be only temporary. Next week new groupings may be in order.

New schoolhouse design eschews the old pattern of a string of classrooms along one or both sides of a corridor with varied shapes and sizes. The first changes substituted the T and the U for the eggcrate. Hexagonal, circular, semicircular, wedge- or fan-shaped, and other shapes keep cropping up repeatedly. These shapes are not vagaries of architects' imaginations. They are the result of study and interaction of teachers, educators, and design engineers. Buildings centered around hubs of materials centers are not uncommon. The shape of the building is often critical. The point is that it is built for learning. Yet educational specifications, when and if drawn, usually leave the teacher out of the planning! Teacher and students are supposed to make do with what is given them. What would happen if classrooms, per se, disappeared entirely to give way to loft-type zones of malleable space? How would teachers and students design their learning environment?

OUTFITTING CLASSROOMS

Teachers should no longer be expected to move classes from their regular classrooms to an auditorium or a room labeled *Audio-Visual*. To be effective, materials must be used by teachers and students in their regular classrooms at the time the materials fit into planned lessons. Qualified school architects and instructional media coordinators can provide valuable advice about structural and functional designs for classrooms in new buildings, in order to plan for using audio and visual equipment. Since school buildings are built to last for many years, it is also worthwhile to bring older buildings up to date with new media developments by renovating or remodeling them.

In both the design of new classrooms and the renovation of old classrooms, the following factors must be considered:

Light Control   Two essential considerations in light control are electrical wiring and room-darkening. In the first instance, attention should be given to the installation of proper amperage because extended use of electrical and electronic equipment may overtax an ordinary wiring job. Electrical outlets should be conveniently located, either in recessed walls or surface mounted. A desirable feature would be on-off switches with three connections at the front and rear of the classroom near projector locations, plus light dimmers if possible. The necessity to use long extension cords should be avoided.

Window placement and arrangement may or may not be a possible change in the remodeled school, but in both new and old classrooms the matter of room darkening must be considered. Makeshift darkening facilities should be unnecessary. Two satisfactory means of controlling outside light are fireproofed fabric draperies and full-closure venetian blinds.

Acoustical Control   Unwanted sound can be as annoying as unwanted light. In the past little or no attention was given to this phase of classroom environment either in new or old buildings. Much can be done by building designers to soften or eliminate noise and reverberation. Acoustical wall and ceiling treatments, carpeting of floors, and the proper use of draperies at windows and walls are the usual ways of handling sound. Concealed wiring from speakers to projectors is recommended. Built-in or wall-mounted speakers should be installed in conventional and multipurpose areas. (At this point it might be well to reread the section on "Wired Listening Stations" in Chapter 5.)

Temperature Control   The temperature of the room can be somewhat controlled by appropriate size and placement of windows. A far better method of temperature control is air conditioning. It is inexcusable to force students to sit in chilly or hot, stuffy rooms for screening, listening, or studying.

Equipment Control   One of the elements in equipment control, as has already been indicated, is that speakers should be wall mounted or built in. Projection screens should also be wall mounted. The portable screen should serve only for temporary purposes. Computer terminals and TV outlets should be provided in new and remodeled buildings.

Furniture Control   Outmoded furniture should be removed from equipment lists. Up-to-date, movable furniture should be installed. Carrels should be installed in appropriate areas.

Storage Space   Schools and homes share the need for storage space in much the same way and for the same reasons. Proper storage space facilitates good and neat housekeeping, prolongs the working life of equipment (simple or sophisticated), assures that equipment is in its proper place, and is a good safety precaution.

Chalkboard and Display Space   In planning for chalkboard and display space, such criteria as flexibility, location, lighting, and size should be considered.

Work Space   Suitable work and production space is necessary both for teacher and students.

Color Control   Appropriateness and variety of color ought to be given high priority.

THE TEACHER'S ROLE

Some fortunate teachers find themselves working in modern school buildings blessed with good lighting, ventilation, artistic coloring, low noise level, attractive school furniture, and all the other desirable physical features. Others must work under exactly opposite conditions. Most teachers probably will find themselves between the extremes.

Psychological as well as physical factors are part of the environment, and the psychological is harder to transform than the physical. School boards can see the physical environment but not the psychological. The student is aware of both. Good teachers earnestly try to provide their students not only with attractive classrooms but with a positive learning environment.

Teachers have it within their power to do almost anything they wish with the environment—their classroom. To a bare, lifeless room the teacher can bring warmth and vitality. Chalkboards, desks, and chairs can be kept clean and uncluttered. Bulletin boards can be centers of color and interest. Maps, globes, posters, and book jackets can clutter or can add a touch of liveliness. Unsightly corners or walls can be covered with corrugated paper and become spots for posters and displays. Science corners and book nooks captivate many students. One imaginative teacher introduced into her classroom a THIS WEEK center. The center became a weekly "changing museum" of fresh ideas on topics of current interest. It took a lot of work to keep this hungry monster satiated week after week, but after a few weeks the students asked to do the work. They formed committees and with teacher-approved topics filled the spaces with interesting and informative materials.

Teachers should take a good hard look at any pictures which may hang on their walls. Although pictures of Sir Galahad, Lafayette, or Napoleon certainly do not lack value, travel posters may be more appealing to students. Why not borrow some artwork from the art department occasionally? Although the quality of the art is a matter of taste, the students will appreciate the change.

You can also call on your district's learning resources center for the loan of art prints, kits, artifacts, dioramas, posters, and whatever is available in your subject area. If nothing fits very well, just get some color, perhaps nothing more than a band of flags of the United Nations. Museums are also excellent sources of materials, as are newspapers, airlines, railroads, and other businesses and industries.

Setting Standards for the Environment

To further facilitate the creation of a good learning environment, standards are needed. Administrative personnel need standards for the selection and purchase of media for school buildings and media centers, while teachers, librarians, supervisors, and curriculum specialists need standards for selecting the most appropriate learning materials to use in presenting particular content, or for tailoring programs that will insure maximum development of groups or individuals. Such standards must be applicable to both hardware and software.

Standards, however, can be no more than guidelines. They cannot be static because school programs cannot be static. No categorical formula can ever be laid down with finality: educational programs vary, hence quantitative standards vary. A listed standard may be quite pertinent for one school, but too lenient or too drastic for another. To be realistic, standards should be rooted in the theories of learning which prevail in a district and in the economic support available to the district.

Recognizing the need for flexible media standards, one must ask who is to formulate the standards and what authority exists for their enforcement. Standards set up by an individual are usually suspect; consequently more acceptable standards are promulgated by committees, councils, or similar groups. Professional bodies who work in the instructional media field are the logical ones to provide the yardsticks. After long and intensive conference and study, the Department of Audiovisual Instruction (now Association for Educational Communications and Technology) and the American Library Association published a set of recommendations in 1969. These associations felt that a dual set of standards was needed, one for schools with *basic* or conventional school programs and another for schools with *advanced* programs "with instructional approaches as individualization of instruction and independent study." It must be kept in mind that these recommendations are for media centers in individual schools, and are, therefore, in addition to recommendations for collections at the district media headquarters. The report also makes the statement, "It is recognized that in certain types of innovative programs even the advanced level will will need to be exceeded."[1]

The publication of the standards met with mixed reactions. As a result, the committee responsible for them set about immediately to rework or revise the list. Since that publication a joint committee of the California Association of School Librarians and the Audio-Visual Education Association of California published a set of standards.[2] This latter set of standards is quite detailed and covers matters of staff and services, facilities, materials (including print), and equipment. In keeping with the national standards of DAVI-ALA, the California standards provide for two levels of development called Phase I and Phase II, the latter designating what more advanced school programs should provide. The standards also furnish different ratios and quantities for elementary and secondary schools.

Table 4 is an excerpt from that list.

In much of the final selection of media for learning purposes, teachers will of necessity make their selections from those media provided by their districts. By experience and training teachers will in most instances know what resources they will wish to use. But, in many instances, and particularly where newer media exist, they will seek help from such colleagues as principals, supervisors, media specialists, curriculum experts, and other specialized personnel. For best results a wide range of options should be allowed.

The Students' Role

Students, who are a prime source for locally produced learning materials, should be involved in creating a learning envi-

1. *Standards for School Media Programs* (Chicago: American Library Association; Washington, D.C.: National Education Association, 1969), p. 44.
2. *Standards for the Development of School Media Programs in California* (Burlingame, Calif.: California Association of School Librarians and Audio-Visual Education Association of California, 1970).

TABLE 4.   Recommendations for Projector Distribution*

	Phase I	Phase II
16-mm sound projector	1 per 4 teaching stations plus 2 in the media center	1 per 2 teaching stations plus 5 in the media center
8-mm projector	1 per 3 teaching stations plus 1 per 25 students	1 per 3 teaching stations plus 1 per 15 students
Filmstrip projector	1 per 3 teaching stations plus 1 per 25 students	1 per teaching station plus 1 per 15 students
Sound film-strip projector	1 per 10 teaching stations plus 1 per 200 students	1 per 5 teaching stations plus 1 per 100 students
Overhead projector	1 per teaching station plus 1 per 500 students	1 per teaching station plus 1 per 300 students
Opaque projector	1 per school or 1 per 25 teaching stations, which-ever is greater	1 per school or 1 per 15 teaching stations, which-ever is greater

*Standards for the Development of School Media Programs in California, pp. 26–30.

ronment. They should plan bulletin boards and make graphics, pictures, models, and decorations and arrangements in general. Try asking the members of a class how they would like to rearrange their classroom. New arrangements, resulting in new environments, usually accompany new units of work.

At this point in your professional life you may not have had an opportunity to create your own classroom learning environment. When such an opportunity comes, you may be amazed at the effect a good environment can have on students' learning. Be assured that your supervisor will be alert to the *environment* you create!

The next chapter will examine the learning resources center as a source for instructional materials. At this point, using the words "creating a learning environment" in the most literal sense, we need to consider procedures which teachers, students, and other staff members can follow to provide learning materials by producing and reproducing those materials themselves. (Our study of individual media has already included *specific* suggestions for local production and reproduction.)

LOCAL PRODUCTION OF MATERIALS

Equipment designates apparatus and usually refers to items of major expense. *Materials* designates those less expensive items which are sometimes called "supplies." For practical purposes, in budgets, expenditures of a permanent nature frequently are classified as equipment and those of a more temporary nature as materials or supplies. Erickson, author of a leading text on instructional media administration, distinguishes between them in this way:

> ... The term *capital outlay* in the writer's budgetary situation applies to the cost of land and nonstructural improvements to land, the cost of equipment such as tools and machinery, vehicles, and items of apparatus, media equipment, and materials, all of which have to be reported in the annual inventory. ... The term *supplies* refers to all commodities and materials, including consumable items that are not carried on the inventory of fixed assets.[3]

In an earlier volume on administration, Erickson spoke of the differences in these terms:

> A given item of material should be considered as a concentration, system, or body of content of potential value when put to work. On the other hand, equipment should be recognized as the means of presenting such content, or in the case of the bulletin board and the chalkboard, the means of displaying it; and in the case of the camera, of assembling it.[4]

Equipment is usually complicated, expensive, and bulky, and no one thinks of it as something that is made locally.

3. Carlton W. H. Erickson, *Administering Instructional Media Programs* (New York: Macmillan Co., 1968), p. 558.
4. Carlton W. H. Erickson, *Administering Audio-Visual Services* (New York: Macmillan Co., 1959), p. 131.

Schools may produce many materials, but they seldom produce equipment. Students will construct charts, graphs, shadow boxes, and the like, but not slide projectors or television receivers. This is not to say that students cannot produce some of these things if given enough time, spare parts, and direction, but such production would ordinarily be a waste of time.

Teachers always have made many of the learning materials they use in their teaching. The first blackboards probably were made by teachers, as were maps, writing materials, science materials, and many other things. Instructional materials may be produced locally by students, the staff of the learning resources center, parents, or local craftsmen who make a few small materials on order.

ADVANTAGES OF LOCAL PRODUCTION   It might be asked why school personnel should produce learning materials. Perhaps teachers and pupils are too busy with other duties to spend time on making things. Doesn't the public recognize the value of learning materials enough so that it is willing to purchase them? Why aren't they acquired through regular budgetary procedures?

Teachers gain valuable insights from producing some of their learning materials. As they produce materials, they inevitably evaluate them, a process which, as we have seen, increases teaching efficiency. The preparation of materials also enables the teacher to visualize content and to put it into that form which best suits his teaching conditions. It is natural for anyone who has created something to take pride in that creation. Although teachers may complain about the time spent in producing materials, they usually enjoy the work and resent any attempt to force them to forgo this effort.

Local production also tends to ensure a freshness not found in mass-produced materials. The teacher who provides taped copies of today's news program from radio or who produces handmade maps or transparencies to interpret the news not only has potentially good learning materials but has materials which cannot be kept up-to-date in any other way.

At times local production can save money. The ingenuity and the many willing hands available for such jobs can be more productive than commercial staffs. As we have seen throughout our study of media, local production also furnishes an avenue for student instruction. Through participation in materials-production projects, new understandings, challenges, and opportunities for creativity are provided.

Commercial materials are mass-produced for mass sales, and often do not fit specific local needs. A school can find commercial learning materials galore on the general benefits of pure drinking water or soil conservation, but materials which treat local problems are more effective. What could possibly be more effective for students who live in a logged-over area in Minnesota than photographs or transparencies of cut-over land, or for students in Pennsylvania than pictures of area blighted by strip coal mining?

Teachers can save time and effort by putting some of the materials they make year after year for their classes into semipermanent form. Worthwhile artistic charts, models, and tapes might well replace some of the flimsy, quickly made things which serve for one lesson and are then discarded only to be remade at a later date when the topic or unit is taught again. Records of recitals, speeches, graduation exercises, special events, or pictorial records of sports, festivals, plays, and the like may be valuable later. Even a record of an ordinary field trip may provide material of great potential. Photographs, photostats, or microfilms of newspapers, special bulletins and announcements, or documents should be considered as valuable as the books and documents in the school library and even harder to replace than many lost books.

School production can help interpret the school and its program to the community. Exhibiting a dynamic learning program will never hurt the passage of a school bond issue. Conversely, school production can help interpret the community to the school. It may lead to understandings and appreciations which might otherwise be overlooked.

DETERRENTS TO LOCAL PRODUCTION   Despite the apparent advantages of local production, a nationwide study[5] sub-

5. Gene Faris, John Moldstad, and Harvey Frye, *Improving the Learning Environment* (Washington, D.C.: United States Department of Health, Education, and Welfare, Office of Education, Government Printing Office, 1963.)

sidized by the United States Office of Education found that educators cite as considerable deterrents, the lack of time, space, supervisory time, in-service education, equipment, interest, and knowledge. Such factors as lack of administrative support, lack of production personnel, lack of budget, and lack of materials, were found to be lesser obstacles.

When to Produce Materials Locally

How does one decide whether to rely on available commercial products or to produce materials at the local level? Six useful criteria are these:

- finances available
- staff's ability and time to do the job properly
- commercial production of the material
- tools and facilities available for the job
- unusual student learning opportunities provided by local production of the material
- public interest in the schools which might be promoted by local production of the material

Who Produces What

Some materials are best produced by individuals, others by groups. Some productions will be simple, such as flash cards and number games; some will be complex, such as models, dioramas, silk-screen reproductions, and costuming of historical figures. Who can best produce what is suggested in Table 5, which is derived from the nationwide study mentioned earlier. That study found that, in cities having a centralized local production center to service the entire school system, learning resources specialists seem to take the lead on visual materials production, though classroom teachers are significantly involved.

Many schools have formally organized production programs. The study mentioned above found that most of these programs are system-wide, though some are limited to individual building centers and some are associated with educational television stations. Greatest use of system-wide centers

TABLE 5. "Who Produces Visual Instructional Materials in Your Preparation Center?"—Responses by School-System Learning Resources Specialists

Producer	NUMBER OF RESPONSES INDICATING:		
	Most Extensive Producer	Second Most Extensive Producer	Third Most Extensive Producer
Classroom teacher, with the assistance of the audiovisual specialist	22	29	5
Learning resources specialist, in consultation with the classroom teachers	38	14	12
Student assistants, under supervision of the audiovisual specialist and in consultation with the classroom teachers	7	7	14
Professional artist, in consultation with the television teachers	1	1	0
Professional artist, in consultation with the classroom teachers	1	1	1
Television teacher, with the assistance of the learning resources specialist	0	4	0
Learning resources specialist, in cooperation with the building coordinators	1	0	0
Secretary, in consultation with the learning resources specialist	1	2	1
Subject matter supervisor	2	0	0
Professional artist, in cooperation with learning resources specialist	6	1	0
Learning resources specialist, in cooperation with a curriculum specialist	3	1	0

is by audiovisual departments, but, when centers are established in buildings, the most extensive users are classroom
teachers.

A footnote to these remarks about local production of
learning materials is that production is done mainly "during
regular school hours," with "after school" a close second.
Far below these are before school, during noon hour, during
summer, and on weekends. (As mentioned, all the data in
the study refer only to production in organized centers.)

Work Areas for Local Production

In schools, the logical work centers are learning resources
centers, classrooms, teacher preparation or work rooms,
lounges, industrial-arts shops, and home-economics centers.
Furthermore, much local production is done in the homes of
teachers and students.

Disposition of Locally Produced Materials

Locally produced materials which have more than passing
value should be catalogued and housed, as are other learning
materials. Some will be stored and distributed from the
learning resources center or library; others will be decentralized and placed in individual school buildings. Many city
school systems are now producing such excellent learning
materials, that, after production, they might well place, for
example, their films or filmstrips on the market through a
commercial distributor.

LOCAL REPRODUCTION OF INSTRUCTIONAL MATERIALS

We turn now to the matter of *re*producing or duplicating
materials. Of interest here are printed materials including
mimeographed data, transparencies, magnetic tapes, videotapes, slides, filmstrips, and mounted flat picture sets. In the
main, reproduction of these materials is relatively simple,
depending somewhat on the volume of duplication needed,
although special equipment may be necessary in some cases.
Videotaping calls for special equipment, as does the repro-

duction of slides and filmstrips, but there are no particular problems involved with this equipment. The same is true of magnetic tape duplication, whether the need is for reel-to-reel or cassette types. Attention was called to high-speed tape duplication in the chapter on audio materials. Most district learning resources centers have this equipment available.

Transparency production and duplication has reached great proportions and sweeping variety, as we suggested earlier in the chapter on graphics. An inventory of production methods, techniques involved, and the equipment required was listed in the chapter on pictorial materials. The materials were separated and categorized as to those which could be made impromptu in the class or handmade prior to the class, and those involving machine processing. Only the machine processes are suitable for the duplication of numerous copies. Some of these processes are complicated, and those teachers who are interested should consult any of the numerous manuals on transparency production. It should also be repeated that classroom teachers will do well to consult their audiovisual personnel for assistance. But, unless the learning resources center personnel have the skill, time, and facilities, certain jobs should be "farmed out" to commercial concerns.

Print Materials

The noncommercial mimeographing, dittoing, and multilithing of print materials has reached staggering proportions. The uses range from secretarial, administrative, public relations, and classroom instruction to innumerable ancillary ones. Our interest here is confined to teachers and students. Teachers from kindergarten through university have need for multiple copies of plans, exercises, directions, outlines, new data, and other pertinent information.

Teacher workrooms are generally equipped with one or more machines for producing "handout" materials. Brief directions on the use of the machines are about all that is needed to do most routine copy work. The more complex machines such as offset printers, certain photocopies, and xerographic units, instead of being located in the teachers' workroom, may be found in the central administrative

TABLE 6. Eight Types of Duplicating Methods, Compared

	Spirit Duplicator	Gelatin Hectograph	Mimeograph (Stencil)	Diazo (Chemical Process—Ammonia Fumes)
Chief Use	classroom and office	limited	use ranges from few copies to several thousand	making transparencies, lesser use in making paper prints; sizes range from small to quite large (blueprints and plans for engineering drawings, etc.)
Equipment or Materials	inexpensive machine; paper	special paper, typewriter ribbons, pencils, inks	mechanical or electric duplicator; waxlike stencils; paper	diazo printer and ammonia developer (pickle jar will do for small uncritical jobs)
Operation	hand or electrical	hand (may also be handmade)	hand or electrical	chiefly hand
Skills Required	simple	simple	slightly more than for spirit duplicator or gelatin hectograph	special training, but not difficult
Cost	less than 1¢ per print unit	less than 1¢ per print unit	less than 1¢ per copy unit	moderate, about 3¢ per copy unit
Maximum Number of Copies	about 250 (on long-run masters)	up to 50	5,000	limited, probably no more than ten
"Master" Copy	paper stencil with colored carbons; typed or handwritten/drawn; some are ready-made commercially	typed or handwritten/drawn	wax stencil; typed or handwritten/drawn with stylus; can also be prepared electronically with a "scanner"	coated transparent film, translucent tracing paper
Color	usually purple (others possible)	several	usually black; others possible	numerous, but chiefly blue on white

Thermal (Heat-sensitive Paper)	Photocopy (Chemical or Heat Process)	Electrostatic	Offset Printing
making copies of practically any pictorial illustrations: charts, graphs, magazine articles, reports, student papers, newspaper cartoons, etc.	limited and specialized: transparencies, pasteups, books	limited and specialized	administrative and extended uses; professional needs
chiefly desk-top models which use heat generated by infrared lamp, special thermal paper	cameras; printers; photographic paper	the best known electrostatic process is xerography by which copies are made by action of light on electrically charged photoconductive surface; image is then developed with special *toner* powder	elaborate, usually located in district office or industrial arts department
hand or electrical; very fast	chiefly hand	chiefly hand	electrical; fast
simple	training required, but some uses are simple	trained personnel	training
about 5¢ per copy unit (thin paper)	about 10¢ per copy	equipment expensive; materials moderate	1¢ plus plate costs
50; not recommended when many copies are needed	50 or so	100 or so	very large
typewritten or handmade on any kind of paper, using any marking tool having a "carbon base" (pencil, india ink, etc.)	negative and positive paper	charged paper	paper masters and metal plates
several, but limited	black	colors	colors limited

offices, the commercial department, or the industrial arts department. A brief elaboration of each type of machine appears in Table 6.

Picture Transfers or Lifts

Related to the development of transparencies is the process of lifting ink pigments from clay-coated papers and causing the ink to adhere to transparent film while retaining the original ink pattern. As an example, suppose a teacher or a student wishes to have a transparent copy of a picture from *Life* magazine. The picture is adhered to a rubber cement or adhesive-coated sheet of acetate, and later the paper is soaked away from the transparency. After drying, the picture is either laminated in plastic or given a thin plastic spray coating. The process has limited use and the quality of the product can be disappointing.

Copyright Restrictions

It is worth noting, again, copyright involvements in the matter of reproducing printed materials, film and other pictorial materials, videotape recordings, programmed lessons, test booklets, musical scores, dramas, recordings, and related communications. The federal copyright law has been under study and revision for several years. Librarians and teachers generally favor fewer restrictions on educational materials, but publishers, authors, artists, and other creative people feel the need for certain protective restrictions.

Present technology makes it possible to copy voluminous materials, including entire books, in a matter of seconds or minutes. Furthermore, the quality of copy is usually quite good. Without copyright protection, entire chapters or books could be duplicated for free distribution! But the matter of "fair use" arises here. What is "fair use"? This book and practically all others have a statement on the copyright page which goes something like this: "All rights reserved. No part of this book protected by copyright hereon may be reproduced in any form without written permission of the publisher." Copyright, in most cases, is held by the publisher.

A teacher, school district, or organization desiring to repro-
duce copyrighted materials must seek written permission to
do so, and should give full credit to the source as required.

We mentioned television and videotape reproduction, either
as such or as part of a newly designed larger production, in
Chapter 7. Here, it should be noted that copying TV or
videotape materials for any purpose whatsoever—whether for
educational purposes, for use without fee, or for sale—is not
legally possible unless permission has been granted by the
manufacturer.

In sum, the best use of learning materials is greatly facilitated by the existence of a creative learning environment.
Harold Gores, President of Educational Facilities Laboratories, has stated this point well:

> Acknowledging at long last what business and industry have
> known for a generation—that quality of environment affects
> productivity—educators and their architects are specifying sur-
> faces and materials and equipment which will help the school
> help the child to learn. . . .
> If the child (or his teacher) is forced to expend energy to protect
> himself against environmental irritations, whether thermal, sonic,
> visual, or esthetic, his total capacity to respond is lessened. If
> educational opportunity for all children is to be maximized,
> comfort is a necessary condition.
> So, too, is amenity. The environment in which the school child
> spends his days teaches him what his community thinks of
> education—and what it thinks of him. What he experiences
> there, no less than what he learns there, shapes his expectations
> of himself and his fellowman. The school that serves its society
> well will nourish the child's spirit and dignity, not his mind
> alone.[6]

6. Harold B. Gores, "Educational Change and Architectural Consequence," in Frederick G. Knirk and John W. Childs, *Instructional
Technology—A Book of Readings* (New York: Holt, Rinehart, 1968),
pp. 176-77.

Chapter 9

The Learning Resources Center

BEHAVIORAL OBJECTIVES

After studying this chapter, the reader will be able to:

1. Identify the personnel typically found in a centralized learning resources center and describe their duties and training.
2. List five services of the learning resources center other than centralized administration and distribution of media.
3. Given twelve instructional materials, and given a specific school district, state whether distribution of each material is best centralized or decentralized, and support the choices.
4. List three ways in which learning resources are administered and distributed in a decentralized system.
5. Name five ways in which teachers interact with the learning resources center.
6. Describe the library's role in the learning resources center.

This discussion of the learning resources center has as its focus the classroom teacher. Other books are available on planning, organizing, and operating such a center, but very few address themselves to helping the teacher actually *use the resources* that the center provides.

It is useful at the outset to clarify the role of the learning resources center vis-à-vis the classroom "learning environment" which was the subject of the preceding chapter. In the final analysis, the environment that teacher and students share in their own classroom is the foundation for all learning. And the preceding chapter presented a host of possibilities for enriching that environment. Today, however, most teachers (particularly those in large or centralized school districts) can draw upon a source outside their own expertise when shaping and expanding their students' learning environment. That source is the learning resources center: it is, literally, a central repository of teaching materials and services which no single teacher could possibly accumulate (let alone store!) by himself.

The city of Los Angeles, for example, provides some 150,000 square feet of floor space to house its instructional materials and equipment, and no estimate can be made of the additional space needed for the materials housed permanently in nearly every school building in the district. San Diego utilizes nearly 100,000 square feet of space at its central instructional materials center (IMC) to house its collection of hardware and software. Rural teachers will have similar resources furnished by the county educational administration.

As a general rule the larger districts have greater facilities and programs, but even the smaller districts have either independent services and centers or have integrated services with a county or parish media center.

To help teachers become better teachers, most school districts provide them with a wide variety of materials and equipment. Under certain conditions this service is decentralized, with the material and equipment deposited in each school building. This is true of materials and supplies that are in constant use, are expendable, and are relatively inex-

pensive.   Other expensive materials which are not used constantly are best moved from building to building.   These
materials are stored in a central location and are distributed
to buildings in the district on request.   Both types of service
are found in most districts, varying according to the needs of
the schools and the philosophies of the administrative
officials.

Table 7's listing of representative media and materials will
show what is commonly centralized and what is decentralized.

TABLE 7. Distribution of Learning Materials

Instructional Materials Usually Centralized	Instructional Materials Usually Decentralized
A certain number of all kinds of hardware to be held as a supply pool. From this pool teachers or schools may draw equipment for replacement at times of breakdown or overhaul, for in-depth use, or for use in experimentation and research	All kinds of equipment for projection materials (slides, films, etc.), recording and playback of audio materials, television monitors and videotape machines
	Prerecorded and blank tapes
Specialized equipment: certain cameras, professional quality recorders, etc.	Prerecorded disc recordings
	Study prints
Professional lettering sets, binding devices, shading (example, air brush)	Transparencies
	Slides and filmstrips
Most 8- and 16-mm films. (The comments of the committee which prepared the *Standards for School Media Programs* illustrates the difficulty of setting an absolute policy in this area: "Acquisition of 16-mm films at the building level would depend upon extent and frequency of use of individual film titles in the school, upon the availability of a system media center and its collection of film resources, and upon other factors." p. 31.)	Films with recurring use, especially those for specific courses
	Models for specific courses
	Charts for specific courses
	Lettering sets (Leroy, etc.)
	Duplicating devices
	Programmed lesson materials
Tape duplication equipment	Supplies for production of instructional materials
Film cleaning and renovating equipment	Cameras (as needed)
Instructional kits	Maps and globes
	Dioramas, replicas, etc.
Realia display cases	Resource files

It must be kept in mind that there is no absolute rule for separation of materials. Each school system adopts an arrangement which best fits its philosophy, finances, personnel, and needs.

Centralized services are administered, of course, from the learning resources center, which purchases, stores, and distributes materials and equipment to teachers and students.

Decentralized services, on the other hand, are administered in each building. Ordinarily, a large room or several adjoining rooms are set aside and called an A-V or an I.M. center. The administration will quite likely be vested in a regular teacher who is given a certain amount of released time to requisition materials and equipment, check these items in and out, do minor repairs, give informal assistance to teachers in the building, provide leadership in his area, train and supervise a crew of student assistants, and numerous other duties as they develop locally and as time is made available. The person in charge of the building center will probably be called the building coordinator, and he may serve continuously, or the office may rotate to other faculty. In some buildings no teacher wishes to take the job. This is usually occasioned by the fact that school policy does not provide him with enough time to do the job, nor is he given sufficient responsibility and recognition. In these, or indeed, in many cases the materials and equipment coordination might be handled at the department level or grade level by the supervisor responsible. The key person implementing a good media program at the building level is the coordinator.

Learning resources centers range from those with the barest of materials and equipment to those which are complete and up-to-date. The author once asked a beginning teacher who was browsing through a city learning resources center if she could find what she needed. The enthusiastic reply was, "I find everything I need here. This is a teacher's paradise." Generally the learning resources center furnishes teachers with materials and equipment, services, and counsel.

New teachers in any school district should acquaint themselves as early as possible with the amounts and types of services and materials the district can furnish. Actually, most districts inform the new teachers about what they can expect. This information may be given verbally at general teachers' meetings at the opening of the fall term, in bulletins and newsletters, or by personal word from the director or a member of his staff.

If teachers do not find the equipment and materials they want, they should make their needs known. Administrative officers are usually amenable to such requests, and if funds are available, the materials will in all likelihood be forthcoming. Quality teaching is the goal.

Equipment and materials are useless unless the teachers know about them, and usually catalogues and lists are available. The catalogue is a primary source in locating available instructional materials. If the materials sought are not in the center and are not forthcoming in the near future, other sources should be explored. These include rental from commercial and university film libraries, loan from industry or governmental agencies, and purchase.

Services furnished by the learning resources center range from in-service teacher workshops and conferences to catalogues, newsletters, bulletins, and personal consultations. Teachers who do not know how to operate equipment often are taught by the learning resources staff. Throughout all this service, attention is given to the theory and the utilization techniques of concrete learning materials so that learning materials will be *properly prepared*, *wisely selected*, and *intelligently used*.

It is useful to get into the habit of going to the learning resources center occasionally. There are always new materials to be seen, new ideas to be had from talking to members of the staff, new exhibits and displays to think about (and possibly to imitate in the classroom), and fresh challenges to be carried away. In the preceding chapter, extended attention was given to the local production of materials. Most learning resources centers are also active in providing this kind of service.

It cannot be emplasized too strongly that the classroom teacher profits from close cooperation with the learning resources center. Many of the learning materials and the attention-getting devices which he or she would like to use are available or can be implemented through the center. As more and more technological developments are applied to instruction, cooperation is a necessity (for example, in such matters as the use of television, videotaping, dial-access, computerization, film production, and others).

A survey of instructional resources both as to availability and to utilization shows some interesting results. Compare the statistics in the Table 8, and then consider the question: do we use what we have?

In addition to the availability and utilization of equipment

TABLE 8. Availability and Use of Instructional Media*

Media	PERCENT OF TEACHERS HAVING RESOURCES AVAILABLE			PERCENT OF TEACHERS USING RESOURCES		
	All Teachers	Ele-men-tary	Second-ary	All Teachers	Ele-men-tary	Second-ary
Phonograph	92.8	95.8	89.4	79.0	92.8	63.3
Silent-filmstrip projector	92.3	93.1	91.4	81.2	89.0	72.2
Charts and maps	84.8	88.1	81.1	77.4	85.0	68.7
16-mm motion picture projector	84.5	80.3	89.2	74.3	74.1	74.6
Overhead Projector	83.3	79.3	87.8	61.5	59.3	64.1
Audio-tape recorder	78.4	76.6	80.4	53.8	61.2	45.5
Opaque projector	72.8	68.7	77.3	49.4	54.0	44.2
Sound-filmstrip projector	54.4	45.4	64.5	43.9	40.8	47.6
Educational TV broadcasts	36.3	47.8	23.4	26.1	40.1	10.5
Programmed inst. materials	34.9	36.3	33.3	28.6	31.3	25.5
Commercial TV broadcasts	31.0	33.5	28.1	13.5	16.2	10.4
8-mm motion picture projector	27.2	21.2	33.9	16.0	15.4	16.6
CC-TV	11.1	12.5	9.5	7.0	10.2	3.4
Computer-based teaching terminals	3.2	2.6	4.0	1.4	1.0	1.9

*Adapted from "Instructional Resources in the Classroom," NEA Research Bulletin, 45 (1967): 75–76.

by teachers, one might raise the question of just how much effort each school district puts into keeping its learning resources center up-to-date. Keeping up with current innovations costs money and districts may hope to "get by" on what was purchased in past years, particularly in periods of budget stringency.

The concept of being up-to-date can also be applied to inservice teachers. What effort do the learning resources center and the "establishment" make to keep teachers abreast of new materials, equipment, and techniques? New developments are in some ways almost overpowering to the nonspecialist. Teachers are no exception. It therefore behooves the school administration not only to provide the new instructional developments but to familiarize teachers with their function and use.

TEACHERS' OBLIGATIONS TO THE LEARNING RESOURCES CENTER

Teachers should recognize that service is a two-way street: they have obligations to the center, just as the center has obligations to them. Teachers can cooperate with center personnel by:

- returning materials promptly
- being willing to share ideas
- observing rules and regulations
- assisting in evaluation of materials
- taking proper care of all equipment and materials

COOPERATION WITH BOOK LIBRARIES

Clearly, the technology explosion has given new dimensions to communications programs and services. This development has meant more equipment, greater sophistication of equipment, more personnel, more counsel with classroom teachers, and more funds.

Libraries, too, have felt the knowledge explosion. It is said today that more than 2,000 pages of books, reports, and newspapers are printed every minute. The task of keeping

Fig. 32. A far cry from school libraries of the past, the school's instructional media center furnishes a wide variety of print and nonprint resource materials to meet the varying needs of individual students. (Photo, courtesy Long Beach, California, Unified School District.)

abreast of this explosion of print materials is staggering. But librarians' tasks are no longer limited to buying, cataloguing, and checking out of books. The many kinds of learning materials tend more and more to overlap, or else to abut and supplement each other. Book publishers are producing films and recordings. Motion picture producers are turning out supplementary books integrated with their film materials. Programmed learning materials involve many sorts of instructional materials. Both librarians and learning resources directors or coordinators meet with and counsel teachers on the selection and use of materials.

Providing assistance to teachers in matters of instructional materials and methods appears to be dichotomized. Libraries and learning resources centers seem to be competing with each other for funds in a race which involves the duplication of personnel, materials, and services. A more rational idea is that there should be *one* learning resources center which has responsibility for the administration of *all* instructional materials—print, electric, electronic, mechanical, and otherwise. Although this concept is given wide lip service, it is slow in implementation. One of the many examples of cooperation, however, is the recent publication of a joint booklet, *Standards for School Media Programs*, which was mentioned in Chapter 8.   Numerous organizational frameworks which unify services are also appearing across the country. A simple organization may follow the pattern shown in Figure 33.

In public schools some such organization may place the director of instructional materials at the level of associate superintendent, and in college or university at the dean's level.   In the past directors and supervisors of the various departments probably tended to be overly concerned with development of their own domains and did not give enough concern to the totality of the system. Currently prevailing educational philosophy merges all these units into an integrated educational consortium. The facilities should include specialized spaces for independent study, small-group interaction, and large-group or aggregate instruction. In the individual learning units, space and facilities should be provided for laboratories, workrooms, seminar rooms, areas for screening and listening, areas for reading, and areas for working with tools and materials of many kinds. Media specialists will become more closely enmeshed with the learning process and will assume new roles. Library and audiovisual assistants may very well find themselves assigned to teaching teams.

It is therefore not surprising to find librarians and media personnel merging their functions and efforts. A casual pe-

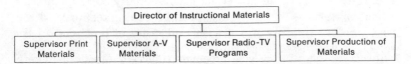

Fig. 33. Typical organization of a learning resources center which includes a book library.

rusal of preservice course outlines for both groups shows that each is receiving training in the aspects of both areas. Frequently, the courses in both fields are found in the school or college of education. Furthermore, several states unify the fields by placing them under the direction of one person. In California, for example, the title of this office is the Bureau of Audio-Visual and School Library Education. New organizational formats across the country tend to combine learning materials services.

The book *Standards for School Media Programs* (1969) has been mentioned several times in this text. This report is in itself an example of cooperation of media specialists and librarians. The booklet was fashioned by a committee of fourteen representatives of the Department of Audiovisual Instruction and fourteen representatives of the American Association of School Librarians. Two objectives motivated the project: "(1) to bring standards in line with the needs and requirements of today's educational goals, and (2) to coordinate standards for school library and audiovisual programs."

The report is directed at schools with a K-12 organization, having 250 or more students. Emphasis is placed on media centers, media resources, and media staff. Definitions included are: *media center*—"A learning center in a school where a full range of print and audiovisual media, necessary equipment, and services from media specialists are accessible to students and teachers"; *media resources* (or just *media*)— "Printed and audiovisual forms of communication and their accompanying technology"; and *media staff*—"The personnel who carry on the activities of a media center and its program."[1] It should be noted that *center* here refers to that found in individual school buildings. The *system* media center or learning resources center is only incidentally treated in this booklet. It is considered a center which is supplemental and supportive to the centers in the individual buildings.

---

1. *Standards for School Media Programs* (Chicago: American Library Association; Washington, D.C.: National Education Association, 1969), p. xv.

MEDIA PERSONNEL

Media staff, defined above, consist of (1) a *specialist*, *certificated*: someone with broad professional education in media, usually an experienced teacher and/or supervisor in some level of instruction or curriculum; (2) a *specialist*, *non-certified*: someone who is a professional but does not hold a teaching credential—for example, a specialist in television; (3) a *media technician*: a staff member who has specialized training in such areas as photography, graphics, and equipment control; and (4) a *media aide*: someone with secretarial or clerical competencies.

Duties of the media staff are covered by the titles and definitions just listed. Individual school systems delimit or expand these duties as circumstances direct. Variations are often dictated by the school's educational philosophy, size, organization, and financial resources.

Penfield, New York, a district with a school enrollment of 6,000 students and 350 teachers and administrators (encompassing six elementary schools, two junior high schools, and one senior high school), reports that each elementary school contains a media center staffed by one media specialist and one half-time media aide. At the junior high schools, one and a half media specialists are employed in each building plus a part-time media technician and a full-time media aide. The senior high school center is integrated in its operation and space with the district media center. Two media specialists and one media aide are responsible for this operation. At the district level, the staff consists of one full-time media generalist, one fifth-time media specialist, and one and a half media aides, one media technician, and one staff assistant is employed.

Certification or credentialing is an issue that has been bandied about for several decades. Only a few states require special certification of the media specialist, although in contrast, certification for librarians is quite common. Certification would tend to professionalize media work. Numerous colleges and universities offer specialized and graduate courses in media administration. Some provide programs leading to M.A. and Ph.D. degrees.

Institutions, foundations, associations, and the federal government have been active in sponsoring institutes and workshops across the country to upgrade or extend the education and training of media personnel. Although these programs are not related to certification or degrees, they are of tremendous importance to the profession.

SECONDARY FUNCTIONS OF THE CENTER

Of course, the chief function of the learning resources center is to assist teachers in solving learning problems. As an ancillary service, however, most centers perform secondary services such as: providing information for parents about school programs and services, promoting bond drives and tax overrides, assisting in community campaigns of various sorts, and helping PTAs.

In addition to the services noted above, the director might be expected to speak to and work with hospitals, service clubs, and similar organizations. Activities of this sort foster public support for the entire school program. No school would consider undertaking a bond campaign or similar drive without using the full force of its media resources. Alert media administrators seek to show their materials and services at such school functions as "open house," "parents' night," and similar occasions. They may also contribute articles from time to time for local news media—press, radio, television. The extent to which the media specialist and the learning resources center concern themselves with public relations will depend upon the philosophy of the school district and the leadership of the media coordinator.

SELECTED REFERENCES

Accountability in Education

Baker, Robert L. and Schutz, Richard, Southwest Regional Laboratory for Educational Research and Development (eds.). *Instructional Product Development.* New York: American Book and D. Van Nostrand: 1971. See especially the following components: *Constructing Objectives of Cognitive Behavior, Managing Classroom Contingencies, Developing Instructional Specifications,* and *Stating Educational Outcomes.*

Bloom, Benjamin S.; Krathwohl, David R.; and Masia, Bertram B. (eds.). *Taxonomy of Educational Objectives: Handbook I, Cognitive Domain* (1956); and *Handbook II, Affective Domain,* (1964). New York: David McKay.

Kemp, Jerrold E. Instructional Design: A Plan for Course and Unit Development. San Francisco: Fearon, 1971.

Mager, Robert F. *Preparing Instructional Objectives.* Palo Alto, Calif.: Fearon, 1962.

Media As an Outgrowth of Social and Technological Change (Chapter 1)

FURTHER READING

Alcorn, Marvin D.; Kinder, James S.; Schunert, Jim R. *Better Teaching in Secondary Schools.* 3rd ed. New York: Holt, Rinehart and Winston, 1970. Chs. 8-9.

Bretz, Rudy. *A Taxonomy of Communication Media.* Englewood Cliffs, N.J.: Educational Technology Publications, 1971.

Criteria Relating to Educational Media Programs in School Systems. Washington, D.C.: Department of Audiovisual Instruction of the National Education Association, 1966.

Gibbons, Maurice. *Individualized Instruction: A Descriptive Analysis.* New York: Teachers College Press, Columbia University, 1971.

Haney, John B. and Ullmer, Eldon J. *Educational Media and the Teacher.* Dubuque, Ia.: Wm. C. Brown, 1970. Chs. 1-3, 9.

Levine, Daniel U. "The Reform of Urban Education," *Phi Delta Kappan,* 52 (February 1971): 328-333.

Martin, Reed and Blaschke, Charles. "Contracting for Educational Reform," *Phi Delta Kappan*, v. 2 (1971): 403–405.

Quantitative Standards for Audiovisual Personnel, Equipment and Materials in Elementary, Secondary, and Higher Education. Washington, D.C.: Department of Audiovisual Instruction, National Education Association, 1966.

Silberman, Charles, E. *Crisis in the Classroom.* New York: Random House, 1970.

Standards for School Media Programs. Chicago: American Library Association, and Washington, D.C.: National Education Association, 1969.

To Improve Learning. A Report of the Commission on Instructional Technology. Washington, D.C.: United States Government Printing Office, 1970.

Weisgerber, Robert A. (ed.). *Instructional Process and Media Innovation.* Chicago: Rand McNally, 1968.

Willower, Donald J. "Educational Change and Functional Equivalents," *Education and Urban Society* (August 1970): 385–402.

RELATED NON-BOOK MEDIA

I Walk Away in the Rain, film, 11 min., color, sound. Holt, Rinehart and Winston. An open-ended film built around the problem of motivating a highly capable adolescent who exerts minimal effort in school work. Accompanied by a guide.

Individual Differences, film, 24 min., b & w, sound. McGraw-Hill. A teacher's praise leads a boy to discover that to be different is not to be wrong. A filmstrip by the same name is also available.

Information Explosion, The, film, 34 min., b & w, sound. Ohio State U.

More Different Than Alike, film, 33 min., color, sound. NEA. Portrays various school systems which have developed unique and creative school programs.

New Design for Education, A, film, 28 min., color, sound. Stanford. Shows research designs and ideas relating to scheduling, theories of learning, etc.

Portrait of the Inner-City School: A Place to Learn, film, 18 min., b & w, sound. McGraw-Hill. Shows conflicts between conventional school techniques and the culture patterns of inner-city students and suggests positive approaches.

Problem of Pupil Adjustment, film, b & w, sound. McGraw-Hill. Part I—*The Stay-In*, 19 min., Part II—*The Drop-Out.* Companion films which emphasize the need for curriculum adjustment.

Providing for Individual Differences, film, 23 min., b & w, sound. Iowa State U.

Quiet Revolution, The, film, 28 min., color, sound. Stanford, distributed by NEA. Depicts a number of staffing problems in five different schools.

Rafe: Developing Giftedness in the Emotionally Disadvantaged, film, 20 min., b & w, sound. Bailey Films.

Remarkable Schoolhouse, A, film, 25 min., color, sound. McGraw-Hill. Walter Cronkite narrates this view of contemporary schools and modern technology.

Revolution in the 3R's, film, 50 min., b & w, sound. Public Media. Describes how the school system is being revolutionized by various new teaching methods such as the Summerhill plan and the "New Math" program.

Room for Learning, A, filmstrip, 94 fr., accompanied by a 12 min. phonodisc at $33\frac{1}{3}$ rpm. Bailey Films, distributed by NEA. Discussion and illustrations of multimedia classrooms.

Tense: Imperfect, film, 12 min., color, sound. Holt, Rinehart and Winston. An open-ended film concerned with a middle-class teacher and a class of culturally different students.

Time for Talent, film, 23 min., b & w, sound. NEA. Classroom and community efforts to provide for talented students.

You're No Good, film, 28 min., b & w, sound. National Film Board of Canada, distributed in United States by McGraw-Hill. Suitable for stimulating discussions with potential drop-outs and delinquents of antisocial behavior.

Walls, film, 10 min., color, sound. Holt, Rinehart and Winston. "A sensitive young teacher has tried to expose his high school class to the type of independent study which will be expected in college."

Communication As Part of the Learning Process (Chapter 2)

FURTHER READING

Alcorn, Marvin D.; Kinder, James S.; and Schunert, Jim R. *Better Teaching in Secondary Schools*. 3rd ed. New York: Holt, Rinehart and Winston, 1970. Chs. 8–11.

Frymier, Jack R. and Hawn, Horace. *Curriculum Improvement for Better Schools*. Worthington, O.: Charles A. Jones, 1970.

Gagné, Robert M. *The Conditions of Learning*. 2nd ed. New York: Holt, Rinehart and Winston, 1965.

Kuh, Katherine. "Eames and Mythic Monster," *Saturday Review*, 54 (1971): 34–35.

McLuhan, Marshall. *Understanding Media: The Extension of Man.* New York: McGraw-Hill, 1964.

Postlethwait, S. N.; Novak, J.; and Murray, H. *An Integrated Approach to Learning.* Minneapolis: Burgess, 1964.

Smith, Karl U. and Smith, Margaret. *Cybernetic Principles of Learning and Educational Design.* New York: Holt, Rinehart and Winston, 1966.

RELATED NON-BOOK MEDIA

Bridge for Ideas, film, 24 min., b & w, sound. USC. Shows how communications media act as bridges for ideas. Illustrations involve radio, films, television, language, and miscellaneous channels.

Can Individualization Work For You? film, 4 min., b & w, sound. Special Purpose Films. Presents Dr. John Goodlad as he talks about changes in school organization, curriculum, and methods of teaching—emphasis on individualized instruction while retaining group systems.

Communications Primer, A, film, 20 min., color, sound. Ray and Charles Eames. Illustrates how steps in the communications act occur and how they affect our lives. An essay in design.

Communications Theory and the New Educational Media, series of films produced by Robert W. Wagner, Ohio State U., under grant from United States Office of Education (OE-3-16-020). Titles are: *The Information Explosion, Perception and Communication, The Process of Communication, The Teacher and Technology*, and *The Communications Revolution.* Running time for the series (called a "Galaxy") is $4\frac{1}{2}$ hrs.

Crisis in the Classroom, film, 16 min., b & w, sound. Doubleday Multimedia. Discusses positive motivation.

Eye of the Beholder, The, film, 25 min., b & w with some colored sequences, sound. Stuart Reynolds. Dramatizes 12 hrs. in the life of an artist who becomes involved in a murder. Shows how we perceive what we want to perceive.

More Different Than Alike, film, 35 min., color, sound. NEA. Depicts unique and creative techniques for individual learning such as data-processing systems, self-instructional programs, and student-planned schedules.

Teacher's Aides—A New Opportunity, film, 21 min., b & w, sound. United States National Audiovisual Center of the National Archives and Records. Training for para-professional aides for preschool services.

To Bring Learning Alive, film, 18 min., b & w, sound. Indian Government. Explains some inherent drawbacks in systems where books alone are used.

Using Pictorial Media (Chapter 3)

FURTHER READING

Andersen, Yvonne. *Teaching Film Animation to Children.* New York: Van Nostrand Reinhold, 1971. (A companion film is available.)

Bell, Geoffrey. *8mm Film for Adult Audiences.* Paris: United Nations Educational, Scientific and Cultural Organization, 1968.

Eboch, Sidney C. *Operating Audiovisual Equipment.* Rev. ed. San Francisco: Chandler, 1968.

Electography Producers Manual—Television Techniques for Television Tape Production. St. Paul, Minn.: The 3M Co., 1969.

Gropper, George L. and Glasgow, Zita. *Criteria for the Selection and Use of Visuals in Instruction.* Englewood Cliffs, N.J.: Educational Technology Publications, 1971.

Ingham, George F. "8mm Films for Individualized Study," *The Instructor,* v. 80 (1971): pp. 88+. Jan.

Lidstone, John and McIntosh, Don. *Children As Film Makers.* New York: Van Nostrand Reinhold, 1970. (A companion film is available.)

Kemp, Jerrold E. *Planning and Producing Audiovisual Materials.* 2nd ed. San Francisco: Chandler, 1968. Pp. 161–186.

Media Equipment Operation: Motion Picture Projectors—Wilkit 70. Ogden, U.: Weber State College, School of Education. (Delineates skills in the use and operation of a 16-mm motion picture projector.)

Minor, Ed, and Frye, Harvey. *Techniques for Producing Visual Instructional Materials.* New York: McGraw-Hill, 1970. Pp. 163–227.

Nelson, Leslie W. *Instructional Aids.* Dubuque, Ia.: Wm. C. Brown, 1970. Ch. 12.

Post, Anne. "Blank Film Encourages Creativity," *The Instructor,* (1971): 80:90 Jan.

Standards for School Media Programs. Chicago: American Library Association, and Washington, D.C.: National Education Association, 1969.

Training in Business and Industry, (October 1969): 52–54, 70. (Includes pictures and specifications of all models of machines made by more than a dozen manufacturers.) "Buyers' Guide," v. 6.

Wiman, Raymond V. *Instructional Materials.* Worthington, O.: Charles A. Jones, 1972.

Wittich, Walter A. and Schuller, Charles F. *Audio-Visual Materials: Their Nature and Use.* 4th ed. New York: Harper & Row, 1967.

RELATED NON-BOOK MEDIA

Dry Mount Your Teaching Pictures, film, 10 min., b & w, sound. McGraw-Hill. A how-to-do-it film showing various types of dry mounting.

8mm Film: Its Emerging Role in Education, film. Sponsored by United States Office of Education, distributed by Du Art Films.

Film Tactics, film, 22 min., b & w, sound. Produced as a navy training film. Shows the right and the wrong way to use a classroom film in a navy setting. A classic.

How to Use a Teaching Film, filstrip, 43 fr., color. Basic Skill Films. Demonstrates how a film should be used in the classroom, including room set-up, discussion, re-showing.

Instructional Materials, filmstrip, 44 fr., color. Bel Mort. Points out values of various instructional materials including books, films, maps, recordings, etc.

Magazines to Transparencies, film, 12 min., color, sound. Florida State U. Describes how to make transparencies by color lift process.

Make a Movie without a Camera, film, 6 min., color, sound. Bailey Films. Shows how a motion picture can be made from white film leader without a camera.

Opaque Projector: Its Purposes and Uses, film, 6 min., b & w, sound. U. of Iowa. Covers operation of the standard opaque projector.

Overhead Projector, film, 16 min., b & w, sound. U. of Iowa. Treats operation of the overhead projector and preparation of materials.

Photographic Slides for Instruction, film, 10 min., color, sound. Indiana U. Basic work in 2 × 2 slide making, including the Polaroid.

Study Pictures and Learning, filmstrip, 63 fr., color. Ohio State U. Utilization of study pictures at the elementary and secondary levels.

Unique Contribution, The, film, 30 min., color, sound. Encyclopaedia Britannica. Shows how the classroom film makes a contribution to teaching by means of film clips to illustrate the multi-functions of film. Sequences on time-lapse, microphotography, animation, slow motion, stop motion, and staging.

Wet Mounting Pictorial Material, film, 11 min., color, sound. Indiana U. Simple, clear how-to-do-it film.

Using Graphics (Chapter 4)

FURTHER READING

Art-work Size Standards for Projected Visuals. Rochester, N.Y.: Eastman Kodak, n.d.

Ballinger, Raymond A. *Layout and Graphic Design*. New York: Van Nostrand Reinhold, 1970.

Culbertson, Hugh M. and Owers, Richard D. "A Study of Graph Comprehension Difficulties," *Audiovisual Communication Review*, 7 (Spring 1959): 97–110.

Fujii, John N. *Puzzles and Graphs.* Washington, D.C.: National Council of Teachers of Mathematics, 1966.

Kemp, Jerrold. *Planning and Producing Audiovisual Materials.* 2nd ed. San Francisco: Chandler, 1970.

"Maps with a Capital M," *Educational Media*, 1 (1970): 22.

Minor, Ed, and Frye, Harvey. *Techniques for Producing Visual Instructional Media.* New York: McGraw-Hill, 1970.

Shea, Elizabeth A. "The Graphic Arts Center in the Public School System," *Audiovisual Instruction*, 13 (1968): 356–359.

RELATED NON-BOOK MEDIA

Creating Cartoons, film, 10 min., b & w, sound. Bailey Films. A humorous animation of cartooning of simple character.

Globes: Their Function in the Classroom, film, 14 min., color, sound. Bailey Films.

Graphs, filmstrip, 54 fr., b & w, silent. Society for Visual Education. Shows many types of graphs. Elementary.

Language of Maps, The, film, 30 min., b & w, sound. Ealing.

Lettering Instructional Materials, film, 20 min., color, sound. Indiana U. Freehand and mechanical devices and techniques.

Map Symbols, Dots and Lines, and companion filmstrip *Using Maps and Globes*, filmstrips, 58 fr., color, silent. Society for Visual Education. Elementary filmstrips valuable in lower grades.

Maps—An Introduction, film, 11 min., color, sound. Indiana U. Children create a map of a community and learn to read legends and to do scaling.

Paper in the Round, film, 11 min., color, sound. McGraw-Hill. The many instructional and artistic uses of paper in posters, sculpture, folding, etc.

Using Charts and Graphs in Teaching, filmstrip, 52 fr., color, silent. Basic Skill Films. Numerous types of charts and graphs shown.

Why Man Creates, film, 24 min., color, sound. Kaiser. A stylized graphic film (some photography) which shows man's creations and developments from cave painting days to the present. Provocative.

Using Auditory Media (Chapter 5)

FURTHER READING

Derby, James. "Tape Cassette: Indestructible Tool," *The Instructor*, 80 (1971): 88.

Drowns, Frances. "Individualized Instruction through the Use of Tapes," *Audiovisual Instruction*, 14 (1969): 41–42.

McLuhan, Marshall. "Radio: The Tribal Drum," *Audiovisual Communication Review*, 12 (Summer 1964): 133-145.

Nicholas, Lois K. "Increasing Listening Skills with Tape-recorded Lessons," *Audiovisual Instruction*, 11 (1966): 544.

RELATED NON-BOOK MEDIA

Behind the Radio Dial, tape recording, 15 min., $7\frac{1}{2}$ ips. National Tape depository, Boulder, Colo. Using radio programs in instruction.

Interpersonal Communications, manual, participant's materials, 9 films. Northwest Regional Educational Laboratory, Portland, Oreg. This workshop package is designed to increase interpersonal communication skills and improve perceptual listening and conversational abilities.

Recording, three 8-mm film loops, about 4 min. each, silent. McGraw-Hill. *Operating the Tape Recorder*, *Operating the Record Player*, *Splicing Magnetic Tape*.

Tapes. Overseas tapes may be exchanged through these international correspondence sources: Caravan of East and West, Inc., 132 E. 65th St., N.Y., N.Y. 10021; English-Speaking Union (Pen Friends Division), 16 E. 69th St., N.Y., N.Y. 10021; Letters Abroad, 45 E. 65th St., N.Y., N.Y. 10021; Ruth Terry, International Tape Exchange, 834 Ruddiman Ave., North Muskegon, Mich. 49445; World Tapes for Education, Box 9211, Dallas, Tex. 75215.

Standard Instructional Materials (Chapter 6)

FURTHER READING

American Behavioral Scientist, 10, nos. 2, 3 (1966). (Articles by leading exponents of simulation about simulation games and learning behavior.

Birstwhistle, C. "Aids in the Teaching of Mathematics," *Visual Education*, (1967): 11-15.

Boocock, Sarane S. and Schile, E. O. (eds.). *Simulation Games in Learning*. Beverly Hills, Calif.: Sage, 1968.

Foreign Policy Association. *Simulation Games for the Social Studies Classroom*. New York, 1969.

Nelson, Leslie W. *Instructional Aids*. Dubuque, Ia.: Wm. C. Brown, 1970.

"Selecting Free and Inexpensive Materials," *ERS Reporter*. Washington, D.C.: Educational Research Service, American Association of School Administrators and the Research Division, NEA, November 1966.

Wiman, Raymond V. *Instructional Materials*. Worthington, Ohio: Charles A. Jones, 1972.

RELATED NON-BOOK MEDIA

ABC of Puppets, film, parts I and II, 10 min., b & w, sound.   Bailey Films.

Anatomical Models, film, 15 min., b & w, sound.   Denoyer-Geppert. Shows a variety of teaching models.

Bulletin Boards: An Effective Teaching Device, film, 11 min., color, sound.   Bailey Films.   Uses numerous examples to show planning and construction of good bulletin boards.   Emphasis on elementary schools.

Chalkboard Utilization, film, 16 min., b & w, sound.   McGraw-Hill. Shows five important ways of improving chalkboard utilization.

Community Resources in Teaching, film, 17 min., b & w, sound.   U. of Iowa.   Explains the value of using community resources including field trips.   An early film but still good.

Diorama As a Teaching Aid, filmstrip, 58 fr., color, silent.   Ohio State U.   Construction and utilization.   Stress on elementary and junior high school.

Dry Mounting Instructional Materials, series of 5 films, 5 min. each, color, sound.   U. of Iowa.   Available in 16-mm of Super 8 (magnetic or optical sound).

Field Trip, The, film, 11 min., color, sound.   Virginia State Department of Education.   Shows how a high school class planned and executed a successful trip to the Dismal Swamp.

Flannelgraph, The, film, 27 min., color, sound.   U. of Minnesota.   A master teacher demonstrates for practice teachers the construction and use of the flannelgraph.

How to Make and Use a Diorama, film, 20 min., color, sound.   McGraw-Hill.   Construction and use of simple and complicated dioramas with varied materials.

Market Game: Use of a Simulation Game, film, 30 min., b & w, sound.   Holt, Rinehart and Winston.   Demonstrates the use of this simulation in the teaching of the social studies.

Movement in Time and Space, film, 30 min., color, sound: Peter M. Robeck.   Explains how teachers provide resource materials for growth through drama, dance, dialogue, impersonization, and language exploration.

Museum: The Gateway to Perception, film, 16 min., color, sound.   Atlantis.   Surveys the history of the museum and then shows the many purposes served.

Near Home, film, 27 min., b & w.   British Information Services.   Shows how an elementary school teacher in a small town energized his students by a project which resulted in widespread community involvement.

School Journey, The, filmstrip, 50 fr., color, silent. Basic Skill Films.
Necessary preparations for a successful journey.

Mediated Instructional Procedures (Chapter 7)

FURTHER READING

Alcorn, Marvin D.; Kinder, James S.; and Schunert, Jim R. *Better
Teaching in Secondary Schools*. 3rd ed. New York: Holt, Rinehart
and Winston, 1970. Ch. 11.

Allen, David. "Reach Many Senses with Multi-media," *Educational
Screen and AV Guide*, 48 (1969): 14–15, 29.

Bushnell, Don D. and Allen, Dwight W. *The Computer in American
Education*. New York: John Wiley & Sons, 1967.

Chu, Godwin C. and Schramm, Wilbur. *Learning from Television: What
the Research Says*. Stanford: Stanford U. Press, 1968. United States
Office of Education Contract OEC 4-7-0071123-4203.

Commission on Instructional Technology. *To Improve Learning*. Washington, D.C.: United States Government Printing Office, 1970.

Dorsett, Loyd G. *Audio-Visual Teaching Machines*. Englewood Cliffs,
N.J.: Educational Technology Publications, 1971. (Includes estimates
for various AVTM options and suggestions for desirable properties to
look for in any device on the market or proposed for the future.)

Gordon, George N. *Classroom Television: New Frontiers in ITV*. New
York: Hastings House, 1970.

Hall, Keith A. "Computer-Assisted Instruction: Problems and Performance," *Phi Delta Kappan*, 52 (1971): 628–631.

Heinich, Robert. *Technology and the Management of Instruction*.
Monograph 4. Washington, D.C.: National Education Association,
1971.

Marland, Jr., Sidney P. "A New Order of Educational Research and
Development," *Phi Delta Kappan*, 52 (1971): 576–579.

Meredith, J. C. *The CAI Author/Instructor: An Introduction and Guide
to the Preparation of Computer Assisted Instruction Materials*. Englewood Cliffs, N.J.: Educational Technology Publications, 1971.

Postlethwaite, S. N., et al. *The Audio-Tutorial Approach to Learning:
Through Independent Study and Integrated Experiences*. 3rd ed.
Minneapolis, Minn.: Burgess, 1972.

*Programmed Instruction, Sixty-sixth Yearbook, National Society for
the Study of Education*. Part II. Chicago: U. of Chicago Press, 1967.

Schmande, Juergen. "Technology and Education," in *Issues in American Education*, ed. Arthur M. Kroll. New York: Oxford U. Press,
1970.

Schramm, Wilbur. *Communication Satellites for Education, Science and Culture.* Paris: UNESCO, 1968.

Skinner, B. F. *The Technology of Teaching.* New York: Appleton-Century-Crofts, 1968.

Teachey, William G., and Carter, Joseph B. *Learning Laboratories: A Guide to Adoption and Use.* Englewood Cliffs, N.J.: Educational Technology Publications, 1971.

Weisgerber, Robert A. (ed.). *Instructional Process and Media Innovation.* Chicago: Rand McNally, 1968.

RELATED NON-BOOK MEDIA

Behind the Radio Dial, tape, 15 min., $7^{1}/_{2}$ ips. National Tape Depository. Radio instruction.

Computer Assisted Instruction, filmstrip with tape, 29 fr., color, 8 min.; tape at $7^{1}/_{2}$ ips. Educational Media. Shows CAI recording and assisting in pupil instruction.

Dial Access Information Retrieval Systems, filmstrip with tape, 25 fr., color; 7 min. tape at $7^{1}/_{2}$ ips. Educational Media. Shows the systems at work at Oral Roberts University and Oklahoma Christian College.

Incredible Machine, film, 16 min., color, sound. Bell Telephone. Shows Bell scientists using computer-generated movies, photographs, music, and speech. The musical score and titles for this film were produced by computer.

Large Group Auditoriums, filmstrip with tape, 42 fr., color, 11 min.; tape at $7^{1}/_{2}$ ips. Educational Media. Instruction in large rooms at several universities. Shows multiscreens, rear screens, special consoles, podiums, room dividers, and movable walls. Dial-access and retrieval systems are integrated.

Recording, series of three 8-mm loops, about 4 min. each, silent. McGraw-Hill. *Operating the Tape Recorder, Operating the Record Player, Splicing Magnetic Tape.*

Sign On/Sign Off, film, 20 min., color, sound. Pennsylvania State U. Examines in simple terms the problems and values of CAI as developed in a laboratory at Penn State.

Successful Use of the Language Laboratory, a series of 8 films each about 15 min., sound. Walter G. O'Connor.

Teaching Machine, The,: Learning and Behavior, film, 26 min., b & w, sound. Carousel. Shows the basic animal behavior laboratory studies of Skinner which underlie conditioning behavior by programming.

Teaching Machines and Programmed Learning, film, 28 min., b & w, sound. United World. An interview with Skinner, Glaser, and Lumsdaine.

Television in Education, film, 24 min., color, sound. Bell Telephone. Shows values and uses of open- and closed-circuit TV. Good sequences from Anaheim, Calif., Hagerstown, Md., and Michigan State U.

Television Techniques for Teachers, film, 24 min., color, sound. San Diego Area Instructional Television Authority.

Telstar, film, 27 min., color, sound. Bell Telephone. Early satellite broadcasting with a story of the research, launching, and first direct telecasts between the United States and Europe.

Thinking??? Machines, The, film, 16 min., color, sound. Bell Telephone. Designed to stimulate student interest in the computer field.

Creating a Learning Environment (Chapter 8)

FURTHER READING

Brown, James W.; Lewis, Richard B.; and Harcleroad, Fred F. *AV Instruction: Media and Methods*. 3rd ed. New York: McGraw-Hill, 1969. Chs. 3, 16.

Knirk, Frederick G. and Childs, John W. *Instructional Technology: A Book of Readings*. New York: Holt, Rinehart and Winston, 1968. Pp. 172–193.

Silber, Kenneth H. and Ewing, Gerald W. *Environmental Simulation*. Englewood Cliffs, N.J.: Educational Technology Publications, 1971.

Taylor, Gary R. "The Lone Learner," *Audiovisual Instruction*, (1971): 16:54–55 Apr.

RELATED NON-BOOK MEDIA

Make a Mighty Reach, film, 25 min., color, sound. Kettering. A stimulating review of innovations and emerging school facilities.

Room for Learning, A, filmstrip, 94 fr., color, accompanied by a 12 min. phonodisc at $33^1/_3$ rpm. Bailey Films, distributed by NEA. A multimedia classroom has numerous possibilities.

Setting up a Room: Creating an Environment for Learning, film, color, sound. Campus Film Distributors.

The Learning Resources Center (Chapter 9)

FURTHER READING

Brown, James W.; Aubrey, Ruth H; and Noel, Elizabeth. *Multi-media and the Changing School Library*. Sacramento: California State Department of Instruction, 1969.

Elkins, F. S.; Rabalais, M. J.; and Galey, E. "The Media Director's Job," *Educational Media*, 3 (1970): 6, 15.

Faris, Gene and Sherman, Mendel. *Quantitative Standards for Audio-visual Personnel, Equipment and Materials in Elementary, Secondary, and Higher Education.* Washington, D.C.: Department of Audiovisual Instruction, National Education Association, 1966. Mimeo.

Rufsvold, Margaret and Guss, Carolyn. *Guides to Educational Media.* 3rd ed. Chicago: American Library Association, 1971.

Standards for School Media Programs. Chicago: American Library Association, and Washington D.C.: National Education Association, 1969. (A comprehensive listing of equipment and materials recommended both for individual buildings and for the media center.)

Vannan, Donald A. "Educational Media in the United States," Part I, *Educational Media*, 1 (February 1970): 15, 21; Part II, 1 (March 1970): 14–15.

RELATED NON-BOOK MEDIA

Elementary School Library, film, 26 min., color, sound. Atlantis. Discusses the relationship of library, curriculum, research, and related aspects of the school and involves faculty and administration.

School Libraries in Action, film, 18 min., color, sound. North Carolina U. Shows how school provide books and instructional materials to students and faculty.

Selecting and Using Ready-made Materials, film, 17 min., b & w, sound. McGraw-Hill. Shows a wide range of commercially made materials.

Index

A

Acoustical control, 225
American Library Association, 26, 71, 228
Association for Educational Communication and Technology (AECT), 17, 228
Atlases, 101
Audiovisual, 16-17. *See also* Instructional materials

B

Behavioral change, 19, 33, 34
Behavioral objectives. *See* first page each chapter
Blackboards. *See* Chalkboards
Brevard Junior College, 165
Bulletin boards, 149-152

C

Cameras, 73. *See also* Polaroid; Teacher- and student-made materials
Camping activities, 176-177
Cartoons and comic strips, 92-94
Cassettes, 117-120
Centralized school services, 245-253
Chalkboards, 145-149, 226
Charts, 105-108
Collage, 55
Comic strips. *See* Cartoons

Committee on Instructional Technology, 23
Communications, barriers to, 45-49
Communications act, the, 42
Communications skills and teacher competence, 40
Community resources, 172-173
Compensatory education, 6
Computer-assisted instruction (CAI), 216-219
Conant, James B., 8, 177
Continuous loop, 82, 84
Copyrights, 240
Cross media, 19
Curriculum adjustments and revision, 7, 11, 20

D

Decentralization of schools and services, 9, 245
Demonstrations, 172
Diagrams and sketches, 91-92
Dial-access, 205, 213-216
Dioramas, 162
Displays, 145, 162-164
Dramatic techniques, 165-168
Dropouts, 5, 9
Duplicators, 237-240

E

Educational change, 1-31
8-mm films. *See* Films

Electric boards, 154–156
Electronic classrooms. *See* Learning laboratories
Electronic video recordings (EVR), 196
Elementary and Secondary Education Act of 1965, 13, 21
Encoding, 43–44
Equipment and materials, 15, 230, 231, 247
Exhibits, 162–164
Extemporaneous dramatization, 165

F

Feltboards, 152–154
Field trips, 54, 174–175
Films
  8-mm, 81–85
  full course, 80
  magnetic sound, 82
  modular films, 83
  optical sound, 81
  single concept, 82
  short-/brief-, 83
Filmstrips, 69–75
  double frame, 69
  single frame, 69
  sound, 70–71
Finn, James D., 15, 181
Flash cards, 65–67
Flat pictures, 51, 240
Follow Through Program, 7, 22, 173
Foreign-exchange students and teachers, 176
Free and inexpensive learning materials, 175
Full course films. *See* Motion pictures.

G

Gifted students, 9
Globes, 96, 101–105
Graffiti fence writing, 95
Graphics, 86–87, 110
Graphs, 87–91

H

Hardback books, 15
Hardware, 18, 212
Head start Program, 7, 22, 23, 173
Home study, 63
Hook-and-loop boards, 157

I

Individualized instruction, 15, 35–37, 62
Industry and education, 24, 25
Inner-city schools, 8–9
Innovation, 12–16, 26
Instructional materials centers, 242–253

J

Job Corps Programs, 23, 24, 173

K

Kits and loan boxes, 164–165

L

Language laboratories. *See* Learning laboratories
Lantern slides. *See* Slides
Large group instruction, 35, 62

Learning laboratories, 198-206
Learning resources centers, 18, 111, 164. *See also* Instructional materials centers
Lettering, 108, 111
Libraries, 53, 223, 248
Light control, 225
Listening, 115-116
Listening posts, 130-134

M

McLuhan, Marshall, 39, 73
Magnetic boards, 154
Maps, 96-105
Marionettes. *See* Puppetry
Materials
  community resources, 172-174
  distribution of, 243
  instructional, 11
  local production, 231-241
Media
  defined, 16-17
  guidelines for use, 28-31
  personnel, 252-253
  professional acceptance, 26
  public acceptance, 20
  state action, 25
  students like for, 4
  values, 19
Mediated instructional materials and procedures, 178, 205
MegaHertz (mHz), 184
Microprojectors, 80
Microteaching, 196-198
Models and mock-ups, 159-161
Motion pictures. *See* Films
Motivation, 7, 37, 38, 116
Multi-image, 180
Multimedia, 18, 180-181
Multipurpose boards, 156-157

Multi-screen, 180
Multisensory materials, 19

N

National Defense Education Act (NDEA), 21, 200
National Education Association (NEA), 12, 13, 17, 26, 116
National Educational Television Network System, 23

O

Objects, specimens, samples, 158
Opaque projections, 75-76
Overhead projections, 76-79

P

Pageants, 166
Pantomime, 166
Paraprofessionals, 8, 96
Peer groups, 35
Penfield (N.Y.) Public Schools, 252
Performance contracting, 24
Personnel. *See* Media
Photographs, 53-54, 72
Picture transfers or lifts, 240
Pictures, 63-75. *See also* Flat pictures, Photography, Textbook illustrations
Polaroid cameras, 72, 84
Posters, 94
Pressey, Sidney, 208, 211
Print materials, 237-240
Production. *See* Materials
Programmed learning, 206-213, 218
Projected still pictures, 67-75

Projects to Advance Creativity in Education (PACE), 22
Public address systems, 142
Puppetry, 170-171

R

Radio, 134-138
Random-access and retrieval. See Dial-access; Learning laboratories
Records and recorders, 116-126
Research and development (R&D), 12-13
Resource persons, 174
Role-playing, 167-168

S

San Diego City Schools, 164, 243
Satellite broadcasting. See Television
Schools, 11, 221-226, 228-229
  classrooms, 224-226
  design, 221-224
  environment, 228-229
Schramm, Wilbur, 188, 190
Scrambled book. See Programmed learning
Senses and learning, 38
"Sesame Street," 15, 22, 193
Simulation games, 38, 168-170
Skinner, B. F., 207, 208
Slides, 69-75
Small group instruction, 35, 62
Software, 18, 201, 209
Special classes and schools, 10
Standards for School Media Programs, 26, 71, 79, 228, 244, 250, 251
Stereoprojectors, 80
Study prints, 52
Systems, 11, 18, 27, 181

T

Tableaux, 166
Tachistoscopes, 80
Tapes and tape recorders, 117-130
Teacher- and student-made learning materials, 54, 72, 73
Teaching, dimensions of, 27
Teaching machines. See Programmed learning
Team teaching, 35, 189
Technological and social change, 4, 11, 27
Telelecture, 140
Telemation, 179, 181
Telephone interviews. See Telephone sound systems
Telephone sound systems, 138-140, 176
Television
  broadcast, 182
  closed-circuit, 182, 184
  coaxial cable, 184
  color, 190-191
  copyright, 241
  ETV and ITV defined, 183
  evaluation, 191-193
  Miami-Dade Junior College, 191
  MPATI, 186
  narrowcast, 182
  Public Broadcast Act, 185
  Roanoke Public Schools, 191
  Samoan ETV, 186
  satellite broadcasting, 187
  team teaching, 189
  VHF and UHF, 184
Textbook illustrations, 58
Three-dimensional materials, 158-165
Training aids, 19
Transparencies, 77-79

U

Underprivileged and culturally deprived, 4–7, 8
UNESCO, 17
U.S. Office of Education, 5, 22, 190, 234

V

Videotape recording (VTR), 193–196, 241

VISTA program, 23, 173
Visual literacy, 40, 73

W

Wireless listening stations, 140, 201, 205
Wireless microphones, 141